S. AL-JASSAR
1/03

D1597314

S. AL-GASSAR
1V92

# Ethics and Urban Design

# ETHICS AND URBAN DESIGN

## CULTURE, FORM, AND ENVIRONMENT

Gideon S. Golany
*Distinguished Professor of Urban Design*
*The Pennsylvania State University*

JOHN WILEY & SONS, INC.
New York   Chichester   Brisbane   Toronto   Singapore

This text is printed on acid-free paper.

Copyright © 1995 by John Wiley & Sons, Inc.

All rights reserved. Published simultaneously in Canada.

Reproduction or translation of any part of this work beyond that permitted by
Section 107 or 108 of the 1976 United States Copyright Act without the permission
of the copyright owner is unlawful. Requests for permission or further information
should be addressed to the Permissions Department, John Wiley & Sons, Inc., 605
Third Avenue, New York, NY 10158-0012.

This publication is designed to provide accurate and authoritative information in
regard to the subject matter covered. It is sold with the understanding that the
publisher is not engaged in rendering legal, accounting, or other professional
services. If legal advice or other expert assistance is required, the services of a
competent professional person should be sought.

*Library of Congress Cataloging in Publication Data:*
Golany, Gideon.
   Ethics and urban design : culture, form, and environment / Gideon S. Golany.
     p.   cm.
   Includes bibliographical references and index.
   ISBN 0-471-12274-2 (alk. paper)
   1. City planning—Environmental aspects.  2. City planning—Moral and ethical
aspects.  3. Urban ecology—Moral and ethical aspects.  4. Urbanization—
Environmental aspects—History.  5. Urbanization—Environmental aspects—Case
studies.  I. Title.
HT 166.G597 1995
307.76—dc20                                                                                   95-1333

Printed in the United States of America

10 9 8 7 6 5 4 3 2

TO MY FATHER JACOB, WHO BEQUEATHED TO ME HIS
LOVE AND DEDICATION TO THE BIBLE AND TO ERETZ-
ISRAEL . . . THE LAND OF ISRAEL

# CONTENTS

# PREFACE

This book is a compilation of my work throughout the last decade. With the exception of parts of Chapter Seven, none of this text has been published before; however, some of the drawings were previously used in my other publications. This book has a three-part structure. Part One deals with the historical past; Part Two examines the present; and Part Three considers the future. In some discussions, the past and present or present and future are fused together.

In my view, the strength of this book is in its attempt to view the environment comprehensively. However, this approach has its limitations. It necessitates a broad knowledge of different fields, and, when this is lacking, may therefore lead to the sacrifice of depth of understanding for breadth of analyses. It also requires the ability to communicate effectively with other design team professionals and to be tolerant of their views and take them into serious consideration. Collaboration with a design team offers both challenge and opportunity and is where the comprehensive view is most likely to be found.

This book emerged from a combination of my lectures in the classroom, the comments of my students, discussions with my colleagues at international conferences where I presented some of my thoughts, and the support of my research assistants. I am thankful to them all for their contribution.

My thanks go to my editorial assistant, Ms. Sally Atwood, for her careful handling of the many details related to the text, the bibliographical listing, and the sources. Without her perseverance, this volume would not have been finished on time. My thanks also go to Ms. Yue Li, who drafted most of the drawings. Ms. Yan Yun Zhang facilitated the publication of this book, and I thank her for her support in preparing the translation of the earlier draft of Chapter One for a lecture I presented at the China Academy of Sciences in Beijing, where I was awarded the title of Honorary Professor.

I am deeply thankful to Penn State University, especially to Dr. David Shirley, Senior Vice President for Research and Dean of the Graduate School, and to my Dean, Professor Neil Porterfield, who has continuously supported my scholarly work, for their financial support, which made possible the preparation of this manuscript. Without their help, this and other creative work could not have been accomplished.

My thanks also go to the secretary of my department, Ms. Linda Gummo, for her patient and careful typing of this volume, and to my assistant, Ms. Ruth Vastola, for her help at the final stage of this manuscript's preparation.

They all deserve my deepest appreciation.

Gideon S. Golany
*Distinguished Professor of Urban Design*
*The Pennsylvania State University*

# INTRODUCTION

Throughout this century, more than at any other time, there have been continual and dynamic changes associated with growth in all facets of our environment. We define *environment* as all of the natural landscape as well as the socio-economic-physical and human-made environment surrounding us. With our advanced science and technology, we are confident that we can create a balance between our resources and our needs and that we are able to understand the forces behind these two strata of the environment. Although this may be true, we still lack a full understanding of the reciprocal relationships between these forces. To a great extent, we have been able to produce and control nuclear energy, but we have not yet been able to fully control its threat or effectively dispose of its waste. It is only recently that we have become more aware of the serious danger of the impact the production of chemical materials we consume has on our global and regional environment.

For the sake of discussion, we define *ethic* as the norms and standards constituted by the society to retain order and healthy management in its social and environmental setting. Ethic is the discipline by which we measure what is good and bad, right and wrong, and moral obligations. Ethic is a group of moral principles or a set of values that is essential for human physical and mental survival. As such, ethic applies to community and individual behavior as related to the code of urban setting, to the norms by which we create human-made environment, and to the way we treat the natural environment.

We also are moving toward a greater understanding of the city. The city is the largest and most complicated project ever produced by humankind. It is a living organism that introduces a symphony of complex environment; it has, in many cases, grown beyond our ability to manage it efficiently notwithstanding we enjoy being part of it. Yet, with our religious-like belief in our advanced technology, we as designers have often ignored the achievement of our ancestors as well as the inherent complex social values on which the community rests. It is becoming more and more clear that our challenge is not technology—we have already arrived on the moon—but rather an understanding of the issues that helped previous generations create a social cohesiveness balanced with the environment. During my three decades of scholarly activities, I have come to believe that we cannot design the future effectively without studying and understanding past practice; from this we must draw some lessons. This applies to the social, economic, physical, and natural environments.

In the distant past, "design without designers" was common among indigenous peoples. They used both their observation skills and their intellectual instinct to provide a product that we today view as recyclable, harmonious, sensitive to nature, and creative in its use of local materials. It is true that the scale of our contemporary urban design and architectural creativity is different, which makes construction more difficult and complex, but it is equally true that we have basically lost much of our ancestors' sensitivity to the natural environment because of our deficiency and lack of ethic in urban design and management of urban growth.

We also differ from our ancestors in the method of selection of an urban site and its future expansion. Alternatives for potential urban expansion are certainly limited. In contemporary times, we have extensively used valley lowlands and plains for urban expansion. Consequently, much land suitable for agriculture has been consumed and, therefore, this practice has diminished globally our source for potential agricultural production. This loss is an irreversible process. Historically and geologically, it would take thousands of years to recreate this land for agriculture. Thus, the existing system of urban expansion has been costly in terms of human needs and economics.

There are, however, some feasible solutions for our generation and future generations to consider and accept. Urban design is a trade-off of loses and gains. There are solutions with varying degrees of social and economic viability.

We are heading toward an increasingly dominant urban lifestyle. We can outline five innovative and pioneering alternative frontiers for urban designers and policy makers to consider in future urban expansion.

1. *Sea Frontier.* Developing a floating or below-water city is technically feasible. In fact, throughout history there have been indigenous floating cities in southeastern Asia where established communities live permanently in an aggregate of boats and ships. These settlements today are congested and associated with substandard conditions, a low-income population, and a poor environmental quality of life. On the other hand, a contemporary type of floating city, such as Amsterdam, which resulted from limited land choices for expansion, utilizes a highly sophisticated, expanded regional and national network of waterways. Similarly, indigenous floating villages were built on wooden platforms in the lakes of Switzerland. These floating settlements have eliminated many of the problems associated with the historical spontaneously developed floating settlements.

   With our advanced technology and systems of communication, we can create a livable, modern floating city. In fact, Nikken Sekkie Design Office of Tokyo, Japan, has recently introduced the innovative "Imaginative Floating Circle City," which is a combination of above- and below-water space, for the Bay of Tokyo. The circle of the city is made of assembled floating individual neighborhood units, and different land uses are combined to form a huge circle surrounding a large body of water. A reasonable portion of the city is below sea level to accommodate storage and transportation. The above-water living section of every neighborhood unit is designed to be built in a configuration of terraced slopes on two sides to receive maximum light, sunshine, and ventilation. The city has elaborate and diversified facilities and amenities, with every neighborhood unit enjoying immediate access to the waterfront. The whole design makes the city construction flexible and expandable. It includes water and land transportation as well as an airport.

2. *Mountain Frontier.* Throughout history, for reasons of defense, recreation, preservation of agricultural land, and improvement of the quality of living, humankind has extensively used the slopes of mountains for developing a wide range of urban and rural settlements. Although slope developments may consume a higher initial investment than development in the lowlands, especially for transportation and construction, they have proven to provide healthier conditions than the lowlands by offering more ventilation, less pollution, and better views of the pleasing natural environment.

3. *Below-Ground Space Usage Frontier.* The use of below-ground space is an ancient one and has been practiced extensively virtually all over the world, especially in China, Tunisia, Cappadocia (Central Turkey), and the southwestern United States. Although it has been traditionally associated with low-income communities, it is evident today that with our sophisticated technology and innovative design, geospace (below-ground space) is a promising alternative for a diversity of urban as well as rural land uses complementary to the existing supraspace community.

4. *Colonies in Space Frontier.* This is a new concept that has proven to be technologically feasible. Yet, today it appears to be expensive: Despite the technology that makes it achievable, there are social, psychological, and logistical problems associated with such an endeavor.

5. *Agro-Urban Development Frontier.* The evolution of human settlements since the fourth millennium B.C. has basically produced two types of settlements: the rural one, functioning for agricultural production; and the urban one, consuming food from rural settlements and rendering services and industrial production and management. Today, it seems feasible and desirable to merge these two types into one settlement by designing an agro-urban settlement environment. Newly developed agricultural production is possible in a controlled environment without using soil and by replacing water with fertilized mist. With this innovative method and its sophisticated new technology, we could produce agriculture within the city where a single structure accommodates the functions of living and agricultural production. Such development can save land for recreation and simplify the logistics of transportation of agricultural products.

Another aspect of our cities affects the landscape of our environment. Since the industrial revolution of the nineteenth century, rapid urban growth has made urban design a complex endeavor. The increasing impact of diversified social, economic, and climatic forces has shaped the environment of the city. Moreover, in the technologically advanced countries, the global majority of the population will be dominantly urban for the foreseeable future. This accelerated dynamic change in the city is happening much faster than it has before and requires intelligent and active response to all facets of existing and future urban design and management.

*The urban design message of this book* is diverse and views the urban setting as complex, with increased necessity of environmental ethics for urban design. The first and most important message is that it is the socio-cultural values of past historical experience, rather than our technological achievements, that stand as the great lesson of environmental norms and needs that will guide us in establishing the ethics of future urban design.

Second, justifiably, social liberalism, human rights considerations, freedom of expression, and humanitarianism have
been, and will continue to be, on the increase globally. This
awareness needs to be expressed in the physical form and configuration of urban design. Thus, the aesthetic of physical form
has social value, and the environmental ethic of socio–physical nature should be the focal guideline of urban design. Such
a lesson was introduced to us by Chinese culture when they
designed their ancient cities and community space.

Third, the ethic of the professional interdisciplinary urban
design team is to be compatible with diversified environmental ethical needs. Thus, economic values need not overshadow
the social values of individuals and the community.

Fourth, professionally, urban design is no longer dominated
absolutely by one or two disciplines. It is a distinct profession
in its own right. Yet, it involves interdisciplinary team input
that requires the ethic of common language communication,
and has the vision and pragmatism to balance between aesthetics and function rather than to create urban design driven
by monumentalism.

In short, the message of our environmental ethic is:

- *Future City Design.* Past, present, and future should be
  considered as one continuum. The focus is the ultimate
  design of the city of the future using lessons drawn from
  the past.
- *Past Social Values and Contemporary Technological Practice.*
  Sophisticated technology should neither diminish nor
  eliminate the consideration of social values; nor should
  it ignore the forces that shape our environment and the
  reciprocal balanced relations (interinfluence) between
  social, economic, physical, and climatic forces. Thus,
  the mission of the modern urban design ethic is to provide an equilibrium amid the fusion of technology and
  social values.
- *Vision.* A visionary view of the future city is essential
  for the enhancement of the morals and ethics of the
  environment.

- *Future Urban Frontier.* It is necessary to surge forward toward a new frontier for urban design location with an innovative and unconventional approach.
- *Comprehensiveness.* Comprehensive treatment of urban design should be the basic norm of environmental ethics.

This book is an attempt to introduce some historical as well as contemporary examples of theses concepts and to provide a vision of a future urban environment in order to create a better understanding of the need to harmoniously integrate natural and human-made environments.

This world is the only source of our survival. It is our responsibility to enhance it and to improve the quality of its life.

# 1
## ETHICS OF ENVIRONMENTAL DESIGN

## BACKGROUND

Our generation continuously faces the challenge of rapid changes in society. These include increasingly sophisticated technology, changes in the standard of living, and an acceleration in the consumption of goods and space. Some of these are part of a natural process; others are the result of humanity's collective or individual activities. In short, everything surrounding us or inside us is in a constant state of change, and we are required to cope with it or ignore it. In any case, the impact of these changes on future generations has far-reaching implications for our physical and mental health and well-being.

Also, humanity's intrusion by changing the face of the earth and shaping the surrounding environment is constantly increasing. Although the understanding and the proper design of this intrusion has become the challenge of almost every professional, policy maker, and both natural and social scientists, the bulk of the design of the physical environment still rests on the shoulders of urban designers/planners and landscape architects.

# ENVIRONMENTAL DESIGN: WHAT IS IT?

In a generic way, and for the sake of early discussion, environmental design is the science of shaping the environment surrounding us for the benefit of humankind. God, as the Creator of this world, can be looked upon as an environmental designer. Man, as a dynamic intruder in this world, is also an environmental designer for better or worse.

Urban designers/planners, architects, and landscape architects need to conceive of environmental design as having two basic elements: the natural environment and the human-made environment.

## Natural Environment

The natural physical environment surrounding us is a synthesis shaped by the continuing process of dynamic interactions of the complex of interrelated forces made up of climate, soil, hydrology, flora, fauna, solar energy, tectonics, and others. It is the activities and magnitude of each of these forces that establish the equilibrium and harmony of the natural environment.

Among the components of the natural environment are the following basic elements (Figure 1.1):

1. Climate dynamics
2. Hydrological cycles
3. Tectonic forces
4. Soil evolution
5. Solar energy
6. Flora cycles
7. Fauna activities
8. Site character synthesis

Each of these forces is strong and dynamic in its own right. It is the *symphony* of all these forces that really forms the environment around us.

The natural environment is created by *dynamic*, not static, processes. As such, it is undergoing constant change. However, it is possible to outline some basic characteristic pat-

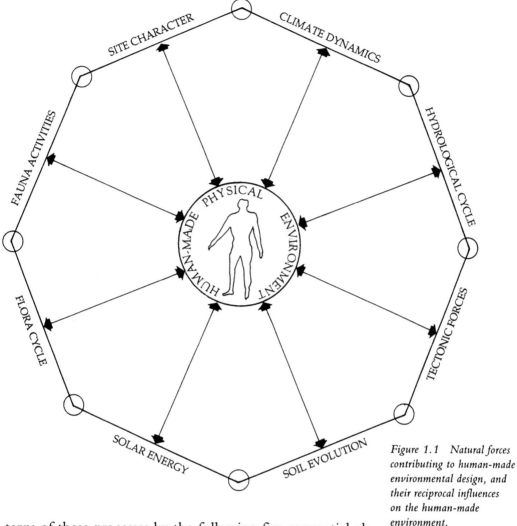

Figure 1.1 Natural forces contributing to human-made environmental design, and their reciprocal influences on the human-made environment.

terns of these processes by the following five sequential elements:

1. *Cycle.* In nature the process of change works in cyclic patterns—diurnal, seasonal, or other short- or long-term time periods. It is the understanding of science that all facets of this earth and the cosmos are under the jurisdiction of these patterns without exception (Figure 1.2).

2. *Interinfluence.* Within the dynamic processes and activities of various forces, there is a complicated multireciprocal pattern of influences.

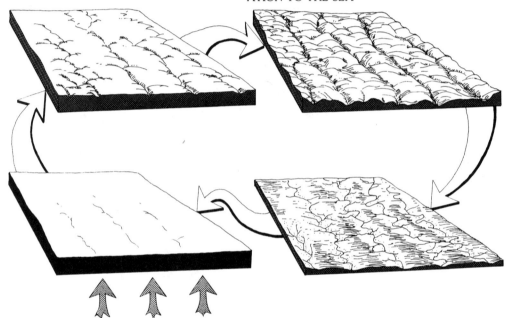

A. **YOUTH:** A PLATEAU AT ITS EARLY STAGES OF EROSION

B. **MATURITY:** INTENSIVE EROSION, EVOLUTION OF THE RIVER NETWORKS, AND LOWERING THE HIGHLAND THROUGH SOIL TRANSPORT-ATION TO THE SEA

D. **NEW EQUILIBRIUM:** NEW CYCLE ENFORCED BY ENDOGENOUS GEOLOGICAL FORCES TO ESTABLISH A NEW PLATEAU

C. **OLD AGE:** FULLY DEVELOPED MAJOR RIVERS ON THE FLATTENED PLATEAU

*Figure 1.2    Cyclical pattern of nature (plateau, soil, and river) throughout youth, maturity, and old age. (Adapted in part and reproduced from Finch, 1957, p. 247.)*

3. *Equilibrium.* Throughout the course of time and space, an equilibrium, or natural balance, is created within and among each of the contributing forces. (Figure 1.3)

4. *New Form.* Throughout the natural dynamic changes and with the intrusion of humanity's constructions, the existing natural balances are disturbed. After a given duration, usually a new form and equilibrium will be created among the forces of each contributing element. This new form can be considered a synthesis of all the contributing forces. In any case, the newly created form will never be the same as the previous one.

5. *Prediction and Control.* In most cases in natural processes, the pattern and output of the equilibrium can be predicted by new technology. Still, there are a few that are not fully predictable, such as seismic movements. It is in the realm of prediction and control—and consequently improvement—that the environmental designer's contribution becomes vital.

## Human-Made Environments

Humanity's intrusion into the natural environmental process is a product of historical and contemporary actions and creativity. Such activities are diverse and can occur both below and above ground, such as in the case of physical construction, agriculture, and social and economic impact. In any case, the synthetic physical environment is considered to be an intervention in the natural environmental process. Such human activities, when not designed properly, often have destructive results for both nature and humankind in that they exhaust vital resources.

Components of human-made environments, similar to those of the natural environment, are diverse as well as complicated. The following components are among the important ones (Figure 1.4):

1. Urban and rural construction
2. Technological growth
3. Economic dynamics
4. Socio-behavioral dynamics

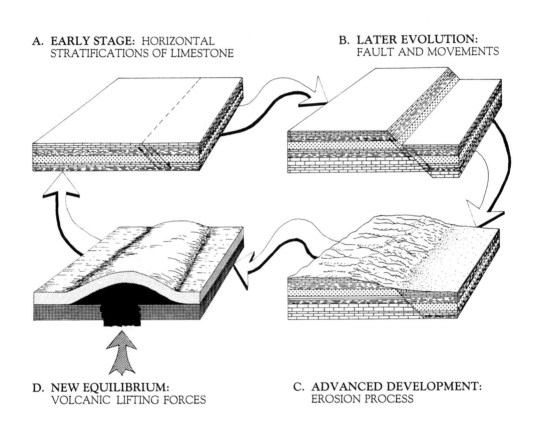

A. **EARLY STAGE:** HORIZONTAL
   STRATIFICATIONS OF LIMESTONE

B. **LATER EVOLUTION:**
   FAULT AND MOVEMENTS

D. **NEW EQUILIBRIUM:**
   VOLCANIC LIFTING FORCES

C. **ADVANCED DEVELOPMENT:**
   EROSION PROCESS

*Figure 1.3   Cyclical impact of a geological fault combined with hydraulic erosion in changing the landscape of the environment. (Adapted in part and reproduced from Finch, 1957, p. 220.)*

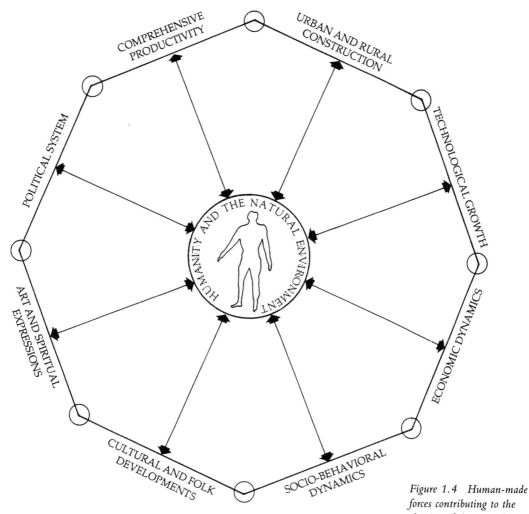

Figure 1.4  Human-made
forces contributing to the
shaping of the natural
environment and their
reciprocal influences.

5. Cultural and folk developments
6. Art and spiritual expressions
7. Political system
8. Comprehensive productivity

The characteristics of human-made environments differ
from those of the natural environment. Here are the basics of
these characteristics:

1. *Technology.* There have been rapid changes in and growth
   of human-controlled technology. The level of technol-

ogy has determined throughout history our ability or inability to change our natural environment. In the Paleolithic era, for example, people had almost no tools and were unable to change any of the natural landscape, while the environment certainly had an impact on them. On the other hand, contemporary technology and anticipated future developments have now enabled us to change our environment radically.

2. *Dynamics.* Rapid, contemporary changes and growth are often beyond our full comprehension and control. The increase and expansion of this growth is a double-sided dilemma that potentially threatens the democratic system. On one hand, growth and development need to take their natural courses. The development and usage of natural resources need increased control and coordination. Also, growth and development result in the intrusion of public institutions into individual privacy. Growth is expressed in the size and form of settlements, in natural population increases, in the consumption of natural resources, and in the compounding of all types of waste materials.

3. *Consumption and Disposal.* Increases in consumption (food, water, and manufactured goods) bring about increased transportation activities on local, regional, and international levels. The national and worldwide distribution of natural resources does not coincide with the distribution of the population. In most regions, humankind consumes more resources and products than are produced locally. The increase of liquid and solid waste disposal has a direct impact on both the human-made and natural environments, and necessitates constant and effective treatments.

4. *Limited Prediction.* In spite of a high level of technology and ingenuity, humanity has a limited ability to predict the precise impact of growth and development on the environment. This is due to a limited amount of information concerning the changes, the dynamics, and the frequency of the changes; a limited understanding of the forces involved and their magnitude; a limited de-

gree of international coordination; and the pressure of socioeconomic groups with different interests.

In summary, any changes in the natural and the human-made environments will directly affect human well-being. These changes and their impact are the concern of the environmental designer.

## Environmental Design

The theory of environmental design is a relatively new subject developed, especially in the United States, by departments of architecture, landscape architecture, urban design, or other related fields. Although it was called by such different names as *nature* or *subsistent resources*, or given religious holiness cover (trees, water, soil, or natural landmark), the environment was, and still is, a subject of concern for communities throughout history. The need for sensitivity to the natural environment was often mentioned in the Bible, which calls for perfect morality and ethics of conduct in regard to agriculture and nature. Today, this concern has become acute because of the rapid accelerated growth in all facets of life, especially in consumption and disposal. By its nature, environmental treatment is an interdisciplinary field requiring a team of experts that has the knowledge and understanding of the contributing forces that shape our physical, social, and economic environment.

Environmental design starts from the very small scale of housing units and ranges to the larger scale of cities and their regions. It is the systematically planned intervention of humankind to improve and enhance the environment through physical design for the optimum benefit of its users with a minimum amount of harm to the natural environment. Environmental design is concerned with achieving a balance between human-made physical creativity and the reciprocal influence of natural forces. Furthermore, the environmental design field is the study of the complex relationship within each of the two environments as well as between the two environments (Figure 1.5). Thus, environmental design is the art of establishing a synthesis between natural and human-

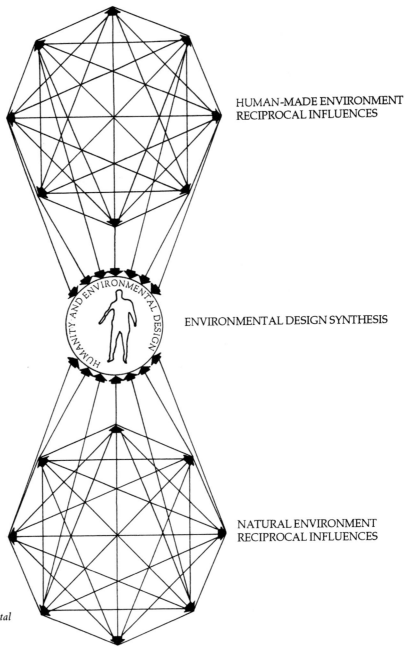

HUMAN-MADE ENVIRONMENT
RECIPROCAL INFLUENCES

ENVIRONMENTAL DESIGN SYNTHESIS

NATURAL ENVIRONMENT
RECIPROCAL INFLUENCES

*Figure 1.5  Environmental design synthesis as an outcome of the comprehensive complexity of reciprocal processes of both human-made and natural environmental forces and their contribution to environmental design.*

made environments. The designer's responsibility is to shape the newly combined environment. As such, environmental design is primarily a preventive method as well as a therapeutic one, and its strategy is intended to protect the health and well-being of the environment and the community. This differs from environmental protection, which is a legal system of rules and regulations established as a tool of governmental institutions for the protection primarily of air, water, and soil. The design team's responsibility is to avoid deterioration and to improve both environments for future generations.

## ORIENTAL AND WESTERN VIEWS OF THE ENVIRONMENT

Environmental concern is an ancient subject. We have reasons to believe that its early rise was associated with the rise of the early human settlements in the form of the village in Mesopotamia around the eighth millennium B.C., when humanity had the technology to shape the environment. Almost every ancient civilization adopted some natural environmental norms throughout its agricultural practice, and constrained humanity's conduct toward the consumption of the surrounding resources. Such conduct was introduced as religious norms, philosophy, and ethics in Judaism, Hinduism, Buddhism, as well as Shintoism (Figure 1.6).

More than any other ancient peoples, the Chinese, followed by the Japanese, have developed strong and distinct environmental ethics of human behavioral conduct constituted in norms and rules toward natural as well as human-made environments. These ethics were expressed in their landscape architecture (gardens), urban design, and architecture; however, it is necessary to comprehend the Sino-Japanese view of the environment versus that of Western practice.

Both the ancient Chinese and the Japanese view of the environment is distinctive and unique to their historical cultures. For the sake of discussion, it can be stated that this was often expressed through four major categories: (1) unity of

Figure 1.6 Isolation and deep contemplation of nature has been a strong ethic dominating ancient religions and their indigenous communities. Mid-air Buddhist Temple on Mount Hengshan, east of Datong city, north of China.

nature, humankind, and heaven; (2) humankind and nature; (3) humankind and heaven; and (4) aesthetics and beautification.

## Unity of Nature, Humankind, and Heaven

Ancient Chinese philosophers viewed the world as centered around three unified elements: nature, humankind, and heaven. Accordingly, there is a clear and confined pattern of relations between these three elements, which provides equilibrium and harmony. Humankind is expected to retain the purity of nature for ultimate survival, and should not influence and change the course of nature. On the other hand, the earth with its resources and cycles affects our well-being. Heaven is the provider of the life cycle, and it is the place where the worshipped ancestors are. Yet, heaven affects the earth as well as our life in a one-way relationship (Figure 1.7). Thus, nature, humankind, and heaven have a relationship that necessitates unity and therefore provides harmony. Accordingly, this pattern should not be disturbed.

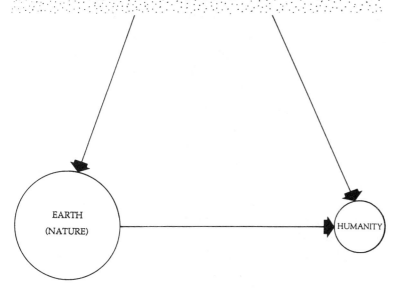

HEAVEN

(COSMOS, GODS, & RHYTHM OF CYCLES)

EARTH
(NATURE)

HUMANITY

*Figure 1.7 Simplified diagram of the ancient Chinese philosophical concept of the unity of heaven, earth, and humanity and their influential relationship. Note the uni-directional pattern.*

Throughout Chinese history, more than in other times and places, architecture, landscape architecture, and urban design have been the art of harmoniously integrating human-made forms with the natural environment. In the past, this was achieved through the historical evolutionary course of cultural symbolism, an attachment to and respect for the natural environment, a philosophy of the ideal behavior of the individual and society, and the elegant use of natural resources for construction.

The sense of nature was also widely expressed throughout Chinese history of urban design. For example, various human-made city objects, such as gates, streets, neighborhoods, and buildings, were identified with names relating to the natural environment and phenomena of the cosmos or the season.

(This is much less the case in Western society.) The Chinese were educated to see themselves as existing in relation to, and not separate from, the earth beneath their feet and the heaven above them.

*Humankind and Nature*

The Chinese view of the environment is unique and has a lengthy history. For the Chinese, the term *environment* is associated with the natural environment, morality and ethics, human behavior, and aesthetics. All of these elements are deeply rooted in the ancient Chinese philosophies of Daoism and Confucianism. The historical Chinese case points out that a society that is attached by proximity to the local natural resources required for its survival is subsequently sensitive to the well-being of its natural environment. Consequently, architecture and village and urban design became indigenous and therefore an integral part of the natural environment, evolving with it but not against it.

Traditional society adapts itself and its patterns of behavior to suit its natural environment, and therefore establishes an equilibrium between the two with minimal or nonexistent conflict. The Chinese view of what is now called *environmental design* was perceived through the norms and ethics of the unity of society and its various parts. Both form a balance (family, neighborhood, community) and exist in harmony with nature.

The Chinese have retained practical views on human-made and natural environments because of their appreciation of the interrelationship between the two. We achieve unity with nature when we recognize that harming even one part of our environment will affect the whole and consequently our survival.

Chinese society, like others that are similar, views humankind and nature as a unity of one system and believes that our survival depends on the survival of nature. This thematic concept evolved from the early stages of agricultural village development until the rise of contemporary metropolitan cities. More than in any other society, the Chinese view the dual unity and equilibrium as a philosophy and repeatedly expressed this in their mythology. The village is the settlement that is most attached to nature—it is the bedrock of the Chinese view of their environment. In Chinese history, the village is dominant and rooted in agricultural evolution and has lasted for many millennia.

*Humankind and Heaven*

The classical Chinese ideology of the environment considers nature, humankind, and heaven as an inseparable unity. Among these three distinct yet dynamic elements there exists a cycle of powerful interrelated forces, some of which are conceivable but not visible, that have a significant impact upon humankind and nature. Heaven is expressed in the form of many forces, including the cosmos, gods, and the cyclic rhythm of their dynamics. Although there is some similarity between the Chinese concept and other early civilizations, the Sino-Japanese philosophy of this subject remains distinct. In any case, its uniqueness has produced and supported a social order and environmental development that is deeply related to agriculture and to humankind's survival. The ancient Chinese pattern of urban design was linked with the idea of the cosmos, its nature, and the practice of agricultural rituals.

Most of the Chinese expressions in mythology, poems, storytelling, and painting were focused on enhancing and promoting natural and heavenly environments. It is this appreciation of beauty, purity, and perfection of the natural landscape that received greatest attention in the arts, and it was around this that their sense of spiritual inspiration and material needs revolved. All of nature's forms are viewed as being in harmony, and their function as offering a definite feeling of tranquillity and ease. Therefore, these conditions contribute to the social quality of life.

## Aesthetics and Beautification

Chinese aesthetics considered nature not only as a basic source of humankind's practical needs but also as a source of our spiritual and artistic inspiration. The Chinese intention was to preserve nature's purity. The adaptation of nature to humanity's needs for the purpose of survival should follow nature's rules rather than our disciplines. In this way, nature and humankind share an integrated coexistence with one another and are indivisible from the unity of the universe. Beautification in the Chinese tradition was expressed primarily, but not exclusively, through the use of nature's symbolism and in gardening. Some of the design distinctions of Chinese gardens include the following: (1) combining bodies of water with land; (2) a concentration on detail and miniaturization; (3) zigzagging pathways; (4) the use of landmark structures, such as pavilions; (5) locating scenic spots within overall garden design; (6) using gardens for multiple functions; (7) introducing variation into the natural scenery; and (8) the ability to stimulate and inspire.

In short, Chinese gardening envisions the natural environment as a source of inspiration and spiritual satisfaction. It provides identification with nature and with a tranquil, pleasant environment.

In conclusion, the Chinese view of the environment has always focused on the natural environment. The social environment, with all its complexities, along with the historical dominance of the Chinese rural environment, was properly adapted to the natural environment. In all Chinese philosophies, there is a cohesive interrelationship among the three basic elements of nature, humankind, and heaven. These philosophies all express the unity of these elements within the universe.

## Environment and Western Practice

Although at first the Western view of the environment as a whole appears to be similar to the Sino-Japanese, in reality contemporary Western practice conflicts with Sino-Japanese philosophy. With the immense scale of contemporary urban dominancy, urban humankind (which forms the majority of the Western world's population) has become detached from nature. Moreover, we in the West do not view nature as a source of our survival. To some extent, these two elements have led to a sense of alienation from nature. Often this is expressed in modern architecture and urban design when it is imposed on the environment. We have just begun to realize the urgent need for principles for developing human-made environments in line with nature's strengths and weaknesses, in order to avoid such catastrophic events as the earthquakes in Armenia and California and the drought in Somalia and Rwanda.

Comparing the pattern of the reciprocal relations between heaven, earth, and humankind of the Sino-Japanese philosophy with the Western pattern, we find conflicting views (Figure 1.8). Although we in the West would agree on the vitality of these three elements and their significance for our survival, we differ in practice on the reciprocal relations between the three elements. According to the indigenous Sino-Japanese philosophy, humankind should not change the face of the earth. Their message to us has been that environmental design and practice should work with nature, not against it. We in the West, with our sophisticated technology and intellec-

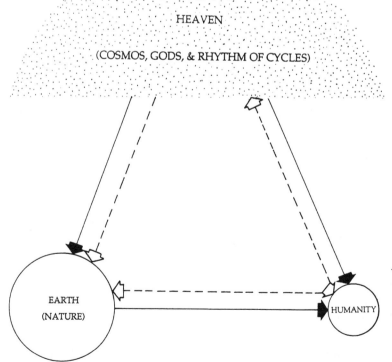

Figure 1.8 Comparison of the reciprocal pattern between the ancient Sino-Japanese environmental philosophy (solid line) and contemporary western practice (broken line). Note the western intrusion of humanity in the cosmos and in earth.

tual innovations, are changing our immediate environment rapidly and often with little, if any, sensitivity. Thus, our practice creates a strong reciprocal relationship between humankind and earth, rather than a one-way (earth-to-humankind) relationship as in the Sino-Japanese view. Similarly, we have interfered with the atmospheric environment and have begun to intrude into the cosmos. Here, too, we are establishing reciprocal relationships between humanity and heaven. Ultimately, changes will occur in the pattern of relationship between the cosmos and the earth. The dynamic growth of our urban and environmental design practice has often trapped us into working against nature (Figure 1.9). Unfortunately, it seems that the contemporary Sino-Japanese practice also has been trapped into coming closer to the contemporary Western practice.

However, environmental design methods can be the foundation for reaching a synthesis between forces and, consequently, establishing an environmental equilibrium by which humankind, earth, and the cosmos can live in harmony and unity.

### Questions for the Future

Finally, a few basic questions should be posed to our urban designers, philosophers, scientists, and policy makers.

1. Do we fully understand the forces that influence our physical and social environment, their reciprocal pattern, and their positive and negative impact on our future well-being?
2. If we understand these forces, are we well equipped with the knowledge and tools needed to control, divert, or improve upon them in order to suit our existing and future needs?
3. What avenues or methods should we pursue in order to design a better future for ourselves and the generations to come?
4. Since any newly created environment is complex and requires diverse expertise and knowledge, and since any new design will have some side effects, are we and our

*Figure 1.9 Example of design without environmental consideration in the Unites States. Two aerial photographs showing the same area in California within ten years. One is from 1956, showing the undeveloped land along the hazardous major San Andreas fault; the other is from 1966, when this same area was developed for housing. (Golany, 1976, p. 70–71.)*

students of urban design, landscape architecture, and architecture well trained and skilled enough to work as an interdisciplinary team in a coordinated urban and environmental design endeavor?

5. Urban environmental design requires the intellectual ability and training to be able to conceptualize a synthesis of diversified concepts brought together for the sake of such design. Have we developed a curriculum to enable future generations of designers to grasp this conceptualization and cope with such a challenge?

6. By which ethics and norms should we conduct our vision and philosophy in the development of future human settlements?

In conclusion, the role of the urban and environmental designer is becoming increasingly vital. It is unfortunate that modern architecture and urban design have, to a great extent, detached themselves from the past. Excuses are made for this new style of modern architecture on the basis of economics and cost benefits and because, in the less technologically advanced regions, it is an attempt to imitate Western styles. The new style is an expression of a change in self-image and in social and individual values. In any case, a balance between the values of the past and present will lead to the norms and ethics of future urban design.

The following chapters are a selection of what I consider successful examples for their time. The message of the past is for us to understand the forces involved in shaping the environment and to find the synthesis when we are designing and shaping the environment. The following chapters deal with the past, present, and future. I hope that this combination will help urban designers and architects in their venture into urban design.

# SELECTED READINGS

ETHICS

Attfield, Robin. *The Ethics of Environmental Concern*. 2nd ed. Athens, GA: University of Georgia Press, 1991.

Beatley, Timothy. *Ethical Land Use, Principles of Policy and Planning*. Baltimore: Johns Hopkins University Press, 1994.

Berry, R. J., ed. *Environmental Dilemmas, Ethics and Decisions*. 1st ed. London: Chapman & Hall, 1993.

Blatz, Charles V., ed. *Ethics and Agriculture: An Anthology on Current Issues in World Context*. Moscow, ID: University of Idaho Press, 1991.

Brown, Noel J. and Pierre Quiblier, eds. *Ethics & Agenda 21: Moral Implications of a Global Consensus*. New York: United Nations Environment Programme, 1994.

Callahan, Daniel and Phillip G. Clark, eds. *Ethical Issues of Population Aid, Culture, Economics, and International Assistance*. New York: Irvington Publishers, 1981.

Clark, John Maurice. *The Ethical Basis of Economic Freedom*. Westport, CT: C. K. Kazanjian Economics Foundation, 1955.

Cooper, Terry L. *An Ethic of Citizenship for Public Administration*. Englewood Cliffs, NJ: Prentice-Hall, 1991.

Coward, Harold and Thomas Hurka, eds.; essays by F. Kenneth Hare, et al. *Ethics & Climate Change, the Greenhouse Effect*. Waterloo, Canada: Published by Wilfrid Laurier University Press for the Calgary Institute for the Humanities, 1993.

Cua, Antonio S. *Ethical Argumentation: A Study in Hsun Tzu's Moral Epistemology*. Honolulu, HI: University of Hawaii Press, 1985.

Denton, Robert E., Jr., ed. *Ethical Dimensions of Political Communication*. New York: Praeger, 1991.

Dotto, Lydia. *Ethical Choices and Global Greenhouse Warming*. Waterloo, Canada: Published by Wilfrid Laurier University Press for the Calgary Institute for the Humanities, 1993.

Dower, N., ed. *Ethics and Environmental Responsibility*. Aldershot, England; Brookfield, VT: Avebury, 1989.

Engel, J. Ronald and Joan Gibb Engel, eds. *Ethics of Environment and Development, Global Challenge, International Response*. London: Belhaven Press, 1990.

Ericson, Edward L.; foreword by Isaac Asimov. *The Humanist Way: An Introduction to Ethical Humanist Religion*. New York: Continuum, 1988.

Ferre, Frederick and Peter Hartel, eds. *Ethics and Environmental Policy: Theory Meets Practice*. Athens, GA: University of Georgia Press, 1994.

Glover, Jonathan et al. *Ethics of New Reproductive Technologies: The Glover Report to the European Commission*. DeKalb, IL: Northern Illinois University Press, 1989.

Goodpaster, K. E. and K. M. Sayre, eds. *Ethics and Problems of the 21st Century*. Notre Dame, IN: University of Notre Dame Press, 1979.

Gunatilleke, Godfrey, Neelan Tiruchelvam, and Radhika Coomaraswamy, eds. *Ethical Dilemmas of Development in Asia*. Lexington, MA: Lexington Books, 1993.

Hart, Richard E., ed. *Ethics and the Environment*. Lanham, MD: University Press of America, 1992.

Kapp, Marshall B. *Ethical Aspects of Health Care for the Elderly: An Annotated Bibliography*. New York: Greenwood Press, 1992.

Lasswell, Harold D. and Harlan Cleveland, eds. *The Ethic of Power: The Interplay of Religion, Philosophy, and Politics*. New York: Distributed by Harper, 1962.

Lipson, Leslie. *The Ethical Crises of Civilization: Moral Meltdown or Advance?* Newbury Park, CA: Sage Publications, 1993.

Marcuse, Peter. *The Ethics of the Planning Profession: The Need for Role Differentiation*. Los Angeles, CA: School of Architecture and Urban Planning, University of California, 1974.

Natale, Samuel M. and John B. Wilson, gen. eds. *Central Issues in Moral and Ethical Education*. Lanham, MD: University Press of America, 1991.

Natale, Samuel M. and John B. Wilson, gen. eds. *The Ethical Contexts for Business Conflicts*. Lanham, MD: University Press of America, 1990.

Pearson, Karl. *The Ethic of Freethought and Other Addresses and Essays*. 2nd ed. (rev.). London: A. and C. Black, 1901.

Rescher, Nicholas. *Ethical Idealism: An Inquiry into the Nature and Function of Ideals*. Berkeley: University of California Press, 1987.

Rolston, Holmes, III. *Environmental Ethics: Duties to and Values in the Natural World*. Philadelphia: Temple University Press, 1988.

Thomas, Evan Edward. *The Ethical Basis of Reality*. London: Longmans, Green, 1927.

Wachs, Martin, ed. *Ethics in Planning*. New Brunswick, NJ: Center for Urban Policy Research, 1985.

Warner, Daniel. *An Ethic of Responsibility in International Relations*. Boulder, CO: L. Rienner, 1991.

ENVIRONMENT

*12th Annual Report of the Council on Environmental Quality*. Washington, D.C.: U.S. Library of Congress, 1981.

Aptekar, Lewis. *Environmental Disasters in Global Perspective.* New York: G. K. Hall, 1994.

Attfield, Robin. *Environmental Philosophy: Principles and Prospects.* Aldershot, England: Ashgate, 1994.

Bartelmus, Peter. *Environment, Growth, and Development: The Concepts and Strategies of Sustainability.* London; New York: Routledge, 1994.

Biosystems Technology Development Program, Office of Research and Development, U. S. Environmental Protection Agency. *Bioremediation of Hazardous Wastes.* Ada, OK: The Agency, 1992.

Caplan, Ruth and the staff of Environmental Action; Foreword by Pete Seeger. *Our Earth, Ourselves: The Action-oriented Guide to Help you Protect and Preserve our Planet.* New York: Bantam Books, 1990.

Carter, Vernon G. and Tom Dale. *Topsoil and Civilization.* Oklahoma City: University of Oklahoma Press, 1974.

Causey, Ann S. *Environmental Action Guide: Action for a Sustainable Future.* Redwood City, CA: Benjamin/Cummings, 1991.

Cooper, David E. and Joy A. Palmer, eds. *The Environment in Question: Ethics and Global Issues.* London; New York: Routledge, 1992.

Dunderdale, J., ed. *Energy and the Environment: Proceedings of a Symposium Organized Jointly by the Inorganic Chemicals Group and the Environment Group of the Industrial Division of the Royal Society of Chemistry,* University of Leeds, April 3-5, 1990. Cambridge, England: Royal Society of Chemistry, 1990.

Dutch Committee for Long-Term Environmental Policy, eds. *The Environment: Towards a Sustainable Future.* Dordrecht, Netherlands: Kluwer Academic Publishers, 1994.

*Environmental and Urban Issues,* 15/2 (Jan. 1988). Boca Raton, FL: FAU/FIU Joint Center for Environmental and Urban Problems, Florida Atlantic University, 1988.

*Environmental Geology and Water Sciences,* 6/1 (1984), 20/3 (Nov./Dec. 1992). New York: Springer-Verlag, 1984, 1992.

Finch, Vernor C., Glenn T. Trewartha, Arthur H. Robinson, and Edwin H. Hammond. *Elements of Geography Physical and Cultural.* New York: McGraw-Hill, 1957.

Fitch, James Marston. *American Building 2: The Environmental Forces That Shape It.* Boston: Houghton-Mifflin, 1972.

Gallopin, Gilberto C. *The Environmental Sustainability of Development and Technological Change in Latin America and the Caribbean.* Santiago, Chile: United Nations Economic Commission for Latin America and the Caribbean (ECLAC), 1990.

Glikson, Artur. *Regional Planning and Development: Six Lectures delivered at the Institute of Social Studies, The Hague, 1953.* Leiden, Netherlands: A. W. Sijthoff's Uitgeversmaatschappij N.V., 1955.

Golany, Gideon S. *New-Town Planning: Principles and Practice.* New York: Wiley, 1976.

Golany, Gideon S. *Environmental Design: A Selected Bibliography.* University Park, PA: The Pennsylvania State University, Dept. of Landscape Architecture, Dept. of Architecture, 1990.

Goodland, Robert et al., eds. *Environmentally Sustainable Economic Development: Building on Brundtland.* Paris: UNESCO, 1991 (1992 printing).

Hall, Ross Hume. *Health and the Global Environment*. Cambridge, England: Polity Press, in association with Basil Blackwell, 1990.

Herfindahl, Orris Clemens and Allen V. Kneese. *Quality of the Environment: An Economic Approach to Some Problems in Using Land, Water, and Air*. Baltimore: Johns Hopkins Press, 1965.

Holdsworth, William J. and Antony Sealey. *Healthy Buildings: A Design Primer for a Living Environment*. Harlow, England: Longman, 1992.

James, Valentine Udoh, ed. *Environmental and Economic Dilemmas of Developing Countries: Africa in the Twenty-first Century*. Westport, CT: Praeger, 1994.

Lake, John V., Gregory R. Bock, organizers, and Kate Ackril, eds. *Environmental Change and Human Health*. Chichester, England: Wiley, 1993.

Marsh, William M. *Environmental Analysis for Land Use and Site Planning*. New York: McGraw-Hill, 1978.

Mattson, Mark T. *Scholastic Environmental Atlas of the United States*. New York: Scholastic, 1993.

McHarg, Ian L. *Design with Nature*. Garden City, NY: Doubleday/Natural History Press, Doubleday, 1971.

McPherson, E. Gregory. "Economic Modeling for Large Scale Urban Tree Plantings." In *Proceedings of the ACEE 1990 Summer Study on Energy Efficiency in Buildings*, 4. Washington, D.C.: American Council for an Energy Efficient Economy, 1990.

McPherson, E. Gregory and Sharon Biedenbender. "The Cost of Shade: Cost-Effectiveness of Trees versus Bus Shelters." *Journal of Arboriculture* 17/9 (1991).

Michelson, William M. *Environmental Choice, Human Behavior, and Residential Satisfaction*. New York: Oxford University Press, 1977.

Millington, Andrew C. and Ken Pye, eds. *Environmental Change in Drylands: Biogeographical and Geomorphological Perspectives*. Chichester, England: Wiley, 1994.

Moeller, Dade W. *Environmental Health*. Cambridge, MA: Harvard University Press, 1992.

Mohan, I. *Environmental Awareness and Urban Development. A Global Study of Environmental Constraints, Pollution, City Planning, Wasteland Development, Social Forestry, Conserving Monuments, and Related Subjects*. New Delhi, India: Ashish Publishing House, 1988.

Montgomery, Carla W. *Environmental Geology*. 3rd ed. Dubuque, IA: William C. Brown, 1992.

Murphy, Raymond. *Rationality and Nature: A Sociological Inquiry into a Changing Relationship*. Boulder, CO: Westview Press, 1994.

National Task Force on Storage Tanks for the Canadian Council of Ministers of the Environment (CCME). *Environmental Code of Practice for Underground Storage Tank Systems Containing Petroleum Products and Allied Petroleum Products*. Ottawa, Canada, 1993.

O'Riordan, Timothy. *Environmentalism*. 2nd rev. ed. London: Pion, 1981.

Office for Official Publications of the European Communities. *Environment*. Belgium: 1992.

*Our Planet, Our Health, Report of the WHO Commission on Health and Environment*. Geneva, Switzerland: WHO, 1992.

Phelps, Matthew P. *Environmental Context Effects and Mental Reinstatement in Recognition Memory: A Global Activation Theory and Approach.* University Park, PA: The Pennsylvania State University, M. S. Thesis, 1993.

Rose, J., ed. *Environmental Health, the Impact of Pollutants.* New York: Gordon and Breach Science Publishers, 1990.

Rudofsky, Bernard. *Architecture Without Architects: A Short Introduction to Non-Pedigree Architecture.* New York: Doubleday, 1964.

Rudofsky, Bernard. *The Prodigious Builders. (Notes toward a natural history of architecture with special regard to those species that are traditionally neglected or downright ignored.)* New York: Harcourt Brace Jovanovich, 1977.

Saini, Balwant Singh. *Building Environment: An Illustrated Analysis of Problems in Hot Dry Lands.* London: Angus and Robertson, 1973.

Serageldin, Ismail and Andrew Steer, eds.; Alicia Hetzner, editorial consultant. *Valuing the Environment: Proceedings of the First Annual International Conference on Environmentally Sustainable Development Held at the World Bank,* Washington, D. C., September 30-October 1, 1993. Washington, DC: World Bank, 1994.

Silverstein, Michael. *The Environmental Factor: Its Impact on the Future of the World Economy and Your Investments.* Chicago: Longman Financial Services, 1990.

Smil, Vaclav. *Global Ecology; Environmental Change and Social Flexibility.* London: Routledge, 1993.

Stanley Foundation. *Environment and Development—Institutional Issues, Report of the Twenty-third United Nations Issues Conference,* sponsored by the Stanley Foundation, February 26-28, 1992. Muscatine, IA: The Foundation, 1992.

Sunkel, Osvaldo, et al. *The Environmental Dimension in Development Planning.* Santiago, Chile: United Nations Economic Commission for Latin America and the Caribbean, 1990.

United States Dept. of Energy. *Federal Environmental Inspections Handbook.* Washington, D.C.: U.S. Dept. of Energy, Office of Environmental Guidance, RCRA/CERCLA Division, 1991.

Veziroglu, T. Nejat, ed. *Societal Issues and Energy/Environment Economics.* New York: Nova Science Publishers, 1991.

Wehrli, Robert. *Environmental Design Research: How to do it and How to Apply it.* New York: Wiley, 1986.

Weinstein, Carol Simon and Thomas G. David, eds. *Spaces for Children: The Built Environment and Child Development.* New York: Plenum Press, 1987.

Weiss, Edith Brown, ed. *Environmental Change and International Law: New Challenges and Dimensions.* Tokyo: United Nations University Press, 1992.

Williams, Colin C. and Graham Haughton, eds. *Perspectives Towards Sustainable Environmental Development.* Aldershot, England: Avebury, 1994.

## SUSTAINABILITY

Angell, D. J. R., J. D. Comer, and M. L. N. Wilkinson, eds. *Sustaining Earth: Response to the Environmental Threat.* Hampshire, England: Macmillan, 1990.

Barbier, Edward B., ed. *Economics and Ecology: New Frontiers and Sustainable Development*. 1st ed. London; New York: Chapman & Hall, 1993.

Biswas, Asit K., Mohammed Jellali, Glenn E. Stout, eds. *Water for Sustainable Development in the Twenty-first Century*. Delhi, India: Oxford University Press, 1993.

Brown, Lester R. "Sustaining World Agriculture." In *State of the World 1987*, edited by Linda Starke. New York: W. W. Norton, 1987.

Brown, Lester R. et al., eds. *Saving the Planet: How to Shape an Environmentally Sustainable Economy*. New York: W. W. Norton, 1991.

Burrows, Brian C, Alan J. Mayne, and Paul Newbury. *Into the 21st Century: A Handbook for a Sustainable Future*. Twickenham, England: Adamantine Press, 1991.

Carley, Michael and Ian Christie. *Managing Sustainable Development*. Minneapolis: University of Minnesota Press, 1993.

Freyfogle, Eric T. *Justice and the Earth: Images for our Planetary Survival*. New York: Free Press; Toronto; Maxwell Macmillan Canada; New York: Maxwell Macmillan International, 1993.

Gupta, N. L. and R. K. Gurjar, eds. *Sustainable Development*. Jaipur, India: Rawat Publications, 1993.

Hailu, Zegeye and Artur Runge-Metzger. *Sustainability of Land Use Systems, the Potential of Indigenous Measures for the Maintenance of Soil Productivity in Sub-Sahara African Agriculture: A Review of Methodologies and Research Results*. Weikersheim, Germany: Verlag Josef Margraf Scientific Books, 1993.

Lyle, John Tillman. *Regenerative Design for Sustainable Development*. New York: Wiley, 1994.

Meadows, Donella H., Dennis L. Meadows, and Jorgen Randers. *Beyond the Limits, Confronting Global Collapse, Envisioning a Sustainable Future*. Post Mills, VT: Chelsea Green, 1992.

National Research Council (U.S.). Committee on Sustainable Agriculture and the Environment in the Humid Tropics. *Sustainable Agriculture and the Environment in the Humid Tropics*. Washington, DC: National Academy Press, 1993.

Nijkamp, Peter, ed. *Sustainability of Urban Systems: A Cross-national Evolutionary Analysis of Urban Innovation*. Aldershot, England: Gower Publishing, 1990.

Okigbo, Bede N. *Development of Sustainable Agricultural Production Systems in Africa*. Ibadan, Nigeria: International Institute for Tropical Agriculture, 1989.

Redclift, Michael and Colin Sage, eds. *Strategies for Sustainable Development: Local Agendas for the Southern Hemisphere*. Chichester, England: Wiley, 1994.

Reid, Walter V. et al. *Biodiversity Prospecting: Using Genetic Resources for Sustainable Development*. Washington, D. C.: World Resources Institute (WRI), 1993.

Sandlund, K. Hindar and A. H. D. Brown. *Conservation of Biodiversity for Sustainable Development*. Oslo, Norway: Scandinavian University Press, 1992.

Stren, Richard, Rodney White, and Joseph Whitney, eds. *Sustainable Cities: Urbanization and the Environment in International Perspective*. Boulder, CO: Westview Press, 1992.

*Sustainable Design: A Collaborative National Park Service Initiative*. Denver, CO: Dept of the Interior, National Park Service, 1992.

Thayer, Robert L., Jr. *Gray World, Green Heart: Technology, Nature, and the Sustainable Landscape*. New York: Wiley, 1994.

The World Conservation Union. *Caring for the Earth: A Stragegy for Sustainable Living*. Gland, Switzerland: IUN/UNEP/WWF, 1991.

Van der Ryn, Sim and Peter Calthorpe. *Sustainable Communities: A New Design Synthesis for Cities, Suburbs, and Towns*. San Francisco: Sierra Club, 1986.

Van Kooten, Gerrit Cornelis. *Land Resource Economics and Sustainable Development: Economic Policies and the Common Good*. Vancouver: University of British Columbia Press, 1993.

Van Lier, Hubert N. et al., eds. *Sustainable Land Use Planning: Proceedings of an International Workshop*, September 2-4, 1992, Wageningen, Netherlands: Elsevier, 1994.

Walter, Bob, Lois Arkin, and Richard Crenshaw, eds. *Sustainable Cities: Concepts and Strategies for Eco-city Development*. Los Angeles: EHM Eco-Home Media, 1992.

ECOLOGY

Archibugi, F. and Nijkamp. P., eds. *Economy and Ecology: Towards Sustainable Development*. Dordrecht, Netherlands: Kluwer Academic Publishers, 1989.

Bailey, Ronald. *Eco-scam, the False Prophets of Ecological Apocalypse*. 1st ed. New York: St. Martin's Press, 1993.

Bramwell, Anna. *Ecology in the 20th Century: A History*. New Haven, CT: Yale University Press, 1989; Council for an Energy Efficient Economy, 1990.

Gilbert, O. L. *The Ecology of Urban Habitats*. London: Chapman and Hall, 1989.

Gliessman, S. R., ed. *Agroecology: Researching the Ecological Basis for Sustainable Agriculture*. New York: Springer-Verlag, 1990.

Gore, Albert. *Earth in the Balance: Ecology and the Human Spirit*. New York: Houghton-Mifflin, 1992.

Lyle, John Tillman. *Design for Human Ecosystems*. New York: Van Nostrand Reinhold, 1985.

McLarney, William D. "Aquaculture: Toward an Ecological Approach." In *Radical Agriculture*, edited by Richard Merrill. New York: Harper & Row, 1976.

McPherson, E. Gregory. "Economic Modeling for Large Scale Urban Tree Plantings." In *Proceedings of the ACEE 1990 Summer Study on Energy Efficiency in Buildings*, 4. Washington, D.C.: American Council for an Energy Efficient Complete Economy, 1990.

Sallares, Robert. *The Ecology of the Ancient Greek World*. London: Duckworth, 1991.

Stearns, Forest, and Tom Montag, eds. *The Urban Ecosystem: A Holistic Approach*. Stroudsburg, PA: Dowden, Hutchinson & Ross, 1974.

Walter, Bob, Lois Arkin, and Richard Crenshaw, eds. *Concepts and Strategies for Eco-City Development*. Los Angeles: Eco-Home Media, 1992.

Waste, Robert J. *The Ecology of City Policymaking*. New York: Oxford University Press, 1989.

OTHER

Bateson, Gregory. *Mind and Nature*. New York: E. P. Dutton, 1979.

Commoner, Barry. *Making Peace with the Planet*. New York: Pantheon Books, 1990.

Corn, Morton, ed. *Handbook of Hazardous Materials*. San Diego: Academic Press, 1993.

Ellsaesser, Hugh W., ed. *Global 2000 Revisited: Mankind's Impact on Spaceship Earth*. New York: Paragon House, 1991.

Hansen, Niles, Benjamin Higgins, and Donald J. Savoie. *Regional Policy in a Changing World*. New York: Plenum Press, 1990.

Lovelock, James. *The Ages of Gaia: A Biography of our Living Earth*. New York: W. W. Norton, 1988.

Lynch, Kevin. *Site Planning*. Cambridge, MA: MIT Press, 1969.

Mollison, Bill. *Permaculture: A Designers' Manual*. Tyalgum, Australia: Tagari Publications, 1988.

Mumford, Lewis. *The City in History: Its Origins, Its Transformations, and Its Prospects*. New York: Harcourt, Brace and World, 1961.

# PART ONE

## LESSONS FROM THE INDIGENOUS PAST

The study of the origin of human settlements and their evolution from one form to another helps us to understand our present cities and to envision our future ones. Thus, the study of the past is needed for the benefit of the future.

From the beginning, the physical evolution of human settlements has been the byproduct of the social order. Throughout history, it was the community's social identity and its ethics that shaped, along with the natural environment, the urban form and configuration. Thus, the social setting came first and later determined the function and the form of the settlements. This process was guided by society's ability to adapt the physical form of the settlement to the natural environment and its constraints. Human beings have steadily designed their indigenous habitats and environment to work with nature and not against it, with the understanding that both life and nature have compatible cycles and need to be in harmony and not in conflict. Also, people recognized that the natural environment is a source for physical survival and mental inspiration, and consequently, it became vital to live in harmony with it.

Humankind's early communal setting was a byproduct of community and public needs. Community cohesiveness needed harmony and the collaboration of individual members and groups for the sake of enhancing continuity, safety, and social order. Adoption of inherited, yet unwritten, social values and norms for individuals and the community provided assurance, security, self-confidence, social identity, and positive community responsiveness. These ethics of social values, dealing with the code of what is good and what is bad, were reflected in people's response to the environment and further expressed through the evolution of the human-made physical environment, which included streets, public open spaces, houses, and the overall city configurations.

This section discusses the genesis of the city and the sociophysical evolution of the pre-city era. Then, the discussion moves to the evolution of the village and the integration of the social environment into a new physical framework of diversified types of villages. It was here with the rise and the evolution of the village that the wisdom of individuals and the community evolved and was shaped into the standards and norms of environmental ethics. Nature fulfilled the promise and expectation of the community as an integral part of pastural and agricultural production, handicrafts and symbolism, and cultural activities. During this period, people did not have the technology to change nature and so lived in harmony with it, with minor changes.

The "urban revolution," which was introduced later, was an innovative setting primarily for nonagricultural practices, such as trade and management, and for political and cultural centers and spiritual monuments. The development of more advanced technology was the beginning of humanity's influence on the natural environment, and therefore, the start of environmental changes. Still, there was much harmony left between humanity and the environment until the nineteenth century, when the impact of technology began to threaten the environment.

Four early distinct urban civilizations—Mesopotamia, Indus Valley, Northern China, and Egypt—are valuable examples of the earliest urban evolution in the ancient world. A common denominator among these four urban civilizations was their location in a hot-dry climate. Still, the rise of these four civilizations was an example of successful adaptation to the environment. Here, too, each of the four urban civilizations developed its own environmental ethic. These four hydraulic urban civilizations based their survival on the ethic of strict water management regulations, on an efficient irrigation system, on the creation of new land suitable for agriculture from the dry, salty desert land, on an intensive and extensive agricultural system, and last, but not least, on social ethics of combined rules and values used to maintain the collaborative system of agricultural production.

Finally, ancient urban civilizations offer primarily lessons of the dominancy of social ethics without sophisticated technology along with a deep sense of environmental ethics. In comparison, our contemporary urban environment offers the dominancy of technology, to which we are submissive, with very little in the way of social ethics.

**2**

# GENESIS OF THE CITY

## PRESETTLEMENTS

Very little is known about how humankind lived before archaeological evidence or written records became available. We can only speculate that people formed small social groups and that these groups were scattered and isolated. Climate and environment influenced their diet, tools, dress, dwellings, and social traditions. There were, of course, linguistic differences and a variety of cultural responses to geographical and other stimuli.

The natural resources of a given region are the basis of humanity's subsistence and survival. Settlements arose within each region as a result of these resources and a variety of elements that developed throughout the time, such as tools and their technology. The earliest civilizations developed in the great alluvial valleys of the Near East. While there is some evidence that the early Egyptian civilization was stimulated by Mesopotamian influences, the rising civilizations in these two areas were essentially independent of each other and developed more or less during the same period. A third civilization began in the valley of the Indus River, and a fourth appeared in northern China in the Wei River Valley.

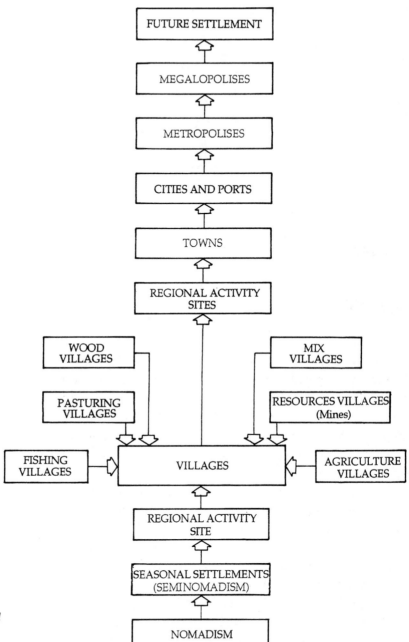

*Figure 2.1 Sequential evolution of human settlements in history.*

The evolution of settlements has been a sequential process: nomadism, seminomadism with seasonal settlements, villages of different types, regional activity sites, towns, cities and ports, metropolises, and megalopolises (Figure 2.1). This process is revealed throughout the archeological records of each human civilization from the Mesopotamian era to our own. The duration, emphasis, and magnitude of each phase differs from one civilization to the next. For example, Mesopotamian cities developed after only a short period of town evolution, while in China, town evolution developed over a longer period before cities came into existence. Moreover, in different cultures each phase matures in different eras. Throughout history, advanced degrees of urbanization have existed and still exist simultaneously with Paleolithic nomadism.

## NOMADISM

Nomadism is associated with the Paleolithic period (Stone Age) and featured food gathering and hunting. There were different degrees of nomadism during Paleolithic times, ranging from small, primitive groups in the early Paleolithic era to more advanced animal domesticating, pasturing societies in the late Paleolithic and early Neolithic eras. We can assume that the classical Paleolithic wandering pattern within a valley unit was focused around four major sites: water (the river), hunting sites (slopes and along the river), food gathering, and shelter (caves) (Figure 2.2). People performed their hunting and food gathering as a community group. Hunting usually took place near the valley's river where the animals watered. The caves selected for shelter were usually located on the slope of the valley overlooking the lowland. The advanced Paleolithic life pattern, after animals were domesticated, led to a wandering cycle where the valley became the center. The sites in this wandering cycle included water resources, hunting pasturing area, and shelter (Figure 2.3).

Nomadism is the oldest presettlement form of socio-economic and societal management. It evolved through a collective search for survival by the small family unit, the extended

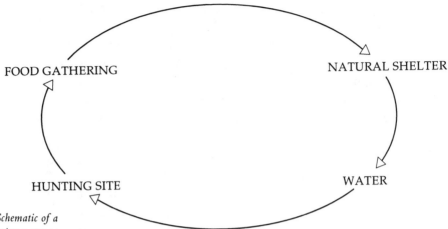

FOOD GATHERING

NATURAL SHELTER

HUNTING SITE

WATER

*Figure 2.2 Schematic of a classical wandering pattern during the early Paleolithic era.*

family frame, and the subtribal and tribal blood-related community. Throughout the ages, nomadism had some distinct characteristics that would later come to influence settlement patterns and land use.

The first of these characteristic patterns was the communal way of life as an economic order. With the absence of personal and community property, the focus of the economy was on daily survival. Many of the tasks of daily life in the tribal society, such as preparation for hunting (making tools and traps, etc.), hunting, fire, and food preparation for meals, naturally led to collective efforts and sharing. Similarly, the early

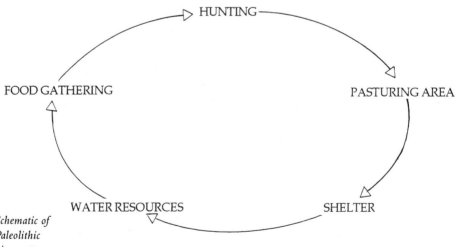

HUNTING

FOOD GATHERING

PASTURING AREA

WATER RESOURCES

SHELTER

*Figure 2.3 Schematic of the advanced Paleolithic cyclical wandering pattern.*

formation of villages by nomads required collective effort for the development of agriculture. Thus, this collective-communal system was strongly reinforced in both nomadism and later in the evolution of the village.

The second characteristic pattern of nomadism was tribal loyalty. History has shown that of all loyalties, the strongest and longest lasting is that among blood relations. These kinship bonds are stronger than economic, religious, or political ties. An enlightening example of such tribal loyalty is the case of the twelve tribes of Israel described in the Old Testament. Most notable is the durability and duration of this loyalty. It was in evidence from the tribes' inception as the sons of Jacob, throughout the four hundred years of Egyptian slavery, the forty years of desert wanderings under Moses' leadership, the settlement process in Canaan under the leadership of Joshua, the judges and the kings, and even later when they were taken by Nebuchadnezzar to Babylonian exile or by the Romans to the Diaspora. The tribes' loyalty to blood ties was extremely dominant and became a tool for social order and management. A second, more contemporary example is the loyalty pattern that exists among Arabian tribal societies in the Saudi Arabian Peninsula, the Syrian Desert of the Fertile Crescent, and in North Africa. Later village settlement patterns were shaped by the homogeneity of the tribe that was enforced by the territoriality of the neighborhood. This pattern of settlement has continued to take place in many cases into modern times (Figure 2.4).

The third dominant characteristic of the nomads was their socio-political system. Tribal societies developed territories and cultural identities through nomadism. Because of these bonds, tribal society evolved its culture with a sophisticated socio-political system of strict, unwritten, yet commonly agreed upon rules, regulations, and norms used as guidelines for individual and community behavior and ethics. This established a unified context for an identifiable self-image, as well as a source of pride and pedigree.

Thus, three forces merged together—the economic, the social, and the political—to ensure the survival of this unity. The evolution from nomadism to seminomadism was encour-

1

2

7    3

8    4

11   9    5

12   10   6

0  100  200  300  400  500M

*Figure 2.4 Tayiba*
*Indigenous Village, Israel,*
*in 1960. Tribal society and*
*spatial territoriality overlap*
*to establish a strong*
*identity. Each pattern*
*represents a tribe. (G.*
*Golany, 1976, p. 185.)*

aged by the discovery of agriculture and its possible storage, which led gradually to semipermanent settlements and later to permanent settlements.

## SEMINOMADISM

The evolution to seminomadism took place during the transition period from the end of the Paleolithic to the beginning of the Neolithic era. Nomadism, in its advanced stage in the late Paleolithic era, relied on three sites in the wandering cycle: the source of water, the source of forage for animals, and shelter. Seminomadism, which is the combination of nomadism and some forms of settlement, developed additional sites, including agricultural production, storage, and marketing sites, all of them related to definite locations (Figure 2.5).

The domestication of animals not only provided a source of energy to augment existing human power, it also required humans to care for, feed, and shelter the animals. The need to feed them resulted in the development of pasturing and the selection of suitable pasturing sites that were included in the wandering cycle. Shelter and protection against attacks by wild beasts were provided by caves or circular stone enclosures. The domestication of animals, the need to feed them, and the innovation of agriculture, then, encouraged the foundation of seasonal settlements, which later led to the creation of permanent settlements.

The seasonal cycle of seminomadism is related to the development of semisettlements. There are two known settlements of this type. One is exclusively used for food storage, and the other is used for one season's living. Examples of seminomadic food–storage seasonal settlements are in evidence in the North African countries bordering the Sahara region. Today, excellent examples of food storage settlements can still be found in southern Tunisia nearby and on the Matmata plateau. These settlements are called *ksars*. My field survey in

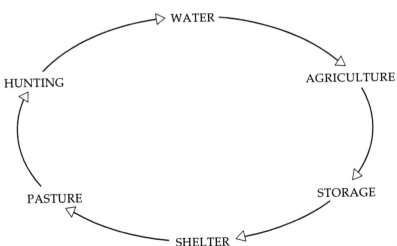

*Figure 2.5 Schematic concept of seminomadic cyclical wandering pattern.*

this area located more than one hundred ksars majestically situated on the plateau or its cliffs and on the narrow lowland strip between the plateau and the sea. Ksars consist of buildings constructed by the tribe for the sole purpose of communal food storage and typically became landmarks within the area of the nomads' wandering pattern. Ksars are made up of individual rooms called *ghorfas*, which are built on several levels and have only one door and no windows (Figure 2.6). The entrances of the ghorfas face onto a central courtyard that has only one gate for access, thereby allowing for protection and defense. The visit to the ksar by the nomadic tribe was part of the wandering cycle pattern that took place before or after the pasturing stage. Since the tribe was in control of its own region, they would leave only one person behind to guard the ksar. Today, many of these ksars are either abandoned or used as tourist attractions and shops.

Seminomadic seasonal settlements have been found in the Ukraine, Kurdistan, northern Mesopotamia, and Persia. The settlements were usually a collection of small conical huts built

*Figure 2.6 Site used exclusively for food storage by nomadic tribes. Front view of Ksar Medenine, Southern Tunisia. Each room is an independent unit and belongs to one family. It can be entered only from the courtyard since there are no doors on the other side. (Golany, 1988, p. 42.)*

on low circular stone walls. Some of the earliest seasonal settlements were in Mesopotamia, located at the upper part of the Tigris and Euphrates rivers in a hilly-to-mountainous region. Dated at approximately 9000 B.C., they are considered to be settlements that were used seasonally to house domesticated animals and to store food from a nearby cultivated area. The most commonly known of these settlements is Jarmo, dated at 7000 B.C., in the Iraqi Kurdistan of today. The settlement is a village consisting of around twenty rectangular huts with several rooms each, and probably housed a population of at least 150 people. Another such settlement is Sarab, near Kermanshah in what is now Iran, and it suggests the seasonal encampments of herdsmen. Two other well-known villages are Hassuna and Tell Halaf, which date back to the fourth millennium B.C. and are located in the northern part of Mesopotamia.

Evidence still remains today of the transition process from nomadism to seminomadism in the Middle East and North Africa where nomad society territories border on settled farming societies. Although the two societies coexist, the fact that these are usually two distinct economic, social, and political settings can occasionally lead to conflict. At the end of the Paleolithic era, such interaction did not exist because the nomad society was the only one that dominated the region.

The regional activity site was the next logical step in the sequence after the development of seasonal villages and the discovery of the system of agriculture.

## REGIONAL ACTIVITY SITE

Seminomadism, with its pattern of seasonal villages, was the first way of living to stimulate the need for a year-round permanent settlement, but such development was a slow evolution. A regional activity site provided the bridge between seasonal and permanent settlements. This site developed because the economy of the seminomadic tribes was a combination of a self-sufficient economy, inherited from the purely nomadic society, and an open one that related to the market of others. The need to market its wool, milk, cheese, and meat, or conduct religious or other ceremonial events to others, required the seminomadic tribes to develop activity sites. Definite and frequent meetings led to the evolution of a site within the region that was convenient to all of the seminomadic population of the area and met their needs. Throughout the course of time, such a site became more than a trade center. It may have been used as a site for assembly or religious ritual, for cultural festival performance, with songs, dance, display of handicrafts, and races, or for any other celebration.

Similar to this previllage regional activity center, there developed later a further-advanced postvillage site as a "regional growth center" to serve the villages for similar purposes. This postvillage site became the link between the villages and the rise of the town type of human settlement.

In most cases, the site of the regional activity center would have some landmarks for identification, such as a well, an old or sacred tree, flat topography, a distinctive land form, shade or protection, or other distinct physical characteristics. The use of such sites throughout history along with the rise of services provided may have led to the development of a semipermanent or permanent form of settlement.

## RISE OF THE VILLAGE

Most archeologists, researchers, and scholars assume Mesopotamia to be the cradle of civilization that gave rise to the village and later to the city. The rise of the village is recorded as having occurred around the time of the eighth millennium B.C. Mesopotamia is an arid region in its southern lowlands and a semiarid region in its hilly north. Many civilizations, with the agricultural village as their foundation, survived and flourished in this region. Village and urban development took place along the courses of the Tigris and Euphrates rivers in the south, as well as in the hills and mountains of the north. This analysis of the rise of the village is based not only on the example of Mesopotamia, but also on many other regions of the world. Village farming communities existed in the Indus Valley as early as 3000 B.C., if not earlier. Some degree of contact between the cities of the Indus and those of Mesopotamia is assumed to have existed.

The major element that brought about the rise of the village was agriculture. The discovery of agriculture introduced a rich, new way of life. The development of agriculture required the consideration of many short- and long-range plans that consume the basic resources of suitable soil and water for agricultural production and required permanent attachment to a particular site. This form of human settlement contrasts with nomadism and seminomadism, which did not necessitate permanent locations. With the rise of the village, we count the beginning of the Neolithic era. In fact, this was the "village revolution."

A few of the elements necessary for the development of agriculture are knowledge, suitable soil, water resources, technology, and community collaboration. In indigenous society, knowledge is gained by daily experience and, most importantly, by observing the environment. Through contemplating nature, people observed the cycles of nature and the cosmos and learned that the cycles were repeated diurnally, seasonally, or annually. The discovery of the cycle in natural crops as related to climatic changes, water resources, soil quality, and the existence of seeds led humans to try to imitate nature and learn about seed selection and the pattern of the cycle, which led to the development of agriculture.

Contrary to hunting and pasturing, agriculture required a long planning process. The basic stages for agriculture include: cultivating, fertilizing, seeding, irrigating, guarding, harvesting, storing, marketing, and consumption (Figure 2.7). Most of these stages are site-related and anchored people to a specific place. The planning, however, is especially cyclical when irrigation is not involved, because it requires a knowledge of seasonal and weather cycles.

River valleys were the most logical places for irrigated agricultural villages to evolve. Suitable soil is usually located along rivers and often contains alluvial deposits from them.

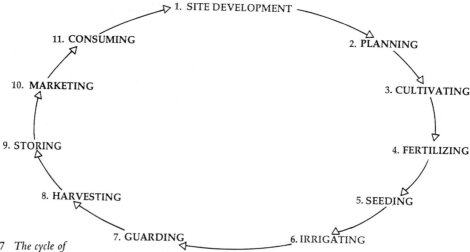

1. SITE DEVELOPMENT

11. CONSUMING

2. PLANNING

10. MARKETING

3. CULTIVATING

9. STORING

4. FERTILIZING

8. HARVESTING

5. SEEDING

7. GUARDING

6. IRRIGATING

*Figure 2.7 The cycle of agricultural production in arid and semiarid climates, which led to the village revolution.*

Although rainfall provided some water, the rivers were the primary secure water resource for the development of agriculture. Since most early rural civilizations developed in dry and semidry climates along major rivers, humans were challenged to develop irrigation systems for agriculture.

Tools for this technology were limited at this stage to primarily wood and bronze and were used predominantly for cultivation and harvesting. The practice of agriculture was deeply affected by the limited technology of the time. The collective system of labor was an attempt to overcome this limitation. The foundation for community collaboration already existed through tribal kinship relationships and its communal way of life. Collaboration was essential, especially for an irrigation and harvesting time table, which permitted the development of water control.

The development of agriculture is the first time in the history of humankind that an attempt was made to influence the natural landscape. It led to the recognition of the necessity to preserve soil, water, and other natural resources. However, people's impact, if any, was very minimal for two major reasons. First was the limited degree of technology. Second was the need to protect the basis for agricultural production by preventing harm to the natural balance of the environment on which the survival of the community relied. It is here at this stage of village evolution where collective norms of environment have evolved. It is in this era where already well-established social ethics merged with the new system of collective agricultural labor management's unwritten code of ethics to form the new ethics of environmental preservation.

The creation of the village was a result of humankind's growing maturity. Sociologically, people needed social closeness and security. The village also provided a place for worship and in some cases an altar was built first and later the village grew up around it. Here, too, the village provided a place for assembly, ceremonial gatherings, and celebrations. Economically, the village strengthened a sense of mutual responsibility, a spirit of cooperation, and an appreciation of common interests. Politically, tribal leadership was strengthened through the village's new collective labor experience and afterward led to regional systems of administration.

In any case, the existence of tribal social balance, the creation of a new economic system of communal agriculture, and the recognition of the need to maintain the natural equilibrium was integrated. These three interrelated forces touch upon all facets of life and, therefore, supported the rise of the early village (Figure 2.8). Collective effort and mutual responsibility for the new economic system of agriculture strengthened the communal life-style of the community. Land, water, forests, and other natural resources in the surrounding area became communal property and were maintained as such. The need to preserve the natural balance of the environment and to exist in harmony with it became a collective responsibility. All in all, the productivity of the village community increased and became more efficient than that of the nomad community. Population density during this period also increased. During this period, a few types of villages evolved.

*Fishing villages* were located near rivers or lakes within the valley. Obviously, this type of village was located in the lowlands and shelters were constructed mostly of natural woods. Since occupancy of this type of village was not dictated by seasonal planning, we can assume that the fishing village was the earliest type of village to develop in the Neolithic era. Although there were some villages that were exclusively fish-

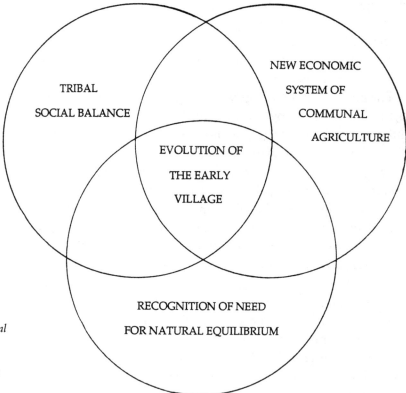

TRIBAL
SOCIAL BALANCE

NEW ECONOMIC
SYSTEM OF
COMMUNAL
AGRICULTURE

EVOLUTION OF
THE EARLY
VILLAGE

RECOGNITION OF NEED
FOR NATURAL EQUILIBRIUM

*Figure 2.8 Conceptual framework for the integration of forces supporting early village evolution.*

ing villages, there could have been others that were developing agriculture simultaneously.

*Agricultural villages* consumed planning and technologically developed tools, were more advanced than fishing villages, and may have been located near a river, in the foothills, on the slope, or in any other part of the valley. The factors that determined site selection were proximity to local/regional resources consumed by the villagers, such as suitable soil and water resources, and protection, drainage, accessibility, and comfort.

*Mining villages* were developed especially in the mountains. The Neolithic era was characterized by the discovery and mining of copper and tin, which contributed to the advancement of technology. During this early period, there may also have been villages that evolved exclusively for the purposes of timber harvesting or hunting.

# REGIONAL GROWTH CENTERS

As the villages of the valley became productive and more mature, regional centers for their common activities evolved. Unlike the regional activity site, which was considered temporary and used occasionally for trading and other cultural activities, the regional growth center became a permanent site that may have evolved from the regional activity site as well as from an existing village or from a new site. However, the impetus for its development was economic needs and the need for transportation, and was the result of the development of the villages of the region. During the early stage, the village was devoted to reinforcing its self-sufficient and self-contained economy and to improving its agricultural production. Later, each of the villages became specialized in agriculture and handicrafts and produced a complementary variety of products. With the development of a surplus, the need for trade arose and led to the beginnings of a regional self-sufficient economy and the regional growth center.

The site of the regional growth center was usually selected because it was geographically central, easily accessible, and comfortable. The site provided adequate space for marketing, for ceremonial events, for assembly, for worshipping, and for other commonly performed regional activities. Such a site gradually accommodated structures for daily needs, especially once marketing moved from a seasonal activity, one day per week, to a continuous daily activity. In many cases, this regional growth center was near the river or a major road where active transportation took place. The center grew up to the size of the village and beyond. Although the main function of its inhabitants was nonagricultural, the center also participated in some agricultural production.

# RISE OF THE TOWN

The original impetus for the settlement of villages was the development of agriculture. The discovery of how to preserve and store food for long periods of time plus improved transportation served as the catalysts for the rise of the town.

Towns as a new type of permanent human settlement began to evolve around the regional growth centers where villagers met regularly to market their surplus goods. Food preservation, which typically was accomplished by dehydrating, salting, smoking, and pickling, and food storage, most often in below-ground spaces, allowed people to move farther away from the site of agricultural production. Therefore, people moved to the trade sites to seek economic opportunities and adventures.

The town served for trade and for the economic needs of the region, facilitated administrative management, and became a center for the arts and political activities. However, in moving to the town, individuals lost the social unity the village was based on.

## RISE OF THE CITY

The evolution of the valley as an economic autarchy brought with it the development of a hierarchy of settlements. The towns within the region developed to different degrees of maturity. This may have resulted from the abundance of their surrounding local resources, the nature of their sites, or the activities of their local people. One or a few of these towns presumably then emerged as large communities and became cities, providing primarily nonagricultural activities.

The earliest cities were established during the fourth millennium B.C. in Mesopotamia. Progress was rapid and by the beginning of the third millennium B.C. urban centers were characterized by improved technology, particularly in the use of metals such as bronze and iron. The city was an independent, manageable unit made up of individuals who moved there from their villages seeking economic and other types of opportunities.

While every civilization's urbanization was caused by different forces of varied magnitude, early cities typically were centers for trade, transportation, and religious, political, and administrative activities, and provided defense for the surrounding villages. The city served the entire valley region, which included villages and towns, and not just consumers in its immediate region as had been the case with towns.

The traditional city, with few exceptions, was small in size. The city was compact and its population density was high since the average urban population was around twenty thousand or less. The basic design principle in ancient urban cities was to put a maximum number of people on a minimum size of land for purposes of defense and as a means to save surrounding agricultural land. Only in recent centuries have cities increased dramatically in size. The main reason for this growth has been improved transportation and a national economy.

With the development of the early city, the social center of gravity moved to the city. The city population, often energetic and enterprising, played a dominant role in the region while the rural population became subservient. The relationship of the village to the city was quite different from its relationship to other rural communities. Among the villages there had always been social and economic interaction. Intermarriage was common, as was the exchange of goods in village markets. With the advent of the city, regional activities shifted from among the villages to primarily between the villages and the city.

Urban centers introduced patterns of social and economic stratification different from those of the village. Villagers shared interests, resources, and responsibilities, and usually belonged to the same tribe or class and lived as equals. In the city, on the other hand, there was little sense of kinship, and few close relationships outside the family unit. While the village was essentially a classless society, the emerging urban centers developed separate population groups and were associated with the rise of new socio-economic classes of traders, merchants, noblemen, and bureaucrats. The city also introduced new values based on economic standards rather than the social kinship values of the village. The city stressed individualism and private property rather than the communal system. Property and possessions tend to establish unconscious jealousy and stimulate possessive, materialistic values that may lead to greed, friction, and conflict. Possessiveness and greed establish polarization, contribute to miscommunication, and enforce the need for protection.

During this period the village became dependent on the walled city for defense and protection of the surrounding region. Consequently, the city collected taxes from the villages to pay for this military protection and to construct a system of defense. When nomadic tribes invaded their regions, farmers fled to the city for protection.

The introduction of the art of writing also played an important role in the evolution of cities. The first examples of writing have been found on clay tablets; through such writing people were able to share knowledge, ideas, and information with one another, and with future generations as well. This exchange of knowledge did much to enhance the development of civilization.

## VILLAGE VERSUS URBAN SOCIETY

Both the village and the city developed their own distinct sets of social values, which were an outgrowth of their environment, economic base, and social evolution. In order to understand these differences in values, we have to first define these two types of settlements.

Historically, the village was a rural, self-employed agricultural society residing at a permanent site and relying primarily on its nearby natural resources. The major function of villages was food production for itself and for the local region. The function of the city was regional as well as local, while its major agricultural needs were provided by its hinterland. The population density per land-use unit was higher than that of the village. Some cities, at their early rise, were partly agrarian in addition to their other major functions, but the city's primary sources of employment depended on nonagricultural resources. The major regional functions of the city were trade, marketing, manufacturing and other industries, business administration, services, cultural and artistic activities, and defense.

Socially, there have been noticeable differences between urban and village societies. Historically, the agricultural village was a socially rooted society. From its early infancy, the village society evolved from tribal, kinship, and blood-related ties, and the settlement process occurred as a joint, community endeavor. On the other hand, urban society evolved mostly from an aggregate of individuals who migrated from rural communities either singly or in families. There also may have been some social or extended family groups among the settlers of the early city. It may be possible that the original agricultural village emerged as the urban center and so preserved some of the early tribal ties, but even then the city, by its nature, stressed individualistic values.

The activities that determined the economic base of the village and the city contributed to the difference in the types of values held by each society. Agricultural activities determined the economic base of the village and because of this the society developed the values of mutual aid through cooperation, a mostly unwritten communal system of social order, and a group sense of pride, confidence, self-reliance, and honesty. These values became the norms for both individual and group behavior, and led to social harmony and equilibrium with a minimum of conflict. The social values of the village society were based on the need for cooperation, which agricultural production demanded. In the village, social values are more strongly rooted and preceded those of materialistic ones. Since the city's society developed primarily out of trade-related activities, its social values tended to be economically based and materialistic in nature. In the city, economically based relationships preceded social relationships.

In conclusion, my observation has been that the more economic and materialistic values are dominant, the more we tend to adopt the city existence as a way of life. When cooperative and communal values are dominant, we tend to prefer the village existence as a way of life. Consequently, it seems that there is some correlation between the increased rate of urbanization in a country and the decreased rate of cooperative social values in that given country.

Last, but not least, the social, economic, physical, and environmental evolution of the pre-city and city genesis would not have matured without the foundation and the existence of norms, codes, standards, and values, which constituted the ethics that were nurtured and manifested by the society. However, it was the synthesis of those values that established the ethics by which these human settlements evolved during this era of the city genesis.

# SELECTED READINGS

Allen, James B. *The Company Town in the American West.* Norman, OK: University of Oklahoma Press, 1967.

Altieri, Miguel A. *Agroecology: The Scientific Basis of Alternative Agriculture.* Boulder, CO: Westview Press, 1987.

Bateson, Gregory. *Mind and Nature.* New York: E. P. Dutton, 1979.

Berkowitz, Bill. *Community Dreams.* San Luis Obispo, CA: Impact Publishers, 1984.

Berry, Brian J. L. and Allen Pred. *Central Place Studies: A Bibliography of Theory and Applications.* Philadelphia: Regional Science Research Institute, 1965.

Branch, Melville C., ed. *Urban Planning Theory.* Stroudsburg, PA: Dowden, Hutchinson & Ross, 1975.

Brown, Lester R. "Sustaining World Agriculture." In *State of the World 1987,* edited by Linda Starke. New York: W. W. Norton, 1987.

Buber, Martin, translated by R. F. C. Hull. *Paths in Utopia.* Boston: Beacon Press, 1958.

Burke, Gerald. *Towns in the Making.* New York: St. Martin's Press, 1971.

Chang, Kwang-chih. *The Archaeology of Ancient China.* 3rd ed., New Haven: Yale University Press, 1977.

Childe, Gordon. *What Happened in History.* Baltimore: Penguin Books, 1967.

Commoner, Barry. *Making Peace with the Planet.* New York: Pantheon Books, 1990.

Corbett, Michael. *A Better Place to Live.* Emmaus, PA: Rodale Press, 1988.

Culther, Lawrence Stephen and Sherrie Stephens. *Recycling Cities for People: The Urban Design Process.* Boston: Cahners Book International, 1976.

De Coulanges, Fustel. *The Ancient City: A Classic Study of the Religious and Civil Institutions of Ancient Greece and Rome.* New York: Doubleday Anchor Books.

Finch, Vernor C., Glenn T. Trewartha, Arthur H. Robinson, and Edwin H. Hammond. *Elements of Geography Physical and Cultural.* New York: McGraw-Hill Book, 1957.

Geddes, Patrick. *Cities in Evolution: An Introduction to the Town Planning Movement and to the Study of Civics*. New York: Harper & Row, 1968.

Givoni, B. *Man, Climate and Architecture*. 2nd ed. New York: Van Nostrand Reinhold, 1976.

Gliessman, S. R., ed. *Agroecology: Researching the Ecological Basis for Sustainable Agriculture*. New York: Springer-Verlag, 1990.

*Global Report on Human Settlements*. Oxford, England: Oxford University Press for the United Nations Centre for Human Settlements (HABITAT), 1987.

Glueck, Nelson. *Rivers in the Desert: A History of the Negev*. New York: W. W. Norton, 1968.

Golany, Gideon S. "Rural Geography of Traditional Village: A Case Study of Tayiba Village." Master's thesis, Israel Institute of Technology, 1967.

Golany, Gideon S. *Earth-Sheltered Dwellings in Tunisia: Ancient Lessons for Modern Design*. Newark, NJ: University of Delaware Press, 1988.

Gore, Albert. *Earth in the Balance: Ecology and the Human Spirit*. New York: Houghton-Mifflin, 1992.

Hatt, Paul K. and Albert J. Reiss, Jr., eds. *Cities and Society: The Revised Reader in Urban Sociology*. New York: Free Press, 1957.

Hughes, Johnson Donald. *Ecology in Ancient Civilizations*. 1st ed. Albuquerque: University of New Mexico Press, 1975.

International Union for the Conservation of Nature and Natural Resources (IUCN), United Nations Environmental Program (UNEP), and World Wildlife Fund (WWF). *Caring for the Earth: A Strategy for Sustainable Living*. Gland, Switzerland: IUCN, UNEP, WWF, 1992.

Kennedy, Declan. "Permaculture and the Sustainable City." *Ekistics* (May 1991): 210-215.

Lovelock, James. *The Ages of Gaia: A Biography of our Living Earth*. New York: W. W. Norton, 1988.

Lyle, John Tillman. *Design for Human Ecosystems*. New York: Van Nostrand Reinhold, 1985.

Mannheim, Karl. *Ideology and Utopia: An Introduction to the Sociology of Knowledge*. New York: A Harvest Book, 1936. Translated from the German by Louis Wirth and Edward Shils.

McHarg, Ian L. and Jonathan Sutton. "Ecological Plumbing for the Texas Coastal Plain." *Landscape Architecture* 65/1 (1975): 78-89.

McLarney, William D. "Aquaculture: Toward an Ecological Approach." Edited by Richard Merrill. *Radical Agriculture*. New York: Harper & Row, 1976.

McPherson, E. Gregory. "Economic Modeling for Large Scale Urban Tree Plantings." In *Proceedings of the ACEE 1990 Summer Study on Energy Efficiency in Buildings*, 4. Washington, D.C.: American Council for an Energy Efficient Economy, 1990.

McPherson, E. Gregory and Sharon Biedenbender. "The Cost of Shade: Cost-Effectiveness of Trees versus Bus Shelters." *Journal of Arboriculture* 17/9 (1991): 233-242.

Mellaart, James. *Catal Huyuk: A Neolithic Town in Anatolia*. Edited by Sir Mortimer Wheeler. New York: McGraw-Hill, 1967.

Michener, James A. *The Source*. Greenwich, CT: A Fawcett Crest Book, Fawcett Publications, 1967.

Minshull, Roger. *Regional Geography*. Chicago: Aldine Publishing, 1967.

Mollison, Bill. *Permaculture Two*. Tyalgum, Australia: Tagari Publications, 1979.

Mollison, Bill. *Permaculture: A Designers' Manual.* Tyalgum, Australia: Tagari Publications, 1988.

Mollison, Bill. *Introduction to Permaculture.* Tyalgum, Australia: Tagari Publications, 1991.

Mumford, Lewis. *From the Ground Up.* New York: Harcourt, Brace & World, 1956.

Mumford, Lewis. *Art and Technics.* New York: Columbia University Press, 1960.

Mumford, Lewis. *The City in History.* New York: Harcourt, Brace and World, 1961.

Mumford, Lewis. *Technics and Civilization.* New York: Harcourt Brace & World, 1963.

Mumford, Lewis. *Technics and Human Development.* New York: Harcourt, Brace, Jovanovich, 1966.

National Research Council (NRC). *Alternative Aquaculture.* Washington, D.C.: National Academy Press, 1989.

Okigbo, Bede N. *Development of Sustainable Agricultural Production Systems in Africa.* Ibadan, Nigeria: International Institute for Tropical Agriculture, 1989.

Oliver, Paul. *Dwellings: The House Across the World.* Austin, TX: University of Texas Press, 1987.

Petrova, Elena. "Rooftop Gardening in Russia." *Permaculture Edge* 4 (April 1994): 8-9.

Plato. *Republic.* Translated by B. Jowett. New York: Vintage Books, Random House, no date.

Possehl, Gregory L., ed. *Harappan Civilization: A Contemporary Perspective.* Bombay, India: Oxford & IBH Publishing, 1982.

Prescott, J. R. V. *The Geography of Frontiers and Boundaries.* Chicago: Aldine Publishing, 1965.

Rapoport, Amos. *House Form and Culture.* Englewood Cliffs, NJ: Prentice-Hall, 1969.

Reissman, Leonard. "The Visionary: Planner for Urban Utopia." In *Urban Planning Theory*, edited by Melville C. Branch. Stroudsburg, PA: Dowden, Hutchinson & Ross, 1975.

Ress, William, E. *The Ecological Meaning of Environment-Economy Integration.* Vancouver, Canada: University of British Columbia, 1989.

Saarinen, Eliel. *The City: Its Growth, Its Decay, Its Future.* Cambridge, MA: MIT Press, 1966.

Schroeder, G. L. "Fish-Farming in Manure-Loaded Ponds." In *Integrated Agriculture-Aquaculture Farming Systems*, edited by Roger S.V. Pullin and Zian H. Schehadeh. Manila, Philippines: International Center for Living Aquatic Resources, 1980.

Schultz, Arnold. "The Ecosystem as a Conceptual Tool in the Management of Natural Resources." In *Natural Resources: Quality and Quantity*, edited by S. V. Ciriacy Wantrup and James S. Parsons. Berkeley: University of California Press, 1967.

Smailes, Arthur E. *The Geography of Towns.* Chicago: Aldine Publishing, 1966.

Stearns, Forest and Tom Montag, eds. *The Urban Ecosystem: A Holistic Approach.* Stroudsburg, PA: Dowden, Hutchinson & Ross, 1974.

Stinner, Benjamin R. and John M. Blair. "Ecological and Agronomic Characteristics of Innovative Cropping Systems." In *Sustainable Agricultural*

*Systems*, edited by Clive A. Edwards, et al. Ankeny, IA: Soil and Water Conservation Society, 1990.

The World Conservation Union. *Caring for the Earth*. Gland, Switzerland: IUN/UNEP/WWF, 1991.

The World Conservation Union. *Caring for the Earth: A Strategy for Sustainable Living*. Gland, Switzerland: IUN/UNEP/WWF, 1991.

Vale, Brenda. *Green Architecture: Design for a Sustainable Future*. London, England; Hudson, NY: UCLA AAUP/ARTS NA, no. 2542.3, 35, 1991.

Van der Ryn, Sim and Peter Calthorpe. *Sustainable Communities: A New Design Synthesis for Cities, Suburbs, and Towns*. San Francisco: Sierra Club Books, 1986.

Walter, Bob, ed. *Sustainable Cities*. Los Angeles: Eco-Home Media, 1992.

Walter, Bob, Lois Arkin, and Richard Crenshaw, eds. *Concepts and Strategies for Eco-City Development*. Los Angeles: Eco-Home Media, 1992.

Weitz, Raanan. *Agricultural and Rural Development in Israel: Projection and Planning*. Jerusalem, Israel: National and University Institute of Agriculture, Bulletin No. 68, 1963.

Wilson, J. "Permaculture's Role in Southern and Eastern Africa." *Permaculture Edge* 4 (April 1994): 17-18.

**3**

# EARLY URBAN CENTERS:
## Mesopotamia, Indus Valley, Egypt, and China

## BACKGROUND

The city is the largest, most complicated project ever conceived in the history of humankind. The city is composed of
historical layers whose physical formation and evolution have
been shaped, interwoven, and entangled by diversified social,
behavioral, economic, climatic, and environmental forces. As
such, the city represents a synthesis of these forces. Above all,
from its inception the city has been shaped and reshaped by
the human vitality that orchestrated the formation of the synthesis of these diversified forces. Moreover, every urban resident, by virtue of his or her existence, contributes at least a
fraction to the city's creation, shape, and atmosphere.

The city can no longer be viewed exclusively as an object
of art as it has been by some architects and a few urban designers. It also must be conceived of as a complex dynamic
living organism with a self-managed system. The city has been
and will continue to be a dynamic, vital, lively organism,
which, like any other organism, has a pulse, a heart, and a
network similar to a human body. Like the body, this organism consists of healthy and decaying portions, and as such it is
continually engaged in a process of self-transformation

throughout its lifetime. It is the role of the urban designer/ planner to understand these forces and their dynamics. In the past and present, the lack of understanding of this process has contributed to the deficiency of the design/planning intended to improve the future. The difficulty in appreciating this process stems from our mental inability to fully understand and precisely predict the complex diversity of our own existing megalopolises. Contemporary urban growth has increased this diversity beyond our comprehension. Another dimension of this transformation process is the contemporary speed at which its dynamics operate. Contemporarily our entire human and environmental landscape can be altered and realtered within one generation. These changes can occur so rapidly that it calls into question our apparently sophisticated ability to predict the evolution of our cities. In a sense, this is a revolutionary process as well as an evolutionary one. The dynamics of change function primarily, though not exclusively, in three intensely interrelated areas: the socio-cultural, technological, and natural environments. A particular deficiency of the new towns concept of this century has been its failure to conceive of the city in these terms at all levels of social class rather than solely at the level of the middle class.

In any case, serious environmental and related social problems have emerged in our present-day urban pattern. The city —historically a center of culture and art and a source of cohesive social networks that promised a pleasant environment with diverse creativity—has gradually lost much of its quality and vitality during this generation. Moreover, especially in the context of Asian cities and that of other developing countries, recent dynamic changes do not promise a better future. It appears that we have lost control of our cities in four critical realms, each of which is a key to other subrealms. These are primarily but not exclusively: environmental and urban social quality of life, urban physical and population growth, urban management and quality of politics, and fiscal deficiency. It is my conviction that the study of past urban patterns of evolution would point to some fruitful and beneficial directions to take in the future.

Urban evolution in history is a subject with a comprehensive nature. A basic knowledge of this subject is required for our generation to bring past experience to bear on present and future development. A lack of understanding of the historical dimension can only limit the creativity of urban designers/planners. Implementation of future urban design improvements should rely heavily on an understanding of the past and present evolution of our cities in a social and environmental context. We should also be alert to the relative dimension of the city's scale in its historic context. This basic approach applies to both developed and developing countries. Yet, every case is unique, and there is no universal formula for solutions that can be implemented.

Urban environmental ethics is the product of two generations of factors that may or may not be fused with each other through urban development. The first is the culture of urban residents by which they conduct their behavior according to norms and standards throughout their urban life, and which gives the ethics their urbanity. The second is the urban designers' input when they designed the neighborhood and the city. This input was dictated by their professional norms, standards, and values, based on their professional beliefs, which determine their ethics. Urban environmental ethics is the product of these two ethics. Indigenous urban design evolved as a system of "urban design without designer," and was in many cases successful in establishing urban harmony. The two ethics, the cultural one of the residents and the professional one of the designers, can overlap to produce the ethics of environmental urbanity and an equilibrium of social quality of life. On the other hand, these two ethics are taking two different paths and producing a low quality of urban environment.

## EARLY URBAN CENTERS

In studying the evolution of settlements and the early rise of cities, four cradles of urban centers development stand out. All located in river valleys, these centers are Mesopotamia,

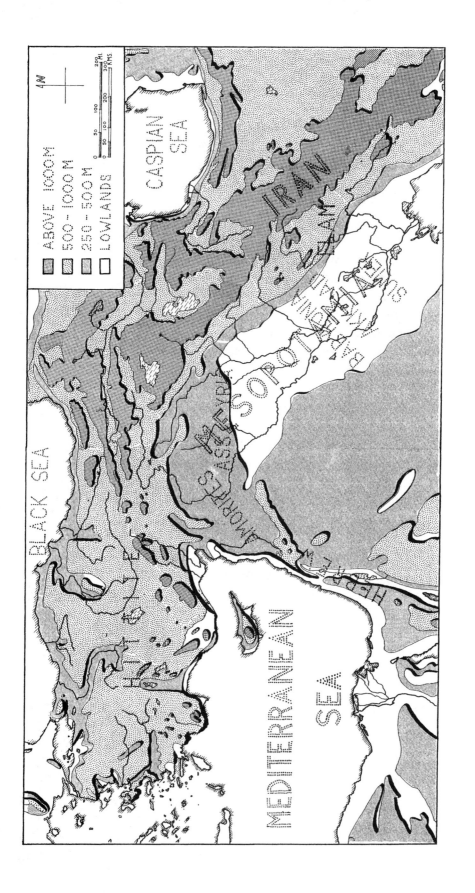

*Figure 3.1   Mesopotamia, the earliest cradle of urban centers, is a fertile valley surrounded by mountains and deserts that forms the eastern wing of the Fertile Crescent. It is the western side of the Fertile Crescent, which runs along the shore of the Mediterranean north to the edge of Turkey, then south to the Persian Gulf.*

the Indus Valley, Egypt, and China. These areas share common characteristics in their environment, climate, and evolutionary process.

## Mesopotamia

Mesopotamia is located in southwestern Asia in the valley of two major rivers, the Tigris and the Euphrates, which run from Turkey to the Persian Gulf (Figure 3.1). Though the soil is fertile, the climate is hot and dry, so all agriculture depends on irrigation. A hot-dry climate is characterized by high radiation, especially in the summer; great amplitude between day and night temperature; and sand and dust storms. Its rain is characterized by being torrential, turbulent, brief, and sparse and often causes flooding because of its intensity and because brief rainfall does not have time to seep into the ground. Aridity results from high evaporation rates that exceed the precipitation rate. Acute dryness causes discomfort for humans, animals, and plants and causes rapid decomposition of materials, including building materials. Decomposition of particles and the absence of vegetation cover combined with the dryness intensifies the destruction of buildings, especially the parts close to the ground.

It is commonly accepted by scholars and archaeologists that the earliest cities appeared around the middle of the fourth millennium B.C. in the southern part of Mesopotamia and probably in the neighboring region Elam in southwest Persia. Later societies, including the Sumerian, Akkadian, and Babylonian, developed urban centers in the same region. It is also commonly assumed that these centers were developed by waves of immigrants who were of Semitic origin. Shortly after the Sumerian centers were developed in the south, the Assyrians developed others in the hilly region of northern Mesopotamia. After the establishment of the urban centers in southern Mesopotamia, centers were developed in the surrounding regions by the Persians in Iran, the Hittites in Turkey, the Amorites in northwestern Mesopotamia, and the Hebrews on the eastern shore of the Mediterranean. While these centers were distinct in their own right, they were influenced by the urban design of the centers in Mesopotamia. This influence was encouraged by the geopolitical location of the Mesopotamian centers, which were in a valley crossroads with easy north–south and east–west movement. Mesopotamia, therefore, became a meeting ground of different cultures and of trade.

Among the important ancient cities of southern Mesopotamia are Ur, Eridu, Larsa, Lagash, Nippur, Kish, Borsippa, Cutha, Sippar, Opis, Adab, Uruk, Kisiga, Babylon, Agade, Ctesiphon, and Seleucia. Among the Assyrian cities of northern Mesopotamia are Assur, Kalhu (or Nimrud), Nineveh, Arbela, and Singara. Most of these cities were recorded in the Bible.

Mesopotamian cities pioneered urban design and established the foundation of the evolutionary process of urban centers. The early generation of these centers evolved as a conglomerate of neighborhoods based on tribal, kinship- or blood-related social groups with a coinciding territory. "Planning," in terms of a prior arrangement of streets and a residential pattern, developed at the periphery of the city well after the nucleus was formed. Although urban design and planning as a preconceived concept did not exist in the early urban revolution of Mesopotamia, it certainly did exist in the public buildings, monuments, religious buildings, and palaces. A great deal of effort and ingenuity went into the ziggurat as a religious and observation tower, the palace of the king, and most importantly, the temple itself (Figures. 3.2 and 3.3).

Public buildings were architecturally monumental, standing well above their surroundings and representing the religious and secular power behind them. These buildings were elevated on a ramp and were significantly higher than the rest of the city's skyline with the ziggurat being the highest of all (Figure 3.4). These monumental buildings were balanced and symmetrically designed and used huge quantities of bricks, as did the city wall.

The determining principle of the city form was to put the maximum number of people on a minimal amount of land. This was the result of the need for defense and for preserving land for agriculture, and also reflected the social need of the residents for propinquity. It also reflected climatic considerations, because compact cities provide more shadowed area

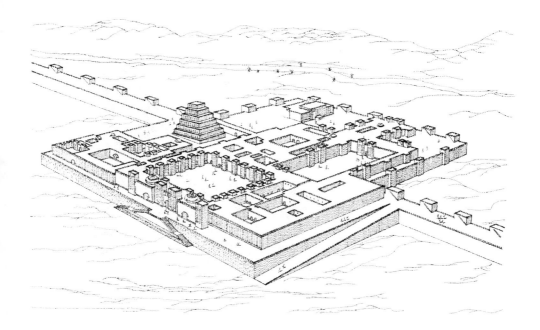

and less area exposed to direct radiation. Thus, the compact city provided cooler streets and dead ends with protection against hot and dusty winds during the day, and, to some extent, retained heat longer than wide open spaces during the evening when it was desirable. Usually the cities were round in shape.

Streets in the ancient Mesopotamian cities were developed in at least three levels. The widest was the main street, leading to the major monumental buildings and dividing the neighborhoods. The second was narrower, penetrating into the neighborhoods, and enabled limited animal transportation. The third, and a very important one, was the dead end, usually surrounded by a conglomerate of houses that were attached side-to-side and back-to-back in a disorganized manner. In most cases, these streets ended in a patio that provided great privacy, safety, and security. We assume the patio entrance was open during the day and closed at night. Drawing from existing examples of ancient neighborhoods, we also can assume that the residents around these dead ends were a homogeneous ethnic group with blood-relation, tribal, or religious ties. These dead-end alleys, as well as second-level

*Figure 3.2 Place's restoration of King Sargon II's palace. Sargon was king of Assyria in the eighth century B.C., during the zenith of the civilization. (Adapted and reproduced from Lloyd, 1945, Figure 16.)*

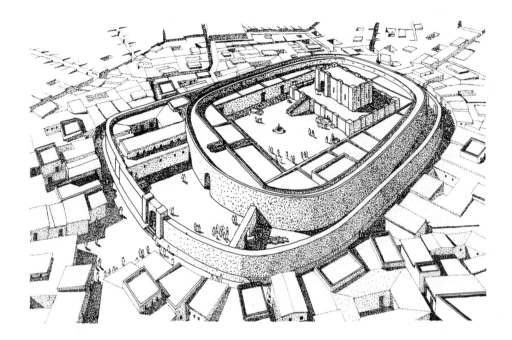

*Figure 3.3 The oval temple at Khafajah built in the third millennium B.C. in southern Mesopotamia is the most thoroughly investigated temple of the Early Dynastic period. (Adapted and reproduced from Delougaz, 1940, frontispiece. Courtesy of the Oriental Institute of The University of Chicago.)*

streets, were very narrow and were curving, or zigzag in pattern. Their design provided privacy and protection from the intense heat and dust storms and from intruders or enemies.

Houses in Mesopotamian cities surrounded a patio and, as mentioned earlier, were attached to each other, side-to-side and back-to-back, leaving only one window side (mostly the second floor, if any) of the house bordering the street. Three sides of the central patio received sunshine while the side facing north received a minimum amount of sun; the patio was surrounded by rooms, some without windows toward the patio. This arrangement allowed for maximum protection and privacy but often led to unpleasant living conditions. Our research findings show that throughout the history of Mesopotamia until the beginning of this century, the design principle of the Mesopotamian house was the patio style surrounded by rooms. The most advanced form of this principle was the Baghdad House.

Because Mesopotamian cities were densely developed due to defense and agricultural needs, they did not have any green or public open space within the city; however, the distance from the core of the city to the open, yet mostly agricultural

space, outside the city wall was an acceptable walking distance. Though large open spaces did exist at the temple or the ziggurat (tower), it was the open space around the city gate that became the focal point of the city. The gate was an architectural, social, and economic entity. It was an architectural landmark for strangers approaching the city. The open area inside the city gate became the site for large social gatherings and also the place where the city elders assembled to settle disputes of the residents. The space immediately outside the gate became a trading site where residents from the surrounding agricultural villages could come and sell their excess goods and handicrafts without incurring the taxes of the city. Immediately surrounding the city walls were agricultural plots that were tended by the residents living at the periphery of the city or in its satellite villages.

*Figure 3.4 This projection drawing shows the restored ziggurat of Nabonidus, the last king of Babylonia in the sixth century B.C. The ziggurat, a temple tower built by the Babylonians and Assyrians, was the highest building in the community. (Adapted from Woolley, 1939, plate 88).*

## Indus Valley

Indus Valley urban centers developed along the Indus River from its Punjab (five) tributaries in the Himalayan Mountains

U.S.S.R.

CHINA

AFGHANISTAN

HARAPPA

PAKISTAN

MOHENJO
DARO

INDIA

ARABIAN SEA

0        200KM

*Figure 3.5 The Indus River Valley in western India and Pakistan—a cradle of ancient urban centers. (Adapted in part and reproduced from Possehl, 1982, p. 16.)*

in the north to its mouth at the Arabian Sea in the south, and from the Rajasthan Hills in the east to the Baluchistan Hills in the west (Figure 3.5). These centers developed around the middle of the third millennium B.C. and lasted until around the middle of the second millennium B.C. Here, too, the climate of this valley is hot and dry. Although there is enough rain to support a pasturing system, all agriculture depends on irrigation. Geopolitically, the Indus Valley was the major crossroads of transportation north and south along the Indus river and east to west from India to Persia. Although our knowledge of the Indus Valley is limited, we assume the origin of the population was Aryan from India.

The first of the valley urban centers, Harappa City, was discovered in 1921 in the Montgomery District of the Punjab. Unfortunately, Harappa City was discovered after most of its stone had been removed to build the nearby railroad; thus much archaeological evidence was destroyed. Another large center, Mohenjo-Daro, was discovered in the southern part of the valley in 1928. Most of our knowledge about urban design in the Indus Valley comes from Mohenjo-Daro, which has been extensively excavated (Figure 3.6).

Indus Valley urban design was characterized by a high standard of design, regularity, hierarchical street design, and, most importantly, an intensive development of high-quality city organization, including municipal services and food supply and sanitation arrangements. The design also was influenced by the environment, climate, local building materials, and site conditions. Mohenjo-Daro, the most intensively studied city, was made up of building blocks of about 366 meters by 183 meters. Like Mesopotamian cities, the buildings were made of baked bricks. Mohenjo-Daro can be considered among the first cities of its time to introduce a systematic, preconceived design.

Two distinctive characteristics of Mohenjo-Daro's urban design are the semigrid systems of its streets and the independent government citadel. The streets themselves were divided into three hierarchical levels: a wide straight street, narrower, almost straight streets running parallel to the major street, and the narrowest streets with some right angles running perpendicular to the first two street levels (Figure 3.7). Dead ends were almost nonexistent.

The unique government citadel was close to the city but completely separated from it and combined many different functions (Figure 3.8). The citadel included a large granary, a college, an assembly hall, public baths, fortifications, and many other public buildings that have not yet been identified.

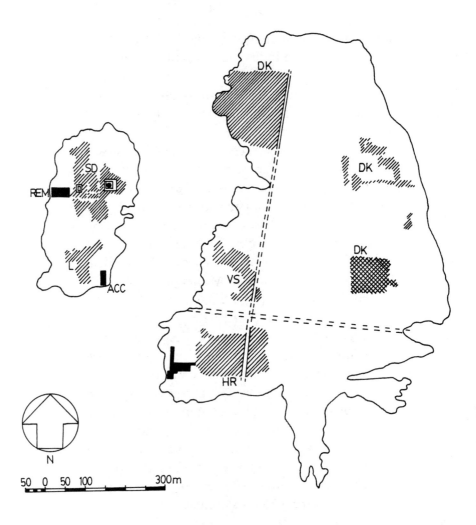

*Figure 3.6 The overall plan of Mohenjo-Daro reveals its unusual design, which separates the government citadel (Stupa at the west) from the rest of the city. Excavated area (HR) shown in hatched lines. (Adapted and reproduced from Wheeler, 1950 p. 27.)*

Homes in Mohenjo-Daro shared some common characteristics with those in Mesopotamia. Again, they were patio-style homes with two stories of rooms surrounding the courtyard, which was open to the sky. Though homes may have lined the main street through the city, access to all homes came from the second- or third-level streets. Our explanation is that access was blocked from the major street to protect residents from nomad raiders who occasionally swept through the city during times of drought, looking for food. Neighborhoods in Mohenjo-Daro apparently were of mixed social and economic classes, since houses of varying sizes were clustered together.

*Figure 3.7  A partial street plan of Mohenjo-Daro (DK area) showing part of the residential quarter. (Adapted and reproduced from Wheeler, The Cambridge History of India, Fig. 9, p. 35, 1953. Reprinted with the permission of Cambridge University Press.)*

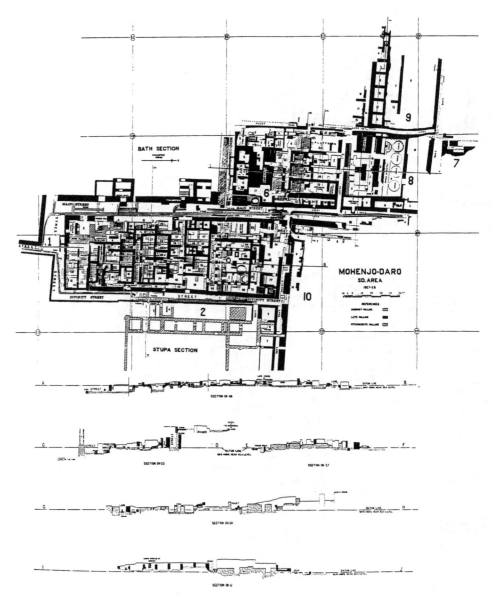

*Figure 3.8 Site plan of the separate government citadel of Mohenjo-Daro. (Mackay, 1938, plate VI.)*

Long before raiders, who presumably were from India, burned the city down in the middle of the second millennium B.C., Mohenjo-Daro was dying geologically. The ground was sinking a little each year, leaving the city subject to flooding from the Indus River, which caused the salinization of the surrounding agricultural land. All of these factors contributed to the decline of the city.

## Egypt

Egypt is a good example of the overwhelming impact the environment can have on urban and social development. Egypt's climate is more stressful than that of Mesopotamia, the Indus Valley, or northern China. The climate is defined, in general, as a hot-dry one with extreme aridity. Rain, if any, is limited to the shore of the Mediterranean in northern Egypt and rarely occurs in the southern part of the country. The Nile, which runs from south to north, was the source of survival. Because of this aridity and scarcity of water, nomadism was confined to the delta region and was nonexistent in central and southern Egypt. Consequently, all human activity was focused exclusively in the cities and villages along the Nile River, leaving no space for a pasturing, nomad lifestyle. However, four small oases exist beyond the Nile to the west, which did support limited nomadism in the western desert of Egypt at El Kharga, El Dakhla, Farafra, and Bahariya. The eastern desert between the Nile and the Red Sea is an extreme environment that offered no oases and, thus, did not provide any conditions for pasturing.

The first impact of this environmental condition was that all cities and villages that developed in ancient Egypt were confined along the Nile River and its only course of throughway between the first cataract and the apex of the delta, and as such were geographically isolated from other cultures (Figure 3.9). Moreover, these cities were never designed with protective walls because there was no threat from either side of the river. The only protective cities developed throughout the history of Egypt were in the delta region or those publicly initiated at the political border between Egypt and the Nubian tribes at the first cataract in southern Egypt.

The second impact of the environment was on the social order, which was primarily influenced by the nature of the Nile River. Settlements developed on the limited strip of alluvial soil deposited along the river's banks. Until contemporary times, when the High Dam was built and the cyclical pattern was interrupted, the Nile brought large quantities of silt enriched by organic materials from eastern Africa and deposited them along the sides of the river. Eventually these

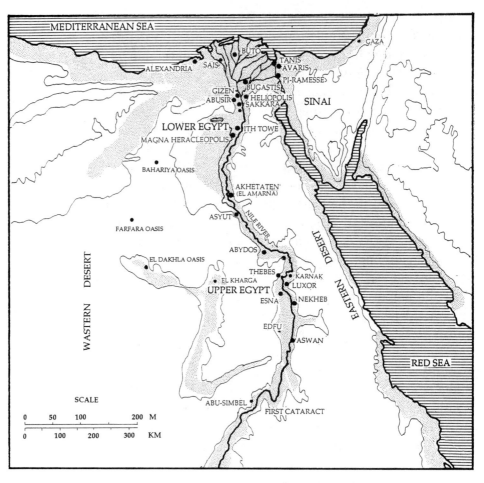

MEDITERRANEAN SEA

GAZA

BUTO

ALEXANDRIA    SAIS    TANIS
                      AVARIS
                      PI-RAMESSE

GIZEH  BUBASTIS
ABUSIR  HELIOPOLIS    SINAI
        SAKKARA

LOWER EGYPT  ITH TOWE

MAGNA HERACLEOPOLIS

BAHARIYA OASIS

AKHETATEN
(EL AMARNA)

ASYUT

FARFARA OASIS

ABYDOS

EL DAKHLA OASIS

THEBES  KARNAK
        LUXOR
EL KHARGA

UPPER EGYPT

ESNA  NEKHEB

EDFU

ASWAN

WASTERN DESERT

NILE RIVER

EASTERN DESERT

RED SEA

SCALE

0    50    100         200  M

0    100    200    300  KM

ABU-SIMBEL

FIRST CATARACT

*Figure 3.9 Ancient
Egyptian urban centers
developed exclusively along
the Nile River from the
first cataract to the delta.*

deposits created levies that were enriched and fertilized by
the annual flooding. The result of this rich soil and arid climate was that agriculture became the only means of survival,
but without the infusion of meat, wool, milk, and cheese that
nomadic societies provided the cities of Mesopotamia and the
Indus Valley.

Egyptian agriculture was exclusively based on irrigation
and all of the economic and social conditions of the civilization resulted from that system. The Nile water was closely
observed and determined the level of taxes the farmers were
to provide the government. In order to secure the continuity
of the irrigation system, a social system developed that, sooner

or later, led to the subjugation of large masses of people in order to operate it. Though irrigated agriculture is intensive and provides more than one crop cycle throughout the year, there were still periods during the year when most farm workers were unemployed. During these times, these laborers were used to work on other projects. It is my opinion that the monumental buildings, great temples, and the pyramids were the byproduct of this system. Thus, a tight social order that essentially subjected a mass of people to a year-round slavery system developed in order to retain the irrigated-agriculture society. The system also ensured the continuation of monumental building projects. A good description of this system is provided in the Old Testament concerning the four-hundred-year stay of the Israelites as slaves in Egypt.

The third impact of the environment was on the survival of city buildings. Except for monumental buildings, temples, palaces, and the like, buildings in Egyptian cities were built exclusively of mud. The rain in Egypt, like rain in any arid region, is torrential and of short duration, which intensified the erosion of these common buildings. Also, the dry, strong winds' deflation accelerated the decomposition of the building materials. As a result, ancient urban neighborhoods that were usually built without foundations left no trace of their layout, so we know little about the urban design of the ancient Egyptian cities. Our knowledge is quite limited even about the single houses and their layout. The Egyptian house, however, had two floors and was simple in its structure. In the city of El-Amarna (Akhetaten), houses were oriented toward the north or west to take advantage of the cool wind. We have some limited information about the workmen's villages, such as in the city of Tell el-Amarna, which was built as a new capital city by Ikhnaton in the second millennium B.C. (Figure 3.10). Workmen's neighborhoods or cities were well planned by the government. The overall pattern was small units attached mostly in linear form with very narrow streets. The structures were geometrically standardized with all units being the same and occasionally were isolated from the other parts of the city. The streets of the ancient Egyptian cities were not paved and there was no drainage system, very little

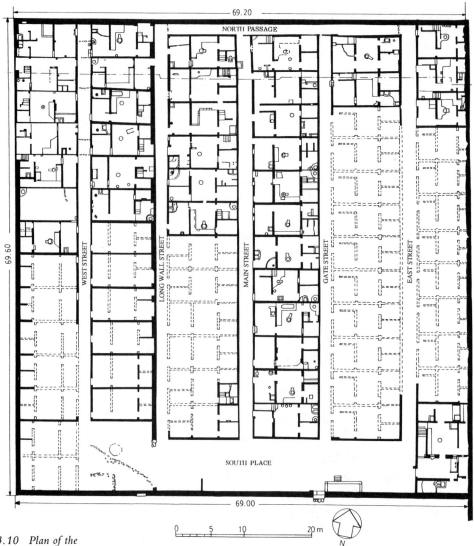

NORTH PASSAGE

69.20

69.60

69.00

WEST STREET

LONG WALL STREET

MAIN STREET

GATE STREET

EAST STREET

SOUTH PLACE

0    5    10              20 m

N

Figure 3.10 Plan of the workman's village at Tell el-Amarna, the new capital city of Ikhnaton and Nefertiti. This is part of one of the most carefully excavated sites of ancient Egypt. (Adapted and reproduced from T. Eric Peet and Leonard Woolley, 1923, plate XVI.)

proper sanitation, and no garbage collection. Garbage was accumulated outside and near the house.

In contrast, we do have vast knowledge about ancient Egyptian monumental buildings, which were usually made of stone. The impressive monumental buildings with heavy masses of masonry against vast open spaces were typical of the ancient Egyptian cities. The temple was the strong nucleus of the city and became the center around which the residential and the commercial complex of buildings developed.

Egypt's geopolitical position is unique. Its influences came primarily from the north along the delta or, in a more limited way, from the south along the Nile. The delta is distinct environmentally and ethnically. Because of the delta's location along a major international thoroughfare running from Asia through North Africa, delta cities were ethnically mixed, heterogeneous, and culturally enriched. Those along the Nile were homogenous in their population. The influence from the south was much more limited. Although the Nile was used as a transportation link, the first cataract prevented it from becoming a major water thoroughfare. Despite its distance from the geographical center of country, the delta became home for almost all of the capital cities throughout the history of ancient Egypt. The cities were developed along the eastern edge of the delta, at its apex, within the delta, or on its western edge. New delta cities built to be capitals included Memphis, Ith-Towe, Avaris, Pi-Ramesse, and Bubastis. Existing delta cities chosen to be capitals were Heracleopolis, Tanis, and Sais. The only capital city developed in the central part of Egypt was Thebes, which had a very brief history. All of these delta capitals were fortified cities. It is also significant that most of the publicly initiated new towns throughout the history of ancient Egypt were developed within the delta region.

In periods of strong centralized government, the ancient Egyptian cities were developed as regional or local centers for cult worship, administration, or trade. The city-state concept, which had early evolved in the delta region, completely disappeared with the unification of southern and central Egypt with the delta.

## China

The cradle of Chinese civilization, which included the urban centers, was in the northern part of China along the Wei He and the Huang He Rivers. This region is located north of Qin Ling Mountains, which run northwest to east and divide China into two distinct geographical regions—the north with a hot-dry climate and the south with monsoon rains. The economy of the north is primarily based on grain, while that in the south is based on vegetables, fruits, and rice. The north, where urban civilization started, is made up of primarily but not exclusively aeolian loess soil. This soil is fertile and, when combined with water available for irrigation, is very productive. The soil is almost uniform and free from stones, which enabled relatively easy digging and the creation of dwellings in the subterranean space. The climate of this region is arid and semiarid and becomes more arid toward the north and northwest, where precipitation can be around one hundred millimeters a year (such as in Gansu and Ningxia provinces Figure 3.11), or a little more than that (such as in Shaanxi or Shanxi provinces), and toward the southeast region with four to five hundred millimeters a year (such as Henan province). The region as a whole has plenty of water along the Huang He and the Wei He Rivers, which enabled the development of elaborate and intensive agriculture.

It is my understanding that the historical Chinese practice of settlement evolution indicates that the town, as a form of settlement, was an intermediate stage between the matured village as a farming settlement and the urban center as a walled housing conglomerate that focused on trade, commerce, transportation effort, manufacturing, politics, religious, culture, and art, and acted as a service center. Urban centers developed, according to some Chinese scholars, around the middle of the second millennium B.C., at the time of the Shang Dynasty (sixteenth to eleventh century B.C.). Its theoretical and practical foundation was shaped during the Zhow Dynasty (eleventh century to 221 B.C.). The peak eras of the ancient Chinese urban centers were during the Han Dynasty (206 B.C.–A.D. 220), and later the Tang Dynasty (A.D. 618–907), and the Song Dynasty (A.D. 960–1279).

The design principles of ancient Chinese urban design were best expressed in the capital cities. Most of these cities were located in central and some in northern China, and were designed by order of the emperor, who usually drafted hundreds of thousands of farmers to construct them in a short time (Figure 3.11). Most of the capitals were built from scratch as new towns and from a preconceived plan prepared by theoreticians, philosophers, and builders (Figure 3.12). Each new city was concerned with improving the site selection, and

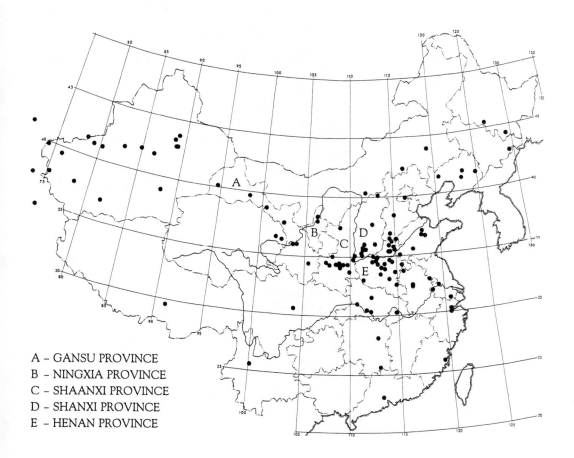

A – GANSU PROVINCE
B – NINGXIA PROVINCE
C – SHAANXI PROVINCE
D – SHANXI PROVINCE
E – HENAN PROVINCE

*Figure 3.11  Chinese capital cities (partial) constructed throughout the country with increasingly sophisticated urban design plans. (Golany, 1994.)*

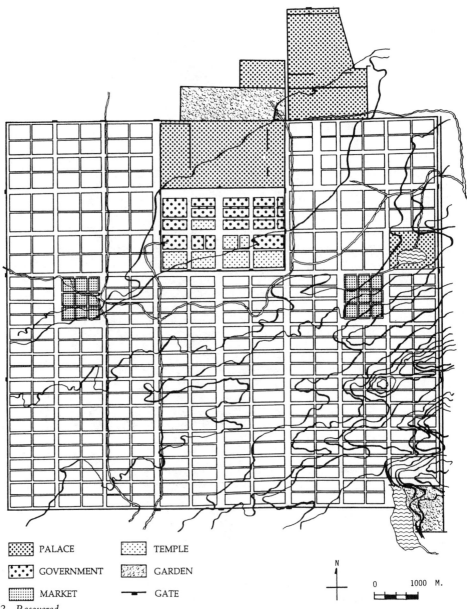

PALACE  TEMPLE

GOVERNMENT  GARDEN

MARKET  GATE

N

0    1000    M.

*Figure 3.12 Recovered figure of Changan City, the Western Capital in the Tang Dynasty (Xian, Shaanxi Province). (Adapted and reproduced in part from Teaching and Research Office in Urban Design, 1982, p. 28, and in part from other sources.)*

with a host of other forces, including religion and cosmology, standards and conventions of the socio-economic classes, and environmental concerns.

Other determining factors that were considered revolved around the triumvirate of elements related to the philosophies of Daoism and Confucianism. These three elements were heaven, earth, and humankind. Cosmology, *Feng Shui* (Chinese art of site selection in landscape and cityscape), *Ying Guo* (system of urban design and management), *Feng Li* (neighborhood design), and other design concepts played an important role in the design and location of important cities and public buildings, as well as in the space allocation for agricultural festivals and the development of buildings used in agricultural/religious ceremonies. Both Ying Guo and Feng Li systems were already developed during the western Han Dynasty (206 B.C.–A.D. 24).

There are numerous design principles evident in the ancient Chinese urban centers. These include the use of open space, the use of below-ground space, the merging of agrarian and commercial facilities, the integration of residential and commercial needs, and aesthetic configurations that enhance the quality of the environment. Chinese urban design recognized that the physical environment contributes significantly to the well-being of society. Courtyards were used throughout the cities as a common public space, and gardening and natural landscaping were combined with bodies of water to enrich the environment. (For more information, see Chapter One.) Within the city, two types of land-use patterns were dominant. One pattern, which was used only in the marketing areas, combined markets on the ground floor with residences on the second floor. In all other areas, residential and commercial buildings were segregated. Chinese cities also were developed to reflect the social pattern of the culture (Figure 3.13). Unity was reflected at all levels, starting with the nuclear family, then on to the extended family, to the neighborhood, and so on. At each level, housing focused around an internal open space enclosed by walls. For example, the family home turned its back on the street and focused around an internal courtyard. The same was true of entire neighborhoods, which were collections of these houses enclosed within a larger wall and arranged around an internal open space that was common to all of the houses. Thus, each grouping created a nesting pattern from the core of the city to its outer edge. Under all circumstances, the city was designed with consideration given to the views of philosophers and with the integration of moral values, natural forces, and

Figure 3.13 Central
courtyard space is a strong
spatial element often
introduced in indigenous
design. It represents family
and community collectiveness
(Beijing, China).

cosmic cycles in the symbols of urban structures. All of the cities were constructed based on a code that the public followed and to which they were committed.

Ancient Chinese cities were quite different from cities developed in the other ancient urban centers of the world. First, they differed in scope, with some of the ancient Chinese cities having a population of one million early throughout their evolutionary process, while in the West the largest known ancient cities barely reached a half-million residents during the renaissance time. The Chinese viewed the city primarily as an agricultural marketing and administrative center, rather than as a symbolic and practical base for expansion into other territories as it was in the West. Also unlike the West, Chinese capital cities were never conceived as eternal monuments, so it was relatively common for new capitals to be built at the request of the emperor. While cities of the West, especially those in Egypt and Mesopotamia, constructed massive buildings that served as monuments, such as the pyramids and the ziggurats, the Chinese instead viewed the city as a whole as a monument. Each Chinese city was designed with coherent creative and artistic interrelationships among the parts and was conceptualized as a collective work of art with harmony and artistic unity as its goal. Despite some massive features, such as the wall and some pavilions, the buildings of the city were low. This approach to the city was influenced by Chinese philosophy and a practical view of the environment. The traditional Chinese ideal has been a society with all of its parts in balance. Regarding nature, the Chinese believe that harming even one part will affect the balance and unity of the whole. Therefore, human-made designs are intermingled with natural elements to produce harmony.

## COMPARISON OF EARLY URBAN CENTERS

In comparing the four case studies presented here, we can outline some of the commonalties of these early urban centers of the world: location and site selection, the river impact, monumental buildings, the cycle pattern, astrology and astronomy, trade, the evolutionary process of settlements, and the impact of the common natural environment.

Location and site selection of the hot-dry climate area are a common denominator among the four case studies. All developed in arid zones with differing degrees of aridity. It's difficult to speculate on the reason for such a selection. One possible explanation is that people were pushed away from the tropical zone by the continuous threat of illness and disease resulting from heavy rain, swamps, dense vegetation, and the difficulty of coping with the discomfort of the rainy, humid tropical climate. It may well be that the high density of wild animals, reptiles, and insects threatened life and health even more. Consequently, people were driven away to the northern edge of the tropical, to the subtropical, and then to the arid zone. Similar pressure may have occurred from the temperate zone falling north of the arid zone because of the stressful cold climate of snow and blizzards that characterizes those zones. Under the latter condition, too, people may have moved south to the semiarid and to the arid zone. In either case, the zones that were left relatively comfortable for humans were the arid and semiarid regions. Ultimately, climatic conditions may have been the major factor in the selection of the location and the evolution of humankind throughout early civilization and city development. We also can speculate that the hot-dry climate of the arid zone, especially that of the Middle East and the Fertile Crescent, provided vast open space, cloudless skies, and views unobstructed by forests, all of which stimulated the imagination and may have led to mystical vision. If this later explanation is acceptable, then it is no wonder that the major religious philosophies and prophecies of this world, including Judaism, Christianity, and Islam, were developed in the arid zone. It may be hard to accept this analysis as an isolated one. It would be more convincing to add other complementary reasons.

Rivers were the source of life and the spine of each of the four civilizations with villages, cities, and transportation developing in a linear pattern along their banks. The river was the source for fishing, drinking-water, transportation, and most importantly, for agricultural development. Without the river and the resulting agriculture, these regions would have been deserts, supporting only the nomad culture. Because there was not enough rain to support dry farming, the evolution of agriculture depended on the river water. The four hydraulic civilizations that evolved along the rivers were superior in their agricultural production, with more than one crop annually, to those that practiced the dry-farming system that relied on seasonal rain and limited them to one crop a year. In all four cases, the development of a sophisticated irrigation system, its maintenance, and the social order required for its continuity became a major force in the society. To maintain the irrigation system there was a need for a strong centralized power structure to control and maintain it throughout the community. Social order, which became the focal point of the administration, was enforced by the religious institution and its subsequent power. This social order took different forms in each of the four cases. The extreme one was in Egypt, where slavery developed to maintain the agricultural system and its irrigation network. A similar yet less extreme system developed in Mesopotamia, where the religious institution was in control of the social order through communal city labor managed by the priest at the time the Mesopotamian cities evolved during the middle of the fourth millennium B.C. Here the religious institution determined the distribution of labor forces, their working schedules, and the rationing of food for their survival. This was a form of an urban communal system that evolved from the village-tribal society and its familiarity with the communal system. In the Indus Valley case, we have limited knowledge of the structure of the irrigation system and the social order related to it. However, the size of the granary found in the government citadel suggests a high taxation system. In the Chinese case, slavery and the later feudal system were developed during the early dynasties in the Wei He valley and along the Huang He River zone and lasted until around 400 B.C. Finally, irrigation control was a common denominator in all four cases. Here, too, there was a need for social order to maintain the system and the survival of those settlements along the river. Moreover, the development of the centralized political power structure gave way to the city-state structure, which emerged during the early stages of these urban developments.

Monumental buildings were another element common to three of the four case studies. Mesopotamia and Egypt seem to be the leaders of the four, which may be the result of their extreme social order and/or the religious commitment that was expressed through the large number of temples and their monumental size. The focus of the Chinese was primarily on palaces and the related buildings of the noble class. Yet, Chinese temples were more related to natural and agriculture cycles than to the idols and goddesses of Mesopotamia and Egypt. However, their temples were relatively more modest than those of Mesopotamia and Egypt.

The Mesopotamian, Egyptian, Chinese, and probably the Indus Valley civilizations observed the cyclic pattern of nature, the cosmos, and humankind, as diurnal, seasonal, annual, or multiannual. Their observation of the cosmic cycle (sun, stars, moon) and equally of the cycle of nature (rain, temperature, rise and fall of the river) led them to the conviction that there must be a cycle in human life, too. All of this enforced religious beliefs in unknown mighty forces and, therefore, enforced the power dominancy of the religious institution.

Also, to understand the cycle phenomena in all four cases, astrology and astronomy developed to a reasonably advanced level. Each of these regions has skies almost free from clouds, which encouraged observation of the stars. For environmental reasons, house roofs in both Egypt and Mesopotamia were flat, and low humidity encouraged their use for sleeping during the summer. Since the streets of ancient cities were dark at night and did not provide any entertainment for the citizens, people spent their time in the evenings at home, often on the rooftops. Consequently, the people watched the stars and eventually observed the cyclic pattern of their movements. Over a period of time, people in these civilizations began to equate movement in the heavens with the events in their lives, and astrology was born. Later, when their observations became more sophisticated and more concerned with understanding the pattern of stars' movements within the cosmos rather than with their relationship to the life cycle, the science of astronomy was born.

A common denominator was also the development of trade within the valley unit and later between the valley and its surroundings. Transportation and urban development were two sides of the same coin in the four case studies. Land and river transportation were adjacent and parallel, and along with the linear urban development supported internal exchange and external trade. The case of Mesopotamia, Egypt, and China were the most typical of this development. However, all four cases became centers of a flourishing economy and of international marketing systems.

In all the four cases, human settlements evolved through the same process of the same sequential stages with little difference in the degree of length of each stage. These stages started with nomadism and continued with the rise of the village and the town before producing and adopting the city form of living. As we have discussed in previous chapters, it was the maturity, the agricultural surplus, the need for exchange, and the rise of the religious and political power structure that brought about the rise of the town and the accomplishment of the urban center.

In Mesopotamia, almost five millennia (beginning eighth millennium B.C.) passed between the rise of the village and the rise of the city. It took a similar length of time to evolve in China, slightly more time in Egypt, and a shorter time in the Indus Valley. It was during this span of time that the form of the town evolved to introduce exchange, trade, and local-regional services.

Finally, the development of the strong sense of the environment and its ethics originated in nomadism and subsequently led to village society. All four urban civilizations must have carried with them a load of social and cultural ethics along the way to urban development. The discovery of the city of Ur and its neighborhood configurations in southern Mesopotamia reveal that sections of the city were inhabited by a cohesive tribal society. However, those inherited ethics took the form of physical design in the streets, dead-ends, and houses. Thus, a fusion of social values, norms, standards, conduct, and behavior together introduced socio-cultural ethics, which determined the physical configuration of the house, the neighborhood, and the city. In a sense, this was "architecture without architects" and "urban design without urban designers." In short, indigenous design of urban configurations emerged from the sense of environment of the culture and not from the drafting table. It was from earlier processes that the environmental ethics for urban design was derived.

In conclusion, all four cases have ultimately produced preconceived thoughtful design from their predetermined sociocultural ethics. In Mesopotamia as well as in Egypt, one central theme of urban design was their concept of the city's monumentality. As for the Chinese, and it seems the Indus Valley people as well, their design was for the masses of people. The ancient Chinese conceived of the city as a whole as a cohesive piece of art, rather than focusing on the singular architectural monuments as the Mesopotamians and Egyptians did.

The evolutionary process of human settlement in all four case studies was almost identical. First came the rise of nomadism, followed by seminomadism, and then the village, regional growth center, town, and city. It was predetermined socio-cultural ethics that sequentially led to the preconceived ethics of indigenous urban design and the rise of the "urban revolution."

# SELECTED READINGS

Adams, Robert McC. *Heartland of Cities: Surveys of Ancient Settlement and Land Use on the Central Floodplain of the Euphrates.* Chicago: University of Chicago Press, 1981.

Allen, James B. *The Company Town in the American West.* Norman, OK: University of Oklahoma Press, 1967.

Bell, Colin and Rose Bell. *Town Planning in Britain From Roman Times to 1900.* New York: Frederick A. Praeger, 1969.

Birenne, Senri. *Economic and Social History of Medieval Europe.* New York: A Harvest Book, Harcourt, Brace & World, 1937.

Blom, Frans and Oliver LeFarge. *Tribes and Temples.* 2 vols. New Orleans: Tulane University of Louisiana, 1926.

Braidwood, R. J. "The Earliest Village Communities of Southwestern Asia." In *Journal of World History* 1, Paris, France, 1 (1953): 278-310.

Braidwood, Robert John. *The Near East and the Foundations for Civilization: An Essay in Appraisal of the General Evidence.* Eugene, OR: State System of Higher Education, 1952.

Branch, Daniel Paulk. *Folk Architecture of the East Mediterranean.* New York: Columbia University Press, 1966.

Brandon, Samuel George Frederick. *Religion in Ancient History: Studies in Ideas, Men, and Events.* New York: Charles Scribner's Sons, 1969.

Burke, Gerald. *Towns in the Making.* New York: St. Martin's Press, 1971.

Christaller, Walter. *Central Places in Southern Germany.* Englewood Cliffs, NJ: Prentice-Hall, 1966.

Commoner, Barry. *Making Peace with the Planet.* New York: Pantheon Books, 1990.

Corbett, Michael. *A Better Place to Live.* Emmaus, PA: Rodale Press, 1988.

Davis, Kingsley. "The Origin and Growth of Urbanization in the World." *American Journal of Sociology* 60:5 (March 1955): 429-37.

de Camp, Sprague L. *Great Cities of the Ancient World.* New York: Doubleday, 1972.

Delougaz, Pinhas. *The Temple Oval at Khafajah*. Chicago: University of Chicago Press, 1940.

Denis, Numa, Fustel de Coulanges. *The Ancient City: A Study on the Religion, Laws, and Institutions of Greece and Rome*. Garden City, NY: Doubleday Anchor Books, Doubleday, 1976.

Dyos, H. J., ed. *The Study of Urban History: Proceedings of an International Round-Table Conference of the Urban History Group at Gilbert Murray Hall*, University of Leicester, September 23-26, 1966. New York: St. Martin's Press, 1968.

Eliot, Henry Ware. *Excavations in Mesopotamia and Western Iran, Sites of 4000-500* B.C. Special publication of the Peabody Museum of American Archaeology and Ethnology, Harvard University. Cambridge, MA: The Museum, 1950.

Elvin, Mark and G. William Skinner, eds. *The Chinese City Between Two Worlds*. Stanford, CA: Stanford University Press, 1974.

Falkenstein, Adam. *The Sumerian Temple City*. Los Angeles: Undena Publications, 1974.

Frankfort, Henri. "The Origin of Monumental Architecture in Egypt." In *American Journal of Semitic Languages and Literatures*, LVIII (1941): 329-58. Chicago: University of Chicago Press, 1884-1941.

Frankfort, Henri. *Kingship and the Gods: A Study of Ancient Near Eastern Religion as the Integration of Society and Nature*. Chicago: University of Chicago Press, c1948.

Frankfort, Henri. "Town Planning in Ancient Mesopotamia." *Town Planning Review* (July 1950): 98-115.

Frankfort, Henri. *The Birth of Civilization in the Near East*. Bloomington, IN: University of Indiana Press, 1951.

Frankfort, Henri. *Ancient Egyptian Religion: An Interpretation*. New York: Harper, 1961.

Gallion, Arthur B. and Simon Eisner. *The Urban Pattern: City Planning and Design*. 5th ed. New York: Van Nostrand Reinhold, 1986.

Geddes, Patrick. *Cities in Evolution: An Introduction to the Town Planning Movement and to the Study of Civics*. New York: Harper Torchbooks, Harper & Row, 1968.

Givoni, B. *Man, Climate and Architecture*. 2nd ed. New York: Van Nostrand Reinhold, 1976.

Gliessman, S. R. ed. *Agroecology: Researching the Ecological Basis for Sustainable Agriculture*. New York: Springer-Verlag, 1990.

Glikson, Arthur. *Regional Planning and Development*. Leiden, Netherlands: A. W. Sijthoff's Uitgeversmaatschappij N. V., 1955.

*Global Report on Human Settlements*. Oxford, England: Oxford University Press for the United Nations Centre for Human Settlements (HABITAT), 1987.

Golany, Gideon S. *New-Town Planning: Principles and Practice*. New York: Wiley, 1976.

Golany, Gideon S. "Baghdad Indigenous House Design: The Jewish Case." Manuscript in review by a publisher, 1994.

Golany, Gideon S. *Urban Design in Ancient China*. Manuscript in progress, 1994.

Gore, Albert. *Earth in the Balance*. New York: Houghton-Mifflin, 1992.

Hall, Peter. *The World Cities*. New York: McGraw-Hill, World University Library, 1969.

Hardoy, Jorge E. *Pre-Columbian Cities.* New York: Walker and Company, 1973.

Hughes, Donald J. *Ecology in Ancient Civilization.* Albuquerque: University of New Mexico Press, 1975.

Hughes, Johnson Donald. *Ecology in Ancient Civilizations.* 1st ed. Albuquerque: University of New Mexico Press, 1975.

International Union for the Conservation of Nature and Natural Resources (IUCN), United Nations Environmental Program (UNEP), and World Wildlife Fund (WWF). *Caring for the Earth: A Strategy for Sustainable Living.* Gland, Switzerland: IUCN, UNEP, WWF, 1992.

Jacobs, Jane. *The Death and Life of Great American Cities.* Middlesex, England: Penguin Books, 1961.

Jawad, Abdul Jalil. *The Advent of the Era of Townships in Northern Mesopotamia.* Leiden, Netherlands: E. J. Brill, 1965.

Kennedy, Declan. "Permaculture and the Sustainable City." *Ekistics* (May 1991): 210-215.

King, Leonard William. *Babylonian Religion and Mythology.* London: K. Paul, Trench, Trubner, 1899.

Kwang-chih, Chang. *Shang Civilization.* New Haven, CT: Yale University Press, 1980.

Lampl, Paul. *Cities and Planning in the Ancient Near East.* New York: George Braziller, 1968.

Leemans, W. F. *Foreign Trade in the Old Babylonian Period, as Revealed by Texts from Southern Mesopotamia.* Leiden, Netherlands: E. J. Brill, 1960.

Lerner, Daniel. *The Passing of Traditional Society: Modernizing The Middle East.* New York: Free Press, 1966.

Lloyd, Seton. *Mesopotamia: Excavations on Sumerian Sites.* London: Lovat Dickson, 1936.

Lloyd, Seton. *Ruined Cities of Iraq.* London: Oxford University Press, 1945.

Lovelock, James. *The Ages of Gaia: A Biography of our Living Earth.* New York: W. W. Norton, 1988.

Lyle, John Tillman. *Design for Human Ecosystems.* New York: Van Nostrand Reinhold, 1985.

Lynch, Kevin. *The Image of the City.* Cambridge, MA: MIT Press, 1967.

Mackay, E. J. H. and D. Litt. *Further Excavations at Mohenjo-Daro.* Delhi, India: Manager of Publications, 1938.

Maspero, Sir Gaston Camille Charles. *The Dawn of Civilization.* New York: F. Ungar, 1968.

McEwan, Gilbert J. P. (Joseph Paul). *Priest and Temple in Hellenistic Babylonia.* Wiesbaden, Germany: Steiner, 1981.

McHarg, Ian L. and Jonathan Sutton. "Ecological Plumbing for the Texas Coastal Plain." *Landscape Architecture* 65/1 (1975): 78-89.

McLarney, William D. "Aquaculture: Toward an Ecological Approach." Edited by Richard Merrill. *Radical Agriculture.* New York: Harper & Row, 1976.

McPherson, E. Gregory and Sharon Biedenbender. "The Cost of Shade: Cost-Effectiveness of Trees versus Bus Shelters." *Journal of Arboriculture* 17/9 (1991): 233-242.

Minshull, Roger., *Regional Geography: Theory and Practice.* Chicago: Aldine Publishing, 1967.

Mollison, Bill. *Permaculture Two.* Tyalgum, Australia: Tagari Publications, 1979.

Mollison, Bill. *Permaculture: A Designers' Manual.* Tyalgum, Australia: Tagari Publications, 1988.

Mollison, Bill. *Introduction to Permaculture.* Tyalgum, Australia: Tagari Publications, 1991.

Morris, A. E. J. *History of Urban Form: Prehistory to the Renaissance.* New York: Wiley, 1974.

Moscati, Sabatino. *The Face of the Ancient Orient: A Panorama of Near Eastern Civilizations in Pre-Classical Times.* Garden City, NY: Anchor Books, Doubleday, 1962.

Mumford, Lewis. *From the Ground Up: Observations on Contemporary Architecture, Housing, Highway Building, and Civic Design.* New York: A Harvest Book, Harcourt, Brace & World, 1956.

Mumford, Lewis. *Art and Technics.* New York: Columbia University Press, 1960.

Mumford, Lewis. *The City in History.* New York: Harcourt, Brace and World, 1961.

Mumford, Lewis. *Technics and Civilization.* New York: Harcourt, Brace & World, 1963.

Mumford, Lewis. *Technics and Human Development.* New York: Harcourt, Brace, Jovanovich, 1966.

National Research Council (NRC). *Alternative Aquaculture.* Washington, D.C.: National Academy Press, 1989.

Naveh, Zev and Arthur S. Lieberman. *Landscape Ecology: Theory and Application.* New York: Springer-Verlag, 1984.

Okigbo, Bede N. *Development of Sustainable Agricultural Production Systems in Africa.* Ibadan, Nigeria: International Institute for Tropical Agriculture, 1989.

Organization for Economic Cooperation and Development (OECD). *The State of the Environment.* Paris, France: OECD, 1991.

Peet, T. Eric and C. Leonard Woolley. *The City of Akhenaten: Excavations of 1921 and 1922 at El-'Amarneh.* London: William Clowes and Sons, 1923.

Petrova, Elena. "Rooftop Gardening in Russia." *Permaculture Edge* 4 (April 1994), 8-9.

Pirenne, Henri. *Medieval Cities: Their Origins and the Revival of Trade.* Garden City, NY: Doubleday Anchor Books, Doubleday, 1956. Translated from the French by Frank D. Halsey.

Possehl, Gregory L., ed. *Ancient Cities of the Indus.* New Delhi, India: Vikas Publishing House, 1979.

Possehl, Gregory L., ed. *Harappan Civilization.* New Delhi, India: Oxford & IBH Publishing, 1982.

Power, Eileen. *Medieval People.* London: Methuen, University Paperbacks, 1966.

Reiner, Thomas A. *The Place of the Ideal Community in Urban Planning.* Philadelphia: University of Pennsylvania Press, 1963.

Reps, John W. *Town Planning in Frontier America.* Princeton, NJ: Princeton University Press, 1971.

Reps, John W. *Views and Viewmakers of Urban America: Lithographs of Towns and Cities in the United States and Canada, Notes on the Artists and Publishers, and a Union Catalog of Their Work, 1825–1925.* Columbia, MO: University of Missouri Press, 1984.

Ress, William, E. *The Ecological Meaning of Environment-Economy Integration.* Vancouver: University of British Columbia, 1989.

Roseland, Mark. *Toward Sustainable Communities: A Resource Book for Municipal and Local Governments.* Ottawa: University of British Columbia, 1992.

Roselle, Walter. "Three Examples of Ancient Babylonian Art." In *Art in America* II (October 1923): 322-327.

Schultz, Arnold. "The Ecosystem as a Conceptual Tool in the Management of Natural Resources." In *Natural Resources: Quality and Quantity,* edited by S. V. Ciriacy Wantrup and James S. Parsons. Berkeley: University of California Press, 1967.

Shatzman Steinhardt, Nancy. *Chinese Imperial City Planning.* Honolulu: University of Hawaii Press, 1990.

Skinner, G. William, ed. *The City in Late Imperial China.* Stanford, CA: Stanford University Press, 1977.

Stearns, Forest and Tom Montag, eds. *The Urban Ecosystem: A Holistic Approach.* Stroudsburg, PA: Dowden, Hutchinson & Ross, 1974.

Stinner, Benjamin R. and John M. Blair. "Ecological and Agronomic Characteristics of Innovative Cropping Systems." In *Sustainable Agricultural Systems,* edited by Clive A. Edwards, et al. Ankeny, IA: Soil and Water Conservation Society, 1990.

Teaching and Research Office in Urban Design, Tongji University, ed. *History of Chinese Urban Construction.* Beijing: China Building Industrial Press, 1982.

The World Conservation Union. *Caring for the Earth: A Strategy for Sustainable Living.* Gland, Switzerland: IUN/UNEP/WWF, 1991.

Trigger, B. J., B. J. Kemp, D. O'Connor, and B. A. Lloyd. *Ancient Egypt a Social History.* Cambridge, MA: Cambridge University Press, 1983.

Vale, Brenda. *Green Architecture: Design for a Sustainable Future.* Hudson, NY: UCLA AAUP/ARTS NA, no. 2542.3, 35, 1991.

Van der Ryn, Sim and Peter Calthorpe. *Sustainable Communities: A New Design Synthesis for Cities, Suburbs, and Towns.* San Francisco: Sierra Club Books, 1986.

Walter, Bob, ed. *Sustainable Cities.* Los Angeles: Eco-Home Media, 1992.

Wang, Zhongshu. *Han Civilization.* New Haven, CT: Yale University Press, 1982.

Weber, Alfred. *Theory of the Location of Industries.* Translated with an Introduction and Notes by Carl J. Friedrich. Chicago: University of Chicago Press, 1929.

Weitz, Raanan. *Agricultural and Rural Development in Israel: Projection and Planning.* Jerusalem, Israel: National and University Institute of Agriculture, Bulletin No. 68, 1963.

Wen, Feng, ed. *The Great Bronze Age of China.* New York: 1980.

Wheatley, Paul. *The Pivot of the Four Quarters.* Chicago: Aldine Pub., 1971.

Wheeler, R. E. M. *Five Thousand Years of Pakistan: An Archaeological Outline.* London: Royal India & Pakistan Society, 1950.

Wheeler, Robert Eric Mortimer. *The Civilization of the Indus Valley and Beyond.* London: Thames and Hudson, 1966.

Wheeler, Sir Mortimer. *The Cambridge History of India.* London: Syndics of the Cambridge University Press, 1953.

Wheeler, Sir Mortimer. *Early India and Pakistan to Ashoka*. London: Thames and Hudson, 1959.

Wilson, J. "Permaculture's Role in Southern and Eastern Africa." *Permaculture Edge* 4 (April 1994): 17–18.

Wiseman, D. J. *Nebuchadrezzar and Babylon*. London: Oxford University Press, 1985.

Woolley, Leonard. "The Ziggurat and its Surroundings." In *Ur Excavations: Vol. V*. London: Oxford University Press, 1939.

Zhang, Yuhuan, Chief Compiler. *History and Development of Ancient Chinese Architecture*. Beijing, China: Science Press, 1986.

# PART TWO

## PRESENT PRACTICE

Urban design is a continuously evolving process and should be practiced as an endeavor characterized by frequent dynamic changes. Urban design, per se, is focused primarily on human beings and is subject to change. Therefore, it is advantageous to view the historical natural dimension of the given site and its people, and to link their past with their present in order to envision the design of their future city.

Urban design differs from urban planning, and is presently defined as that by which we consider primarily, but not exclusively, the three-dimensional physical forms of the city (width, length, and height) along with the forces that shape its social and physical environment. As such, urban design currently is comprised of strong components of aesthetics, landscape architecture, architecture, civil engineering, architectural engineering, technology, and transportation; it optimally includes the influence of the humanistic and social sciences, and the natural environment as well as the constraints of the human-made environment. The dynamics of the city and the complexity of its components make urban design a delicate object that needs to be pursued by a team of interdisciplinary professionals and decision makers. Urban design is a distinct profession in itself, which happens to have many patrons.

This section introduces some views of the systematic-rational methodology of urban design practices used throughout the twentieth century. Also, a comprehensive-interdisciplinary method of urban design, introduced in this section, has been practiced increasingly throughout the twentieth century. Many urban designers and planners throughout the world were guided by these methods. Yet, neither of the two methods has been established universally or has received the full treatment it deserves. It is hard to point out many schools throughout the world that are well acquainted with these methodologies and are effectively providing them in their curriculum. As an educator, writer, and practitioner, I recognize the significant input of the intuitive and imaginative approach to urban design. This approach can complement the rational-systematic and the comprehensive-interdisciplinary methods, but cannot replace them. It is my perception that this deficiency results from the lack of in-depth knowledge and exposure, and from the failure of teachers and practitioners to adhere to rational-systematic methods and to the comprehensive-interdisciplinary method whereby urban designers and theoreticians can synthesize and integrate all factors involved and, most importantly, communicated in the languages of multidisciplines.

Urban design and the natural environment have been strongly correlated and closely related in their evolution from ancient to contemporary times. This refers to site characteristics and environmental analyses, to resource exploitation and management, and to the whole complex of human activities within the given site. There is no universal theory or method that practitioners can use to deal with the relationship between the site and human-condition issues in a comprehensive and integrated way. Yet, we are closer than ever before to having different theories that complement each other and that fulfill the task of developing a comprehensive design method. One of these is Patrick Geddes' theory, which is one of the most enlightening methods of analysis of urban design introduced in the twentieth century. Geddes first viewed the environment as a component of multielements, where human activities took many forms when married with the site. He introduced the multicomponents of both the site and the community activities by classifying and grouping them, and, most importantly, by introducing the synthesis of their multifaceted combinations and their continuous reciprocal sociophysical impact on the evolution of the settlements. The other significance of his theory is its comprehensive theme and its continuum between past, present, and future.

In addition to the introduction of Geddes' theory, we will examine in this second part of the book my research findings on the evolution of human settlements within the valley and the role of the reciprocal correlation between natural and human-made environmental ethics. Human settlements within the valley evolved sequentially from nomadism to villages, towns, and cities, and then to a port. This theory perceives the valley as a unit and recognizes its dynamic entity.

The other enlightening conceptual design of the twentieth century is the case of urban and regional design in Holland. In comparing small countries such as England, the Netherlands, Israel, and Japan, I found throughout my research a strong correlation between the size of the country, its degree of technological development, the limitations of its resources, and the density of its population on one hand, and the sense of the developmental quality of its urban and regional planning/design on the other. In all four of these countries there has been a strong self-consciousness to enhance the quality of design and its codes at the national, provincial, and local levels. That comprehensive treatment was taken very seriously. Of the previously mentioned four cases, I consider Holland one of the most effective and efficient. Holland is a small country with limited resources and a high-density population, which has led designers to view the manufactured as well as the natural environment in their reciprocal relations and complexity. This is a country where land is precious, where more than 50 percent of it exists below sea level, and where the water table level constantly needs to be comprehensively controlled and coordinated at different localities. The land was literally recreated from the sea. It was this ethic of a comprehensive design that became an effective response to the need for enhancement of the Dutch community.

# 4

## COMPREHENSIVE DESIGN

### BACKGROUND

During the early evolution of the human settlements, the equilibrium between people and nature was, indeed, determined by nature itself. During the Neolithic era, and especially in its early stages, human beings did not have the tools to influence nature. Later, when human settlements were established, people did not want to change nature and the environment, because it was the source of their survival. So, nature took its own course from the Paleolithic through the Neolithic, seemingly peacefully and constructively. This equilibrium lasted a long time in the history of human settlements. From the social, economical, physical, and transportational point of view, the intrusion of urban centers into the environment and with it the evolution of technology was a turning point in the development of human settlements. Yet, this intrusion began to influence the natural environment relatively slowly. It is only recently, since the nineteenth century, that humans accelerated the development of technology and urbanization and became able to change their surrounding environment, sometimes for the better, sometimes for the worse. Accordingly, planning and design became more complex and required new, yet innovative design approaches. Comprehensive design is one of those methods.

Comprehensive design is the art of understanding, analyzing, synthesizing, and bringing to focus the patterns by which all of the forces that shape our environment merge together. The ultimate goal of comprehensive design is to improve the environment and make it habitable and pleasing for the user. This process is a complicated one since it requires the completion of sequential stages and a highly-trained designer who understands the nature of each of those forces. In our educational system, we have usually focused, until now, on specialized training, and we have not given much attention to training designers who have the comprehensive understanding of the contributing forces and their reciprocal relations that form our environment. Such designers are expected to be able to form the synthesis, predict the evolution, define the problems, and introduce relevant solutions in urban or regional design. It seems sometimes that the best synthesizer-designer is nature, which takes its own course throughout the evolution of the environment, synthesizes the development, and finally establishes a harmonious equilibrium. Yet, throughout the course of time, nature introduces catastrophic events or deficiencies that can be prevented when good prediction and design precede them. However, the dynamics of today's environmental reality, on one hand, and our need to influence and enhance the course of events, on the other, as well as using our resources in the optimal way, necessitate the collaboration of an interdisciplinary team able to understand and conceptualize the environmental forces, predict their trends, and offer a solution that is optimal, or close to it. Urban design deals with the revelation of natural forces, as well as the revelation of human behavior and needs. The urban designer, like nature, attempts to establish an equilibrium among human beings, and between them and their natural environment.

The following description of the valley theory is an attempt to clarify the process by which all forms of human settlement development have taken place and by which natural evolution and the evolution of humankind were united. A basic understanding of this process will be valuable in the development of comprehensive regional design.

# THE VALLEY THEORY

The valley theory explains the evolution of humankind, as well as the settlements that have been created throughout history within a valley, as a physical, climatic, and environmental unit. The nucleus of my valley theory was developed by Patrick Geddes. My hypothesis on the evolution of human settlements expands on Geddes' ideas and views the valley unit in a comprehensive and sequential context. The comprehensive theory deals with valley evolution from its early stages of human settlement development and continues through the rise and development of the city, and beyond. It also includes the impact of this evolutionary process on the environment.

The theory has two basic principles. The first is that the valley and its watershed boundaries form one whole, cohesive, and self-sufficient economic unit. The second is that from the appearance of humankind until the formation of cities in the valley unit, the evolution was a sequential, step-by-step process.

The valley became most suitable for the evolution of early humankind's settlements because it provided a wide range of natural resources that offer a variety of options for living. These resources include topography, physiography, climate, soil, water, minerals, flora, fauna, and other special features that, taken together, make the valley a self-sufficient unit. The resources have a mutual impact on each other and through the course of evolution produce a natural equilibrium. Topography, physiography, and climate are among the strongest elements featured in the valley unit. Topographically, the valley introduces three major and distinct units with at least three types of climate: the lowland (mostly flat) with a relatively warm climate, the slope (usually with a high gradient) with moderate temperatures, and the highland (usually plateau or mountainous) with cool or cold temperatures. Each produces different crops in different seasons (Figure 4.1).

Physiographically or geomorphologically, the valley introduces a large variety of land forms that are affected by the type of soil, by the geological features below, by the type of

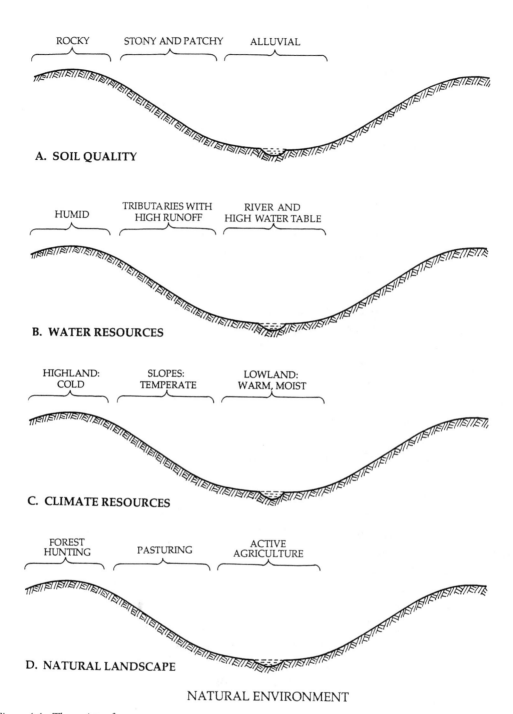

ROCKY      STONY AND PATCHY      ALLUVIAL

**A. SOIL QUALITY**

HUMID      TRIBUTARIES WITH      RIVER AND
HIGH RUNOFF      HIGH WATER TABLE

**B. WATER RESOURCES**

HIGHLAND:      SLOPES:      LOWLAND:
COLD      TEMPERATE      WARM, MOIST

**C. CLIMATE RESOURCES**

FOREST
HUNTING      PASTURING      ACTIVE
AGRICULTURE

**D. NATURAL LANDSCAPE**

NATURAL ENVIRONMENT

*Figure 4.1 The variety of
natural resource landscape
options represented by the
valley unit in a moderate
climate.*

sedimentation, and by other forces. Each unit also has its own characteristics that influence its microclimate, its hydrology network, and its overall natural landscape.

Although it has its own regional characteristics, the climate also is influenced by the physiography of the valley, which establishes different degrees of humidity at different topographical levels and altitudes, and accordingly introduces local climate for each section of the valley. The same can also be said of the wind pattern. The lowland of the valley, for example, features warmth and inversion. Slopes feature moderate temperatures, occasional clouds, increased humidity, and winds. Highlands feature low temperature, frequent clouds, strong winds, and higher humidity.

The hydrological network is a product of both the physiography and the climatic conditions. The quantity of rain and moisture, combined with the physiography and the nature of the soil, will determine the quantity of runoff and the degree of seepage of the drainage system. The more acute the gradient, the greater the runoff and the less the degree of seepage, and vice versa. Similarly, hard or rocky soil increases the runoff and decreases the seepage, and vice versa for soft soil. The hydrological pattern, among such other forces as the character of the soil, influences the type, quality, and distribution of the flora within the valley unit. Also, these, in turn, will influence the fauna types, and their distribution. Finally, all these systems will influence human habitation and its distribution within the valley unit.

The evolutionary process of human settlements began toward the end of Paleolithic nomadism, which was followed by the rise of the Neolithic village. The sequence of settlement habitation patterns within the valley unit was nomadism, seminomadism (seasonal villages), fishing villages, wood villages, mining villages, agriculture villages, regional activity sites, towns, cities, and ports.

In Chapter Two, we discussed nomadism and seminomadism thoroughly within the Paleolithic era. In the following sections, we will expand part of our discussion of the sequential stages of valley maturity from the village to port development (Figure 4.2).

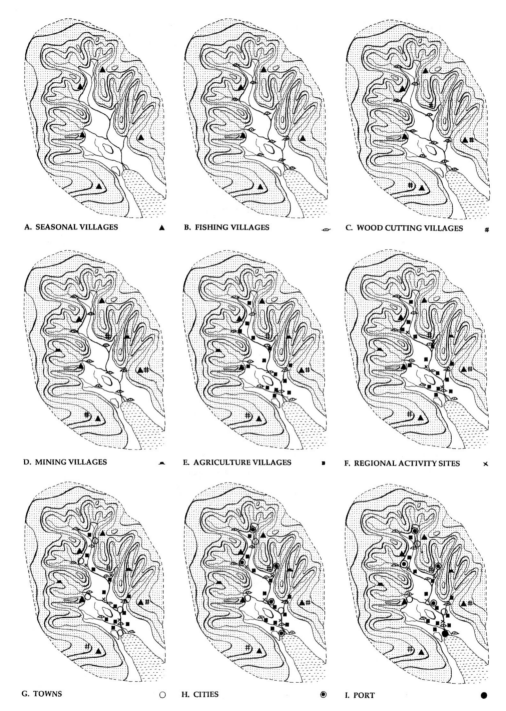

A. SEASONAL VILLAGES ▲   B. FISHING VILLAGES ☞   C. WOOD CUTTING VILLAGES #

D. MINING VILLAGES ◢   E. AGRICULTURE VILLAGES ▪   F. REGIONAL ACTIVITY SITES ✕

G. TOWNS ○   H. CITIES ◉   I. PORT ●

*Figure 4.2 Evolution of human settlements and human-made environments within the valley region unit.*

## Fishing Village

Fishing in the river is one form of food gathering or hunting, which was typical of the Paleolithic era. The river also was used for transportation and for drinking-water. With the introduction of the village during the Neolithic era, the fishing village was probably among the first types to be established. If this assumption is acceptable, we can then envision the development of fishing villages made of a few huts in linear form along the waterfront, while the valley was still occupied by nomads. Fishing villages could have developed independently of, or in combination with, agricultural activities.

## Resource Village

The resource village could have been developed during the early stages of, or throughout, the Neolithic era. The valley unit provided a variety of resources that people consumed, such as wood and metal, and it was logical to expect that the nomads would settle in scattered or clustered huts in the area for collecting the regional resources needed. Most of these resources were located on the slope, and we can assume that resource villages were found there. By virtue of their nature it is most likely that such resources or mining villages were seasonal ones of short duration.

## Agricultural Village

The agricultural village can be considered an advanced form of the fishing and resource villages. It may, in fact, have combined with the fishing village situated along the river, or with the resource village near the creek along the slopes. However, throughout the history of valley development, the agricultural village was the most common and economically active settlement in the valley. The agricultural village took the lead in the socio-economic well-being of the valley. A detailed discussion of agricultural villages is included in Chapter Two.

The next stage in the settlement evolution of the valley was when the agricultural villages established themselves in large numbers occupying most, if not all, of the valley. Villages became mature and different villages specialized in different branches of agriculture, which led to a surplus in their production and the need for trade with others within the valley unit. This developmental growth led to the rise of a regional activity site (temporary), a regional growth center (permanent), towns, and cities, as was explained in Chapter Two.

After the development of the city, when the region as a whole was economically and administratively mature, the valley unit produced a surplus of goods. At this stage, there was need for a new type of regional settlement to function primarily as an exporter and importer with other valley units. This settlement was the port.

## Port Development

To this point, all of the evolution of settlements was contained within the valley and the river's watershed. But, with the many changes that took place during the development and growth of the valley, the boundaries of the region were breached. The primary break occurred at the estuary of the river, where the river meets the sea. The sea became the "new" frontier. It offered opportunities for adventure, exploration, and innovation, as well as the promise of new economic and cultural growth. Consequently, a city was developed at the estuary to function as a port for the exporting and importing of goods and culture.

The port was the next logical step in the sequence of the valley's evolution, and it symbolized an economic maturity and people's desire to expand their horizons. The development of a port was the result of many technological improvements, growing sophistication in land and especially water transportation, continued population growth, the production of a surplus of goods, improvement in political management, advances in trade activities, and the readiness to move from a regional self-sufficient economy to an interregional economy.

The development of a port made the creation of a new interregional system necessary. This resulted in the development of new legal and monetary standards, which were mutually agreed upon among the peoples of the trading regions.

Expanded trade resulted in the creation of a monetary system for the exchange of goods.

In conclusion, the valley unit theory provides a comprehensive design of the evolution of human settlements along with natural evolution in a sequential and coordinated manner, which led to a harmonious environmental equilibrium. People understood that their survival depended on their being in symphony with nature, and they made every effort to support this equilibrium. This environmental ethic evolved out of a deep understanding that people should work with nature, not against it.

## URBAN BORDER ZONE CONCEPT

Concept and theories are usually not universal. Their strength is to explain a limited perspective of a certain condition that may still require another theory to complement the first. In urban design, by virtue of its comprehensiveness, the combination of a few theories may clarify the law and order that governs a given site or regional condition. The valley theory views the given condition of the valley in a comprehensive way. The urban border zone concept is much more limited and views urban development from one narrow perspective.

The urban border zone concept analyzes conditions of two distinct and different adjacently located zones (A and B) that initiate, through their interaction or confrontation, the creation of a superior third zone (C) between the two original zones. Examples of such adjacent zones are:

- Land and sea
- River and land
- Plain or valley and mountain
- Humid and arid
- Soil differentiation

Since every zone A or B is distinct and different in its character and its potential, it is expected that the third zone (C)

*Figure 4.3 Cliff dwellings at the edge between acute slope gradient and the low land making efficient use of the bordering line. Yan' an City, Shaanxi province, China.*

will benefit from the interaction and exchange between the original two zones (Figure 4.3). Land and water zones establish the new zone of ports, metropolitan sites, and fishing villages. A good example of this is the eastern and western coasts of the United States. Humid and arid zones will establish trade cities at their border. An example of this is the Fertile Crescent with the Syrian Desert at its center. In this case, historical trade cities, such as Beershiva, Jerusalem, Beit-Shean, Damascus, Homs, and Aleppo, were developed at the border zone (C) on the rim of the Syrian Desert. Another example is the valley and mountain zones, each of which produce different crops and other agriculture-related products. The valley mostly produces wheat and vegetables while the mountain produces pasturing products, fruits, and other plants. In Europe, many cities were located at the border between the two and grew up using the potential of the two zones.

Cities located at the border zone (C) are characterized by three distinct features:

- *Urban Location*: Urban centers or ports evolve within the zone and serve the adjacent zones. These cities tend to develop a certain order of accumulation of settlements that differ from the pattern of adjacent zones.
- *Urban Size*: These border zone cities are larger than cities falling within the immediate area of either of the adjacent zones.
- *Urban Function*: Cities developed in zone C deal primarily with trade and transportation. In the case of the desert and farming zones, cities located in the C zone are usually developed to be defensible and their size is often predicted by the necessity of defense, which may arise occasionally.

## PATRICK GEDDES' REGIONAL CONCEPT

One of the most comprehensive regional planning models available today was developed by Patrick Geddes. Geddes was a biologist and became one of the earliest environmentalists and urban and regional planners of the West. At the beginning of this century, he understood, before many of his colleagues, that all aspects of the environment are related and that a reciprocal relationship exists between the natural environment and the physical and social environment. Through the course of his work, Geddes developed a comprehensive and systematic way of looking at an environment to improve methods of regional planning for the future. His concept of planning began by looking at the historical past of a region as well as its present before moving into planning for the future.

Since Geddes was aware of the diversity of the geographical conditions of a region as well as of the forces that shape the cultural characteristics of a society, his first premise was that the people (folk), the environment (place), and the local economy (work) are the three fundamental elements that will explain and help us understand the complexity of any region. The second premise of his concept is that each of these elements influences or is influenced by the others. To plan comprehensively and with sensitivity to the environment, Geddes

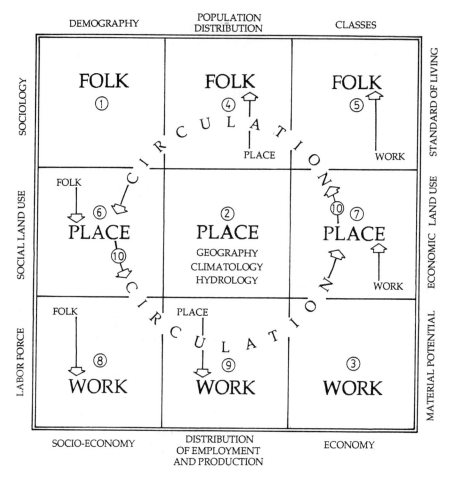

*Figure 4.4 The main subjects to be surveyed in a landscape, according to the Geddes concept of regional design. (Adapted and reproduced from Glikson, 1955, p. 79.)*

believed that a thorough historical and present-day investigation of the region was required by looking at the basic elements and their influence on each other.

In the early 1950s, Artur Glikson of the Israel Institute of Technology in Haifa created a grid of Geddes' elements and described what each block in the grid meant (Figure 4.4). The three main elements are in blocks one, two, and three. Blocks four through nine show how the primary elements influence each other. In each block, the primary element is in large capital letters while the influencing element is in small capitals. From this grid and description of elements, maps would be made of the region to assist in planning. In the following description, numbers one through three explain the basic elements of the survey, and numbers four through ten outline the reciprocal influence of the basic elements within the grid.

1. FOLK—This represents the residents of the region and includes all of the demographic and cultural information.
2. PLACE—This includes all of the physical geographical and environmental features of the region.
3. WORK—This includes the present economic base as well as its potential.
4. FOLK/place—Here the characteristics of the place influence the people, where they live, the type of settlements they develop, and the distribution of the population of the region. This description should also include the differences in settlements that are due to the geographical characteristics and also the health and well-being of the residents.
5. FOLK/work—This describes the influence the type of work available in the region has on the population, including the levels of employment and unemployment, class divisions that result from work, standard of living, labor relations, and the individual share of regional resources.
6. PLACE/folk—Here the influences of the people on the natural environment are considered and include a description of the built areas; the density, type, and dispersion of settlements; the influence of all aspects of society on modifications made to the site; the spheres of influence established by socio-economic forces; and the development of land-use patterns for economic goals, such as agriculture, quarries, or industrial parks.
7. PLACE/work—This area addresses how economic activities change the environment.
8. WORK/folk—Here the influence of the people in the region on the economic base is examined. The relationship between the labor pool and the economic potential of the region as well as how the economic base

is affected by the qualifications of the population should be described.

9. WORK/place—Here the influence of the site on the economic base is examined and should include the types of production, their distribution, and employment opportunities throughout the region, as well as the constraints and potential of the region on the development of its economic activity.

10. Circulation—Mutual influences occur not only between two elements but also among all nine blocks, illustrated by the circle through the grid. This flow expresses the social, economic, cultural, and biological activities in the region and shows the dynamic interaction of the whole system.

Using the grid as the basis of the survey, planners should look at three time periods in the region's history before planning for the future (Figure 4.5). In the first phase, planners should look at the *basic past* (Figure 4.5A), or what the environment was like prior to human intervention. At this stage, the features to be examined are the natural environment and the flora and fauna (organism), and how they all function as a unit within the given environment. The results of this part of the survey will display the original ecological equilibrium of the site and its biological potential.

The second level of the survey should address the *historical past* of the region (Figure 4.5B). This will trace the evolution of humanity's intrusion into the environment and the changing of the natural landscape using the three basic elements of folk, place, and work. It will reveal the gradual development and stabilization of the region that evolved through trial and error. A complete reconstruction of the region according to these two levels will always be difficult but is critical to understanding the region as it is today.

The third phase of the survey focuses on the *present cultural landscape* of the region and should use all sections of the grid (Figure 4.5C). This portion of the survey will help the planner draw conclusions about the population, land use, natural

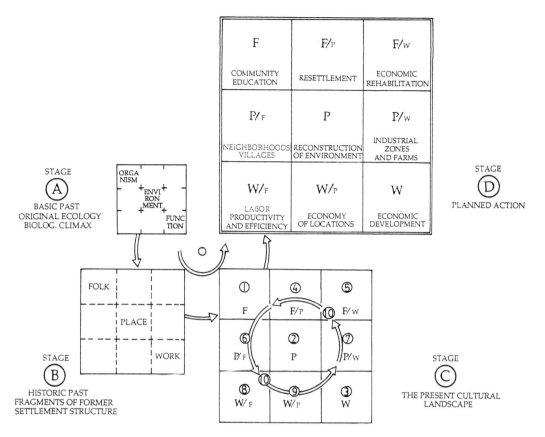

STAGE (A)
BASIC PAST
ORIGINAL ECOLOGY
BIOLOG. CLIMAX

STAGE (B)
HISTORIC PAST
FRAGMENTS OF FORMER
SETTLEMENT STRUCTURE

STAGE (C)
THE PRESENT CULTURAL
LANDSCAPE

STAGE (D)
PLANNED ACTION

Figure 4.5  The main stages of surveying and planning for a region, according to the Geddes concept of regional planning. (Adapted and reproduced from Glikson, 1955, p. 83.)

resources, and forms of settlements and will reveal how the factors of folk, place, and work influence each other.

Once these three steps have been completed, the planner can move on to the *planned action* for the region (Figure 4.5D). Through an analysis of the information gathered in the survey, the planner can enhance the physical, cultural, and economic life of the region. The grid shifts slightly as shown in Figure 4.5D with the three main elements and their interinfluence being redefined for future development.

In conclusion, in spite of limited exposure to historical design methods among designers/planners, Geddes' concept and Glikson's interpretation and expansion of it is one of the most analytical and elaborate concepts in regional design and planning. They introduced the ethics of historical sequences and the ethics of comprehensive consideration of site environment, socio-culture, and labor force. The strength of Geddes' and Glikson's design ethic stems from its comprehensive, systematic, and sequential approach, which establishes reciprocal influences building toward a definite product. It attempts to introduce the historic evolution of the region as the foundation upon which planning/design should be based.

# SELECTED READINGS

Altieri, Miguel A. *Agroecology: The Scientific Basis of Alternative Agriculture.* Boulder, CO: Westview Press, 1987.

Bateson, Gregory. *Mind and Nature.* New York: E. P. Dutton, 1979.

Berg, Peter, Beryl Magilavy, and Seth Zuckerman. *Green City Program for San Francisco Bay Area Cities and Towns.* San Francisco: Planet Drum Books, 1989.

Boardman, Philip. *Patrick Geddes: Maker of the Future.* Chapel Hill: University of North Carolina Press, 1944.

Boardman, Philip. *The Worlds of Patrick Geddes.* London: Routledge & Kegan Paul, 1978.

Botter, Robert Brown. *Ecological House.* New York: Morgan & Morgan, 1981.

Childe, Gordon. *What Happened in History.* Baltimore: Penguin Books, 1942 (1967 reprint).

Culther, Lawrence Stephen and Sherrie Stephens. *Recycling Cities for People: The Urban Design Process.* Boston: Cahners Book International, 1976.

Fathy, Hassan. *Architecture for the Poor.* Chicago: University of Chicago Press, 1973.

Freudenberger, Dean. "The Agricultural Agenda for the Twenty-first Century." *KIDJA, Israel Journal of Development* 7/8 (1988).

Geddes, Patrick. *Cities in Evolution.* New York: Oxford University Press, 1950.

Geyer, John, Robert Kaufmann, David Skole, and Charles Vorosmargy. *Beyond Oil: The Threat to Food and Fuel in the Coming Decades.* Cambridge, MA: Ballinger, 1986.

Givoni, B. *Man, Climate and Architecture.* 2nd ed. New York: Van Nostrand Reinhold, 1976.

Gliessman, S. R., ed. *Agroecology: Researching the Ecological Basis for Sustainable Agriculture.* New York: Springer-Verlag, 1990.

Glikson, Artur. *Regional Planning and Development.* Leiden, Netherlands: A. W. Sijthoff's Vitgeversmaatschappij N. V., 1955.

*Global Report on Human Settlements.* Oxford, England: Oxford University Press for the United Nations Centre for Human Settlements (HABITAT), 1987.

Gore, Albert. *Earth in the Balance.* New York: Houghton-Mifflin, 1992.

*Green Pages: The Local Handbook for Planet Maintenance.* Berkeley, CA: Green Media Group, 1990.

Hamdi, Nabeel. *Housing without Houses: Participation, Flexibility, Enablement.* New York: Van Nostrand Reinhold, 1991.

International Union for the Conservation of Nature and Natural Resources (IUCN), United Nations Environmental Program (UNEP), and World Wildlife Fund (WWF). *Caring for the Earth: A Strategy for Sustainable Living.* Gland, Switzerland: IUCN, UNEP, WWF, 1992.

Isard, Walter. *Location and Space-Economy.* Cambridge, MA: MIT Press, 1956.

Keller, Edward A. *Environmental Geology.* 6th ed. New York: Maxwell Macmillan International, 1992.

Kennedy, Declan. "Permaculture and the Sustainable City." *Ekistics* (May 1991): 210-215.

Kreimer, Alcira and Mohan Munasinghe, eds. *Environmental Management and Urban Vulnerability.* Washington, DC: World Bank, 1992.

Lowe, Marcia. *Alternatives to the Automobile: Transport for Livable Cities.* Worldwatch Paper 98. Washington, D.C.: Worldwatch Institute, 1990.

Lyle, John Tillman. *Design for Human Ecosystems.* New York: Van Nostrand Reinhold, 1985.

McHarg, Ian L. and Jonathan Sutton. "Ecological Plumbing for the Texas Coastal Plain." *Landscape Architecture* 65/1 (1975): 78-89.

McLarney, William D. "Aquaculture: Toward an Ecological Approach," edited by Richard Merrill. *Radical Agriculture.* New York: Harper & Row, 1976.

McPherson, E. Gregory and Sharon Biedenbender. "The Cost of Shade: Cost-Effectiveness of Trees versus Bus Shelters." *Journal of Arboriculture* 17/9 (1991): 233-242.

Mollison, Bill. *Permaculture: A Designers' Manual.* Tyalgum, Australia: Tagari Publications, 1988.

Mollison, Bill. *Introduction to Permaculture.* Tyalgum, Australia: Tagari Publications, 1991.

Morlock, Susan. *Innovation in Subdivision Design.* MLS thesis. Pomona, CA: California State Polytechnic University, 1990.

Mumford, Lewis. *The City in History.* New York: Harcourt, Brace and World, 1961.

Mumford, Lewis. *Technics and Human Development.* New York: Harcourt, Brace, Jovanovich, 1966.

Mumford, Lewis. *The Culture of Cities.* New York: Harcourt Brace Jovanovich, 1970.

Naar, Jon; foreword by Frederic D. Krupp. *Design for a Livable Planet: How You Can Help Clean Up the Environment.* 1st ed. New York: Perennial Library, 1990.

National Research Council (NRC). *Alternative Aquaculture.* Washington, D.C.: National Academy Press, 1989.

Okigbo, Bede N. *Development of Sustainable Agricultural Production Systems in Africa.* Ibadan, Nigeria: International Institute for Tropical Agriculture, 1989.

Petrova, Elena. "Rooftop Gardening in Russia." *Permaculture Edge* (4 April 1994): 8-9.

Register, Richard. *Ecocity Berkeley: Building Cities for a Healthy Future.* Berkeley, CA: North Atlantic Books, 1987.

Reissman, Leonard. "The Visionary: Planner for Urban Utopia." In *Urban Planning Theory,* edited by Melville C. Branch. Stroudsburg, PA: Dowden, Hutchinson & Ross, 1975.

Renner, Michael. *Jobs in a Sustainable Economy.* Worldwatch Paper 104. Washington, D.C.: Worldwatch Institute, 1991.

Ress, William, E. *The Ecological Meaning of Environment-Economy Integration.* Vancouver: University of British Columbia, 1989.

Roseland, Mark. *Toward Sustainable Communities: A Resource Book for Municipal and Local Governments.* Ottawa: University of British Columbia, 1992.

Rowe, Peter G. *Design Thinking.* Cambridge, MA: MIT Press, 1987.

Schroeder, G. L. "Fish-Farming in Manure-Loaded Ponds." In *Integrated Agriculture-Aquaculture Farming Systems,* edited by Roger S.V. Pullin and Zian H. Schehadeh. Manila, Philippines: International Center for Living Aquatic Resources, 1980.

Schultz, Arnold. "The Ecosystem as a Conceptual Tool in the Management of Natural Resources." In *Natural Resources: Quality and Quantity,* edited by S. V. Ciriacy Wantrup and James S. Parsons. Berkeley: University of California Press, 1967.

Serageldin, Ismail and June Taboroff, eds.; sponsors, Government of Norway, et al. *Culture and Development in Africa: Proceedings of an International Conference Held at the World Bank,* Washington, D. C., April 2-3, 1992. Washington, DC: World Bank, 1994.

Stally, Marshall, ed. *Patrick Geddes: Spokesman for Man and the Environment.* New Brunswick, NJ: Rutgers University Press, 1972.

Stearns, Forest and Tom Montag, eds. *The Urban Ecosystem: A Holistic Approach.* Stroudsburg, PA: Dowden, Hutchinson & Ross, 1974.

Stearns, Peter N. *The Industrial Revolution in World History.* Boulder, CO: Westview Press, 1993.

Stinner, Benjamin R. and John M. Blair. "Ecological and Agronomic Characteristics of Innovative Cropping Systems." In *Sustainable Agricultural Systems,* edited by Clive A. Edwards, et al. Ankeny, IA: Soil and Water Conservation Society, 1990.

The World Conservation Union. *Caring for the Earth: A Strategy for Sustainable Living.* Gland, Switzerland: IUN/UNEP/WWF, 1991.

Turner, John. *Housing by People: Towards Autonomy in Building Environments.* New York: Pantheon Books, 1977.

U. S. Department of Agriculture. *Conservation in the 1990 Farm Bill.* Washington, D.C.: The Department, 1991.

Vale, Brenda and Robert Vale. *Autonomous House.* New York: Universe Books, 1977.

Vale, Brenda. *Green Architecture: Design for a Sustainable Future.* Hudson, NY: UCLA AAUP/ARTS NA, no. 2542.3, 35, 1991.

Van der Ryn, Sim and Peter Calthorpe. *Sustainable Communities: A New Design Synthesis for Cities, Suburbs, and Towns.* San Francisco: Sierra Club Books, 1986.

Walter, Bob, ed. *Sustainable Cities*. Los Angeles: Eco-Home Media, 1992.

Walter, Bob. "Gardens in the Sky." In *Sustainable Cities: Concepts and Strategies for Eco-City Development*, edited by Bob Walter, Lois Arkin, and Richard Crenshaw. Los Angeles: EHM Publishers, 1992.

Weitz, Raanan. *Agriculture and Rural Development in Israel: Projection and Planning*. Rehovot, Israel: National and University Institute of Agriculture, Settlement Department of the Jewish Agency, 1963.

Wilson, J. "Permaculture's Role in Southern and Eastern Africa." *Permaculture Edge* 4 (April 1994): 17-18.

Wohlwill, Joachim F. and Willem van Vliet, eds. *Habitats for Children: The Impact of Density*. Hillsdale, NJ: L. Erlbaum Associates, 1985.

World Resources Institute (WRI). *World Resources: A Guide to the Global Environment 1992–93*. New York: Oxford University Press, 1992.

Wright, Gwendolyn. *Building the Dream: A Social History of Housing in America*. Cambridge, MA: MIT Press, 1981.

## 5

# CONTEMPORARY COMPREHENSIVE DESIGN: The Case of Holland

## BACKGROUND

The Netherlands, or Holland, is one of the most densely populated countries in the world. It is characterized by being almost flat lowland with more than 50 percent of the country being two to five meters below sea level (Figure 5.1). Geologically, the country continues to sink into the sea. For many centuries, reclaiming land from beneath the sea level has been a continuous community and national challenge (Figure 5.2). During the twentieth century, the country's challenge has been to retain the balance between rural and urban expansion and to avoid over urbanization and diminishing rural agriculture land. This chapter is intended as an outline of the basic twentieth-century policy that has made Holland such an excellent case study, rather than as a review of the state of the art.

## NATIONAL PLANNING POLICY

The Netherlands' national policy evolved during this century as the result of pragmatic needs, yet its formulation and

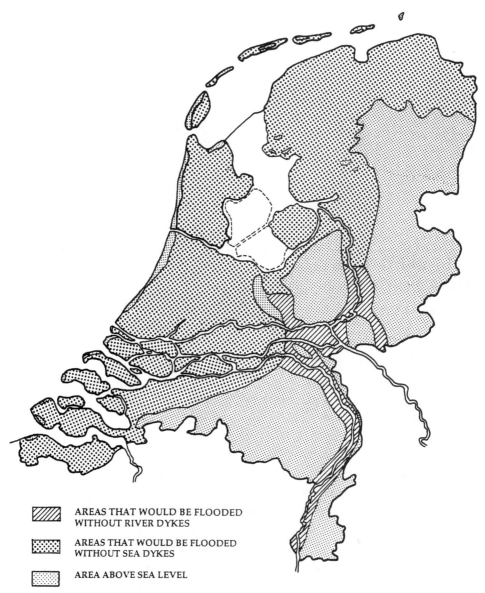

AREAS THAT WOULD BE FLOODED
WITHOUT RIVER DYKES

AREAS THAT WOULD BE FLOODED
WITHOUT SEA DYKES

AREA ABOVE SEA LEVEL

*Figure 5.1 With most of
its land below sea level,
Holland has depended on
its network of dikes both on
rivers and along the coast to
prevent flooding. (Adapted
and reproduced from
Constandse, Wijers, and
de Ruiter.)*

execution can be considered one of the most effective regional and urban planning and design models in the world.
Its foundation was shaped primarily immediately after World
War II and has been subject to continuous modification and
improvement and become increasingly effective. It is for this
reason that we selected Holland as a case study in this volume.

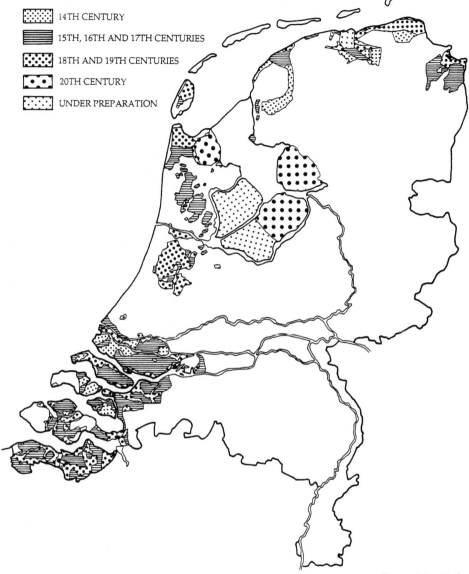

14TH CENTURY

15TH, 16TH AND 17TH CENTURIES

18TH AND 19TH CENTURIES

20TH CENTURY

UNDER PREPARATION

*Figure 5.2   Holland has been reclaiming land from the sea since the fourteenth century through the building of dikes and canals and the continuous pumping of the water. (Source: Adapted and reproduced from Constandse, Wijers, and de Ruiter.)*

A strong national consensus is critical for the success and implementation of a national planning policy. It is my observation that there is a correlation between the size of a country, its natural resources, and population density on one hand, and the degree of national consensus and with it a national policy on the other hand. Basically, the smaller the country the greater the national consensus on policy development.

Consensus is definitely the case in Holland. Most characteristics of the planning policy and its implementation include:

- Comprehensiveness
- Emphasis on physical aspects
- Strong consideration of related factors, such as social and economic aspects of life
- Environmental consideration
- Strong sense of ecology
- Community and individual orientation
- Preservation of green open space and demarcation of urban land
- A sequential relationship at the national, provincial, and local levels in the formulation of design and its implementation

The policy focuses on three major issues—the land reclamation system, conurbation control, and population distribution.

## Land Reclamation System

Motivated by the high density of the population and by the fact that more than 50 percent of the country is below sea level, the Dutch people have established a unique and distinct system for reclaiming land from the sea and converting it to agriculture or settlement use (Figure 5.3). The system necessitates hard work, persistence, and community collaboration, all characteristics common to the Dutch people. It is significant to note that the entire national, regional, and, to some extent, local planning is financed by the government.

The basic concept of the reclamation process is to construct polders by building dikes and by pumping the water out of the area until the water level withdraws to the level of a desired water table. Afterward, continuous pumping is required to prevent the water from returning to its original level over the soil. This continuous effort must be coordinated and requires regional planning for two reasons. First, pumping must be regulated to prevent the line between the North Sea water and the fresh-water table of the reclaimed soil from

*Figure 5.3 New agricultural land resources created from the sea, for existing and future generations, Holland. (Courtesy of the Government of Holland.)*

creeping inland and causing salinization of the water table. Basically, this can be accomplished by low or no pumping on the dunes built as a barrier along the North Sea while increasing the pumping in the central and eastern part of the reclaimed area. Second, the water table must be kept at different levels for different agricultural needs. Thus, there is a careful design and implementation of both the degree of pumping and the type of agriculture practiced on a given site, so that adjacent sites throughout the reclaimed area may have different water tables and produce different crops.

Through centuries of experience, the Dutch people have gained significant and unique experience with hydraulics and the process of land reclamation. Their process is ingenious in its design and development. First, land being reclaimed for agricultural production is confined by a square or rectangular dike. The dike is created by taking soil from the interior adjacent area, which will become the polder. Polders are designed adjacent to each other with a narrow canal between them to collect the water pumped from the polder. The sizes of polders differ; they can be as large as a building, a city block, or even many city blocks together. However, the continuous pumping keeps the land free of water and available for agricultural development.

Land reclamation for urban development is accomplished in a different way. Here, instead of pumping the land completely dry, construction can be accomplished through the use of caissons. These are watertight concrete structures reinforced with iron grids that are used to form the foundation of buildings. Created elsewhere, the caissons are floated to the construction site, where valves in the concrete are opened to allow water into the caisson. The weight of the water forces the caisson to settle, leveled, on the soil below the surface of the shallow water. The building is then constructed using the exposed top of the caisson as the base. Once construction is complete, the caisson is stabilized by the weight of the building, so the water is no longer necessary. The valves are closed, and the water is pumped out of the caisson. As in the countryside, pumping in urban areas is a continual process to maintain the land.

Land reclamation strengthened Holland by providing a good foundation for an agriculture environment and for sophisticated agriculture production. The strong association with and sensitivity to the environment as open green space has helped contain the rise of urbanization and limited the strong competition between urban land use and agricultural land use. Intensified agricultural production has promoted a high regard for the countryside and its role in the national economy (Figure 5.4).

## Conurbation Holland Control

Conurbation (Randstad) is the conglomeration of existing urban and semiurban sites to form aggregate settlement expansion, resulting in a continuous urban environment, mostly linear in form. "Conurbation Holland" is the semicircular pattern of urban and town development in the midwestern sector of the country, starting east of Amsterdam and continuing to the west, then south through The Hague, Rotterdam, and Utrecht (Figure 5.5). This urban crescent form embraces land designated for intensive agriculture.

*Figure 5.4 Land reclamation from sea for new farming expansion of settlers, Holland. (Courtesy of the Government of Holland.)*

This close spatial pattern of urban and agriculture land poses the threat of urban expansion with all its associated problems toward the agricultural center on one hand, and the diminishing or disappearance of the agricultural land and countryside from the immediate urban environment on the other. Considering the small size of the country and the high density of the population, especially in this central section, such development would have a negative impact on agriculture production, social patterns, population distribution (overconcentration in the urban area), transportation, and most

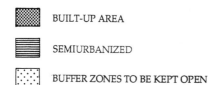

BUILT-UP AREA

SEMIURBANIZED

BUFFER ZONES TO BE KEPT OPEN

*Figure 5.5 Conurbation Holland rings the agricultural land in the western part of the country. (Adapted and reproduced from Constandse in Golany, ed., 1978, p. 58.)*

importantly, on the environment with changes in the soil, air, and the quality of urban life.

The Dutch government and planners realized that unplanned development or the absence of an overall plan and policy would allow this expansion to occur. There was, however, a national consensus on the need to control Conurbation Holland. To cope with this problem, the physical planning body of the country adopted the planning policy that placed strong control on the land use of Conurbation Holland and the agriculture land at its center. The policy called for preventing the expansion of the existing urban area of

Conurbation Holland toward the agriculture land and the disappearance of green open space that existed between the cities themselves.

## Population Distribution

Because the Netherlands is small and densely populated, especially in Conurbation Holland, decentralizing the population is favored to relieve pressure in urban areas and to help improve the quality of urban life. While the Dutch government cannot tell people where they must live to accomplish this, it has encouraged through incentives the shift of the population by the decisions of the Central Planning Bureau, which was formed in 1945 to examine and encourage national economic prosperity.

When the Central Planning Bureau was established, the population of the Netherlands was expected to reach eighteen to nineteen million by the year 2000. That figure has since been revised to fifteen to sixteen million, but with a land mass of less than 12,000 square kilometers, the Dutch still need to be mindful of the population distribution.

A number of strategies have been used by the Dutch government to encourage population decentralization. First, following its creation, the Central Planning Bureau concentrated on expanding the industrial base of the country to cope with the burgeoning population and its need for sustenance. While the bureau could not force new industry to locate in more sparsely populated areas, it could make those locations more attractive by improving the infrastructure, schools, and cultural climate. To an extent, this approach has been successful.

Another position of the government toward population distribution is its support of emigration. The rapid population growth since the end of World War II is a threat to the survival of the Netherlands. Making emigration an option is seen as a support for decentralization as well as an avenue for maintaining good international communications and to spread the reputation of the country abroad. This, in turn, supports and promotes the country's international trade.

The long-term reclamation projects supported by the government also encourage decentralization. The land in the Lake

Yssel polders belongs to the government, and it has encouraged the development of cities and towns on the new land to support a natural population shift. Because full land reclamation takes from fifty to sixty years, using new land to encourage a population shift is not as effective, perhaps, as the first two approaches the government has supported.

Other approaches include strengthening smaller towns to maintain a high quality of life and encourage people to remain there, improving schools in rural areas, and developing new schools and universities with more technical curricula in sparsely populated areas.

Public opinion has, for the most part, supported efforts to decentralize the population. Because Conurbation Holland is a communication and transportation center for northwestern Europe as well as the Netherlands, it will always remain densely populated, but the government's efforts will help contain these cities and keep them from encroaching on the adjacent agricultural space.

## ZUYDER ZEE PLAN

A major element of the planning policy was the development of the Zuyder Zee and more specifically Lake Yssel, located northeast of Amsterdam. The first part of the Zuyder Zee scheme, which had been envisioned in the nineteenth century, was the building of a large dam separating the easternmost area of the Zuyder Zee from the sea and the creation of a fresh-water lake, Lake Yssel. The lake is now fed from the southeast by the water of the Rhine and the Meuse Rivers. The second stage of this plan was the reclamation of parts of Lake Yssel (Figure 5.6). The first area reclaimed was the Wieringermeer Polder in the extreme northwest of the lake, where the reclamation of 50,000 acres was finished in 1930. Next was the construction of the North-East Polder at the eastern part of the lake, which was completed in 1942 and became a model for modern Dutch polder planning during the 1950s. In 1950, the Eastern Flevoland Polder southeast of the lake was started and by mid-1957 most of the reclaimed

*Figure 5.6 (facing page) Five polders created by reclaiming land from the fresh-water Lake Yssel. These polders increased the physical area of the Netherlands by 10 percent. (Adapted and reproduced from* Forum, *1955. Courtesy of the Government of Holland.)*

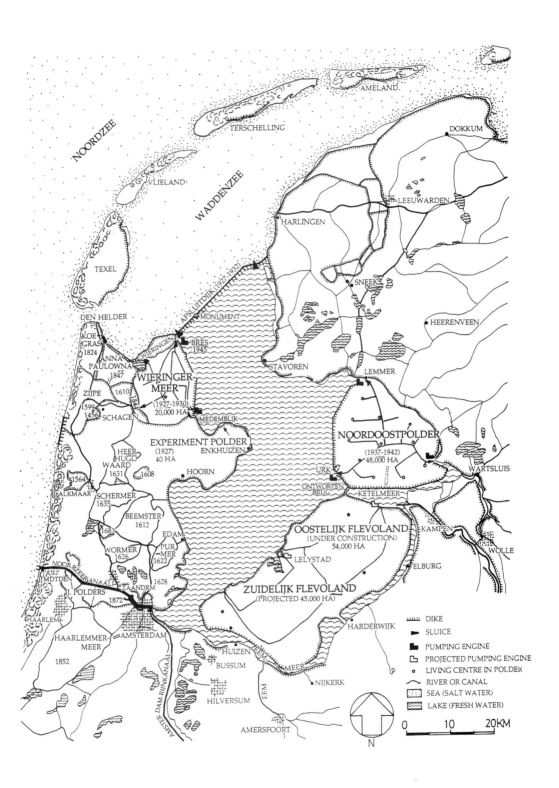

NOORDZEE

AMELAND.

TERSCHELLING

DOKKUM

VLIELAND·

WADDENZEE

LEEUWARDEN

HARLINGEN

TEXEL

SNEEK

DEN HELDER

HEERENVEEN

KOE
GRAS
1824

AFSLUITDIJK (1927-1932)

MONUMENT

ANNA
PAULOWNA
1847

WIERINGEN

BRES
1945

STAVOREN

WIERINGER-
MEER

ZIJPE 1610

LEMMER

1599
1456 SCHAGEN

(1927-1930)
20,000 HA

MEDEMBLIK

NOORDOOSTPOLDER

EXPERIMENT POLDER
(1927)
40 HA

ENKHUIZEN

(1937-1942)
48,000 HA

WARTSLUIS

HEER-
HUGO-
WAARD
1631

1608

HOORN

URK

ALKMAAR 1564

ONTWORPEN
BRUG

KETELMEER

SCHERMER
1635

OOSTELIJK FLEVOLAND
(UNDER CONSTRUCTION)
54,000 HA

KAMPEN

WOLLE

BEEMSTER
1612

1683

EDAM

LELYSTAD

ELBURG

WORMER
1626

PUR
-MER
1622

NOORDZEEKANAAL

ZAANDRM

1628

ZUIDELIJK FLEVOLAND
(PROJECTED 45,000 HA)

IJMUIDEN

IJ. POLDERS

1872

HARDERWIJK

HAARLEM-

AMSTERDAM

HUIZEN

HAARLEMMER-
MEER

BUSSUM

EEM
MEER

AMSTERDAM-RIJNKANAAL

1852

NIJKERK

HILVERSUM

AMERSFOORT

DIKE

SLUICE

PUMPING ENGINE

PROJECTED PUMPING ENGINE

LIVING CENTRE IN POLDER

RIVER OR CANAL

SEA (SALT WATER)

LAKE (FRESH WATER)

0        10        20KM

N

land was already in use. Afterward, 100,000 acres in the southern part of the lake were developed into the Southern Flevoland Polder, which was to be followed by the 148,000-acre Markerwaard Polder northeast of Amsterdam. This last polder was not developed so that Amsterdam would continue to have direct access to Lake Yssel. Despite the polders and further land reclamation from the lake, much of the lake remains. Some of the intentions and achievements of this large-scale development have been to provide green and agriculture open space along with bodies of water close to Amsterdam and Conurbation Holland. In a sense, the polders and Lake Yssel provide alternative green open space to that of the central agriculture land for growth and recreation, and ease the pressure on that space.

### North-East Polder Design

The North-East Polder, which was completely reclaimed from the lake, was considered a successful model of design for its time. The project was started in 1937 and, with the interruption of the war, was finished in 1960. The planners developed the polder in a geometric pattern with the major town of Emmeloord at its geographical center (Figure 5.7). Ten satellite villages were created in a circular pattern so that no resident would be more than 5 kilometers from a village. These villages were a new breed with a standard of living equal to that of a wealthy town. The expected total population of the polder was fifty thousand with a density of about one inhabitant per hectare while Emmeloord's population was expected to be ten thousand. The villages were expected to have an average peripheral area of about ten thousand acres and a population of one to two thousand each. The balance of the population lived in the countryside. New residents were chosen from a high-quality pool of applicants and were selected based on research in regional socio-economic structures, as well as previous experience. They then were settled according to a gradual regional development plan.

The polder was originally planned to be rural in character with its dominant industry being agriculture. Large and small farms were developed with the larger ones being farther away

*Figure 5.7 (facing page) The approximately circular shape of the North-East Polder resulted in a major town at its geographical center surrounded by a circular pattern of ten villages. (Adapted and reproduced from* Forum, *1955. Courtesy of the Government of Holland.)*

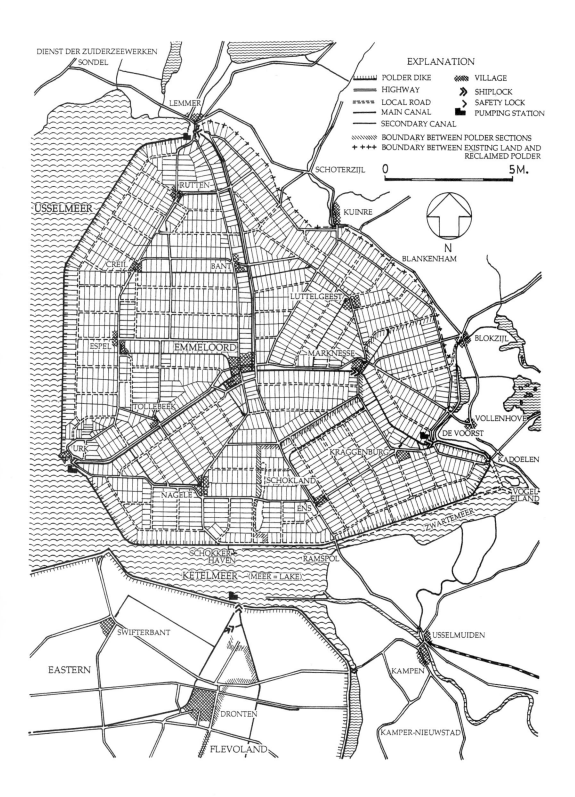

from the villages. Farms of similar size and type were grouped together. The nature of the soil determined, to a large extent, the use of the land. The difference in soil types led to mixed farms with livestock, planned on the edge of the polder where the soil was lighter, while arable farming was planned for the center of the polder where the soil was heavier. Some soil was used for a forest and some was reserved for market gardening and fruit growing.

In conclusion, one strength of Dutch planning is its ethics of comprehensiveness, considering social and economic aspects at the center of its physical design. Yet, without the hierarchical design coordination of the three levels—central government national policy and plan, the provincial master plan, and the local detailed plan—the comprehensive planning would have certainly lost its effectiveness. Also, without the national consensus, at least the one during the three postwar decades, the national and local design would not have been implemented. Since the Second World War, the national sense and awareness of environmental and ecological ethics considerations have been increasing and this has had a positive impact on the evolution of this design. Also, while it is important to notice that the reclaimed land and new settlements have been an intrusion into the natural environment, it is certainly a positive one. It can be considered one of the best urban regional design plans in the twentieth century, and it has led to a successful marriage between the natural environment and the manufactured environment. It certainly has achieved a comprehensive environmental ethic.

# SELECTED READINGS

*A Structure Plan for the Southern IJsselmeerpolders.* The Hague, Netherlands: Rijkswaterstaat Communications, 1965.

Berg, Peter, Beryl Magilavy, and Seth Zuckerman. *Green City Program for San Francisco Bay Area Cities and Towns.* San Francisco: Planet Drum Books, 1989.

Berkowitz, Bill. *Community Dreams.* San Luis Obispo, CA: Impact Publishers, 1984.

Blijstra, R. *Dutch Architecture After 1900.* Amsterdam: P. N. Van Kampen & Zoon N.V., 1966.

Blijstra, R. *Town Planning in The Netherlands Since 1900.* Amsterdam: P. N. Van Kampen & Zoon N.V., 1963.

Botter, Robert Brown. *Ecological House.* New York: Morgan & Morgan, 1981.

Commoner, Barry. *Making Peace with the Planet.* New York: Pantheon Books, 1990.

Constandse, A. K. "New Towns on the Bottom of the Sea." In *International Urban Growth Policies: New Town Contributions,* edited by Gideon Golany. New York: Wiley, 1978.

Constandse, A. K., L. Wijers, and Mrs. N. C. de Ruiter, comp. *Planning and Creation of an Environment: Experiences in the Ysselmeerpolders,* The Hague, Netherlands, 1964.

Corbett, Michael. *A Better Place to Live.* Emmaus, PA: Rodale Press, 1988.

Fathy, Hassan. *Architecture for the Poor.* Chicago: University of Chicago Press, 1973.

Frederick, Douglas D. "Water Resources: Increasing Demand and Scarce Supplies." In *America's Renewable Resources: Historical Trends and Current Challenges,* edited by Kenneth D. Frederick and Roger A. Sedjo. Washington, D.C.: Resources for the Future, 1991.

Freudenberger, Dean. "The Agricultural Agenda for the Twenty-first Century." *KIDJA, Israel Journal of Development* 7/8 (1988).

Geyer, John, Robert Kaufmann, David Skole, and Charles Vorosmargy. *Beyond Oil: The Threat to Food and Fuel in the Coming Decades.* Cambridge, MA: Ballinger Publishing, 1986.

Givoni, B. *Man, Climate and Architecture.* 2nd ed. New York: Van Nostrand Reinhold, 1976.

Gliessman, S. R., ed. *Agroecology: Researching the Ecological Basis for Sustainable Agriculture.* New York: Springer-Verlag, 1990.

Glikson, Artur. *Regional Planning and Development.* Leiden, Netherlands: A. W. Sijthoff's Vitgeversmaatschappij N.V., 1955.

*Global Report on Human Settlements.* Oxford, England: Oxford University Press for the United Nations Centre for Human Settlements (HABITAT), 1987.

Golany, Gideon S.: "Planning and Development in the Netherlands." Thesis. The Hague, Netherlands. Institute of Social Studies, 1965.

Golany, Gideon S. "An Analytical Approach to Optimal Future Location and Distribution of Urban Areas in 'Conurbation Holland' into The Netherlands." Thesis. The Hague, Netherlands. Institute of Social Studies, 1965.

Gore, Albert. *Earth in the Balance: Ecology and the Human Spirit.* New York: Houghton-Mifflin, 1992.

Government Physical Planning Service. *Report on Physical Planning in The Netherlands.* The Hague, Netherlands: Netherlands Printing Office, 1960.

Government Physical Planning Service and the Information Department of the Ministry of Housing and Building. *Physical Planning in The Netherlands.* The Hague, Netherlands: Government Information Service, 1961.

Government Service for Land and Water Use, Ministry of Agriculture and Fisheries. *Rural Development in The Netherlands.* Barneveld, Holland: Barneveldse Drukkerij N.V.

Graftdijk, Klaas. *Holland Rides the Sea.* Barn, Holland: World's Window, Ltd., 1960.

*Green Pages: The Local Handbook for Planet Maintenance.* Berkeley: Green Media Group, 1990.

Groenman, Sjaerd. "Social Aspects of the Demographic Development in The Netherlands." *Planning and Development in The Netherlands* 1/1 (1962): 19-25.

Hendricks, G. *Social Planning and Community Development.* Rijswijk, Holland: Ministry of Cultural Affairs, Recreation and Social Welfare, 1967.

Information Bureau of the Ministry of "Verkeeren Waterstaat" in cooperation with the Service for the Execution of the Zuiderzeeworks. *The Zuiderzee Works: The Work of Half a Century Told in Five Minutes.* The Hague, Holland: Van Loon, no date.

Information Department of the Ministry of Transport and "Waterstaat" in cooperation with The Delta Department of "Rijkswaterstaat." *The Netherlands and the Water.* The Hague, Netherlands: Government Printing Office, 1967.

Information Department of the Ministry of Transport, Water Control, and Public Works, in conjunction with the Board of the Zuyder Zee Works. *The Zuyder Zee Works: Fifty Years of Toil Described in Five Minutes.* The Hague, Netherlands: The Netherlands Government Information Service, 1967.

International Union for the Conservation of Nature and Natural Resources (IUCN), United Nations Environmental Program (UNEP), and World Wildlife Fund (WWF). *Caring for the Earth: A Strategy for Sustainable Living.* Gland, Switzerland: IUCN, UNEP, WWF, 1992.

*Location of Industry in The Netherlands: Census of Occupations 1930.* The Hague, Netherlands: Government Service for Physical Planning.

Lovelock, James. *The Ages of Gaia: A Biography of our Living Earth.* New York: W. W. Norton, 1988.

Lowe, Marcia. *Alternatives to the Automobile: Transport for Livable Cities.* Worldwatch Paper 98. Washington, D.C.: Worldwatch Institute, 1990.

Lyle, John Tillman. *Design for Human Ecosystems.* New York: Van Nostrand Reinhold, 1985.

McHarg, Ian L. and Jonathan Sutton. "Ecological Plumbing for the Texas Coastal Plain." *Landscape Architecture* 65/1 (1975).

McLarney, William D. "Aquaculture: Toward an Ecological Approach," edited by Richard Merrill. *Radical Agriculture.* New York: Harper & Row, 1976.

McPherson, E. Gregory. "Economic Modeling for Large Scale Urban Tree Plantings." In *Proceedings of the ACEE 1990 Summer Study on Energy Efficiency in Buildings* 4. Washington, D.C.: American Council for an Energy Efficient Economy, 1990.

McPherson, E. Gregory and Sharon Biedenbender. "The Cost of Shade: Cost-Effectiveness of Trees versus Bus Shelters." *Journal of Arboriculture* 17/9 (1991): 233-242.

Mollison, Bill. *Permaculture: A Designers' Manual.* Tyalgum, Australia: Tagari Publications, 1988.

Morlock, Susan. *Innovation in Subdivision Design.* MLS thesis. Pomona, CA: California State Polytechnic University, 1990.

Mumford, Lewis. *The City in History.* New York: Harcourt, Brace and World, 1961.

Mumford, Lewis. *Technics and Human Development.* New York: Harcourt, Brace, Jovanovich, 1966.

National Research Council (NRC). *Alternative Aquaculture.* Washington, D.C.: National Academy Press, 1989.

Noordam, B. W. *When the Tide Turns: The Netherlands' Struggle Against the Water.* The Hague, Netherlands: N. V. Uitgeverij W. Van Hoeve, 1963.

"Noordoostpolder 1955." *Forum* X (1955): 1-2.

Okigbo, Bede N. *Development of Sustainable Agricultural Production Systems in Africa.* Ibadan, Nigeria: International Institute for Tropical Agriculture, 1989.

Petrova, Elena. "Rooftop Gardening in Russia." *Permaculture Edge* 4, (April 1994): 8-9.

Register, Richard. *Ecocity Berkeley: Building Cities for a Healthy Future.* Berkeley: North Atlantic Books, 1987.

Reissman, Leonard. "The Visionary: Planner for Urban Utopia." In *Urban Planning Theory,* edited by Melville C. Branch. Stroudsburg, PA: Dowden, Hutchinson & Ross, 1975.

Renner, Michael. *Jobs in a Sustainable Economy.* Worldwatch Paper 104. Washington, D.C.: Worldwatch Institute, 1991.

Ress, William, E. *The Ecological Meaning of Environment-Economy Integration.* Vancouver: University of British Columbia, 1989.

Roseland, Mark. *Toward Sustainable Communities: A Resource Book for Municipal and Local Governments*. Ottawa: University of British Columbia, 1992.

Rowe, Peter G. *Design Thinking*. Cambridge, MA: MIT Press, 1987.

Schroeder, G. L. "Fish-Farming in Manure-Loaded Ponds." In *Integrated Agriculture-Aquaculture Farming Systems*, edited by Roger S. V. Pullin and Zian H. Schehadeh. Manila, Philippines: International Center for Living Aquatic Resources, 1980.

Schultz, Arnold. "The Ecosystem as a Conceptual Tool in the Management of Natural Resources." In *Natural Resources: Quality and Quantity*, edited by S. V. Ciriacy Wantrup and James S. Parsons. Berkeley: University of California Press, 1967.

*Second Report on Physical Planning in The Netherlands: Part II, Future Pattern of Development*. The Hague, Netherlands: Government Printing Office, 1966.

Stearns, Forest and Tom Montag, eds. *The Urban Ecosystem: A Holistic Approach*. Stroudsburg, PA: Dowden, Hutchinson & Ross, 1974.

Stinner, Benjamin R. and John M. Blair. "Ecological and Agronomic Characteristics of Innovative Cropping Systems." In *Sustainable Agricultural Systems*, edited by Clive A. Edwards, et al. Ankeny, IA: Soil and Water Conservation Society, 1990.

The World Conservation Union. *Caring for the Earth: A Strategy for Sustainable Living*. Gland, Switzerland: IUN/UNEP/WWF, 1991.

Turner, John. *Housing by People: Towards Autonomy in Building Environments*. New York: Pantheon Books, 1977.

Vale, Brenda. *Green Architecture: Design for a Sustainable Future*. London; Hudson, NY: UCLA AAUP/ARTS NA, no. 2542.3, 35, 1991.

Vale, Brenda, and Robert Vale. *Autonomous House*. New York: Universe Books, 1977.

Van der Ryn, Sim and Peter Calthorpe. *Sustainable Communities: A New Design Synthesis for Cities, Suburbs, and Towns*. San Francisco: Sierra Club Books, 1986.

Walter, Bob, ed. *Sustainable Cities*. Los Angeles: Eco-Home Media, 1992.

Walter, Bob. "Gardens in the Sky." In *Sustainable Cities: Concepts and Strategies for Eco-City Development*, edited by Bob Walter, Lois Arkin, and Richard Crenshaw. Los Angeles: EHM Publishers, 1992.

Wilson, J. "Permaculture's Role in Southern and Eastern Africa." *Permaculture Edge* 4, (April 1994): 17-18.

World Resources Institute (WRI). *World Resources: A Guide to the Global Environment 1992–93*. New York: Oxford University Press, 1992.

Wright, Gwendolyn. *Building the Dream: A Social History of Housing in America*. Cambridge, MA: MIT Press, 1981.

# PART THREE

## FUTURE FRONTIERS FOR URBAN DESIGN

In the previous two sections, we examined the past and present ethics of urban design. In this third part of the book, our concern is to explore the ethic of the future city. The introduction of this book outlined some innovative concepts explaining the role of the city location and the themes of urban design, and pointed out five pioneering frontiers for future urban expansion consideration: the sea frontier, mountain frontier, geospace (below-ground) frontier, colonies in space frontier, and agro-urban-development frontier.

This third part will focus on climatic consideration and urban design, soil thermal performance, and the geospace city concept as a future frontier. The common denominator among these three subjects is thermal performance, human perception, and an innovative, pioneering concept.

Climatic consideration in urban design is a forgotten subject. Indeed, there has been significant research that has produced a design of a single house with the climatic consideration in mind. Many architects, architecture engineers, civil engineers, and others have contributed to the enhancement of the thermal performance of a house for cooling or heating. However, the treatment of urban design is totally different. To the best of our knowledge, there is no literature that introduces a total urban design with climatic consideration. In contemporary times, in highly developed countries as well as in developing countries urban design forms and configurations have been similar, if not identical, regardless of the climatic conditions of the region. In the cold-warm-humid regions, we designed Boston, London, Ottawa, Paris, Peking, and Tokyo with the same basic patterns, forms, configurations, and morphology we have in the hot-dry climate of Phoenix and Tucson, Los Angeles, Ankara, Tehran, Cairo, and Perth and Melbourne. In contrast, the indigenous cities of the hot-dry climates, where "urban design without urban designers" evolved, the inhabitants introduced effective urban design forms and configurations to meet their needs for comfort. This indigenous design input pattern considered the city holistically as well as its parts, such as streets, heights of buildings, urban peripheral zones, public open spaces, the location of the water bodies within the urban context, and other land uses with the climatic consideration in mind. The study of these indigenous cities of the past can help modern urban designers plan cities to be cooler or warmer through proper site selection, land-use forms, location of land use within the city, and overall urban configuration. The value gained is not only the economic savings in energy consumption, but more importantly, the physiological and mental comfort and health of the urban dwellers, their productivity, and social and physical well-being. This section presents this issue for consideration by future urban designers.

Soil thermal performance between the surface and minus ten meters in depth is our concern from the urban design point of view because of the stability of the temperature during a given season at the depth of ten meters and its diminishing fluctuation within this range of depth between zero and minus ten meters. However, the new knowledge gained recently on soil thermal behavior at different levels of depth certainly opened a new frontier for future urban design that necessitates an innovative challenge. The benefits of a cool temperature in the summer and warm temperature in the winter make below-ground spaces usable for almost all types of above-ground urban land uses, such as the conventional uses of storage and parking, agricultural production, and refrigeration. Below-ground spaces also offer many other newly discovered advantages. Some of these advantages were known to our ancestors and used widely. One enlightening example was the use of below-ground space for grain storage in China more than a thousand years ago. It was more efficient than our modern above-ground silos. Another example is the recent observation that less time is required for recuperation from external surgery in below-ground than in above-ground spaces. In any case, the implication of our knowledge about soil and thermal performance introduces a variety of significant opportunities for urban design.

In conjunction with this subject, this third section also introduces, the system of a future geospace (below-ground) city to relieve our contemporary congested urban environment. This concept has two goals. One is to release the above-ground city from the pressure of the traffic impact and present urban land uses. The other is to have the glory of a fully natural environment penetrate into the city's center to replace the above-ground traffic arteries, with all of the positive implications in fusing urban human-made environment and natural environment. Indeed, below-ground space has been used to some extent throughout the history of humankind, and in this century within large urban centers as well. Our concept is one that embraces, for the first time, the whole variety of complex city land uses with below-ground space complementing, but not replacing, the existing supraspace city. We believe that the implementation of this concept will evolve steadily and become widespread throughout future decades. One of the visions behind it is the challenge and the opportunity to use below-ground space for dwellings within the slopes, encompassing innovative design, where full sunshine and light will penetrate deep into the house. In short, this text calls for the fusion of a conventional supraterraneous city with the proposed geospace city.

The theme of this book is future urban design. To fully comprehend this theme, it is essential to be aware of the ethics of the past and the present. Just as the root of the present is the sequential product of the ethics, of the past, the future should be part of the cultural ethics of the past and the present.

# 6

## URBAN DESIGN MORPHOLOGY AND THERMAL PERFORMANCE

   Urban design is one segment of comprehensive design that demands immediate attention. Throughout this century, urban designers and planners have often ignored climatic considerations and the natural environment when designing future growth. This has led, in some cases, to barely tolerable conditions. Today there is increased pressure on designers to solve these problems as well as avoid them for the future.

   The urban designer's commitment is to understand the existing and anticipated forces behind urban evolution, their dynamic pattern, and their reciprocal influences. To do so requires a great range of knowledge from a large number of disciplines in order to translate them into design tools and formulate and develop them into urban design concepts and forms. The modern urban designer has been under constant demand to define urban problems and to introduce relevant alternative solutions that respond primarily to human needs and comforts. The range of interdisciplinary input is very wide and includes social sciences and humanities, science and technology, and urban climatology, and embraces all aspects of life. Although this heavy reliance on research findings of other disciplines introduces both a challenge and some limits, the urban designer is still required to have the basic and broad knowledge of these disciplines and their mutual relations. Without this basic knowledge urban designers will fall short of fulfilling their primary commitment.

## BACKGROUND

There is a strong correlation between urban climate and the urban design physical configuration and form pattern. The prime responsibility of the urban designer is to introduce the type of urban morphology that improves the city's thermal performance and human outdoor comfort in a given site climate. Urban design with climatic considerations deals with the wholistic morphology of the city, as well as with urban details such as street width, form, configuration and orientation, building heights, city compactness or dispersion, urban open space, integration or segregation of land uses, and other related physical issues.

In the United States, as well as in many other countries of the world, we have mistakenly introduced the same urban design morphology in temperate climates as well as in hot-dry or cold-dry climates or humid regions with almost no reference to climatic conditions. We have justified this by a variety of reasons, among them economical or political. We really have not considered the impact of such design on the health of the inhabitants and the social price we pay under such circumstances. The purpose of this discussion is to outline the complexity of the problems posed by climate conditions as well as the solutions, to enable the modern urban designer to prepare the configuration of the urban design plan.

## TYPES OF CLIMATES

From the urban design morphology point of view, and for the sake of our discussion, we can classify the climate in six major types. Each of these climates has its own basic profile (Table 6.1):

TABLE 6.1

*Main Climatic Types and Their Basic Profiles*

| MAIN CLIMATIC TYPES (1) | EXAMPLES (2) | BASIC PROFILES (3) |
|---|---|---|
| Hot-humid | Equatorial Zone | Hot diurnally & seasonally with minor temperature range<br>Heavy rain<br>More comfort at high elevation |
| Cold-humid (temperate) | Northern United States & Southern Canada | Snowy<br>Windy, blizzard conditions<br>Very cold nights |
| Hot-dry | Middle East & North Africa, Most Australia, & Southwestern United States | Intense solar radiation<br>Large temperature amplitude between day & night<br>Dusty storms<br>Torrential rain<br>Low cloudy days<br>Intense dehydration<br>High salinization<br>Evaporation exceeding precipitation |
| Cold-dry | Inland Plateau, Central Asia, Central Siberia | Stressful & uncomfortable<br>Strong dry cold wind |
| Seashore Strips | Exist especially along the desert coasts of Peru and Northern Chile, the Kalahari in southwestern Africa, along the Atlantic Coast of Moroccan Sahara, northwestern Coast of Mexico and Somalia in Eastern Africa | Windy and stormy<br>Breeze system<br>High humidity<br>Erosive |
| Mountain Slopes | Lower slopes, middle slopes, high slopes | Windy & increasing air circulation<br>Higher relative humidity than the lowland as elevation increases<br>Provide healthy & moderate climate<br>Enhance attractive view |

1. Hot–humid, such as the equatorial zone
2. Cold–humid (temperate), such as northern United States and southern Canada
3. Hot-dry, such as most of the Middle East, Australia, and southwestern United States
4. Cold-dry, such as inland plateaus, central Canada, and central Siberia
5. Seashore strips, which exist in numerous cities and accommodate a reasonably large portion of the world population
6. Mountain slopes, which include lower slopes (largely populated), middle slopes, and high slopes

For the clarification of our discussion, we grouped the major climatic regions that are responsive to our needs for the morphology of urban design. There can be more subgrouping of these major climatic regions. Each of these climatic areas is a distinct one, unique in its climatic pattern, and requires special urban design solutions. Yet, there can be design solutions suitable to more than one type of climatic area, in spite of their distinct differences, such as the cold-dry and hot-dry climate. We prefer to call these two climate types stressful climates.

Each of the six climate types introduces a distinct thermal performance pattern, diurnally and seasonally, with the special combination of its temperature, wind and relative humidity (Table 6.1). In addition, each urban site has its own natural and human-made character, which in turn influences the climate. Any design response would need a careful basic understanding of each of those climates.

## DESIGN RESPONSE

In reviewing the main characteristics of each of the six climate types, I intended to outline the distinct features of each and emphasize those aspects and climatic problems related to urban design. Each climate type has its complex problems that the urban designer is expected to respond to and resolve. However, there is no universal solution and each case is to be examined individually. In the following sections, we will examine the basic principles that can guide the urban designer with climatic considerations in mind. Study and consideration of the climatic character of an area and an introduction of proper design should be in two major levels: one on the level of the city site selection and the other on the level of urban configurations.

## Site Selection

The most crucial stage throughout the process of urban design in any given climatic region, and especially that of the stressful climate zones, is the site selection method and criteria used for the city or a neighborhood. Site selection of the city has an impact on the health of the residents, energy consumption, overall city thermal performance, comfort, economy, and community stability. Once the site is selected and developed, it will be an irreversible decision.

An optimal site is almost unachievable. However, an interdisciplinary team with a sophisticated, rational, quantitative, and comprehensive method should be expected to lead throughout this process. Still, the result might well be a trade-off and a compromise among all the criteria considered for the site selection.[1]

Here are some basic rules and guidelines related to thermal performance:

- *Altitude.* For every 100-meter increase in elevation there will be a 1°C decrease in temperature and visa versa (Figure 6.1). Thus, higher elevations are certainly preferable, especially for a hot-humid and hot-dry climate city.
- *Wind Temperature.* Ventilation is essential for a hot-humid climate city. Also, although ventilation is not desired in a hot-dry climate as it is in a hot-humid one, we can state that, generally, wind coming from a body of water, such as a lake or sea, or winds at the higher elevations, are cooler than those in the neighboring lowland.

EVERY 100 M. DOWN OR UP
SLOPE THE WIND TEMPERATURE
INCREASES OR DECREASES BY 1°C.

*Figure 6.1 Because of the heating and cooling effects of the adiabatic winds, urban location is more favorable on the upper rather than the lower slopes in hot-dry or hot-humid climates.*

- *Evaporative Cooling.* In hot-dry climate location adjacent to a body of water temperatures can decrease significantly if the residential site is positioned properly to receive the prevailing wind direction. Thus, an evaporative cooling process will take place.

- *Urban Ventilation.* In a hot-humid climate, air movement and urban ventilation become an essential element for reducing temperatures within the urban environment. It is important that the hot-humid city receive air flow on its site.
- *Slope.* Location above the valley level diminishes the health risk associated with inversion and provides air circulation. The lowland of a valley is conducive to inversion and to low air ventilation, and when combined with air pollution produced by cars and industries it constitutes a serious threat to the health of the inhabitants.
- *Seashore Breeze.* When ventilation is essential (such as in hot-humid climates), location along the seashore is desirable, provided that the streets are designed to receive ample ventilation during the summer. This rule is applicable in both hot-humid and in hot-dry climates.
- *Flood.* In hot-humid, hot-dry, and cold-humid climates the risk of flood is a real threat when the location is in the lowland or the valley. In the case of a hot-dry climate, the rain is torrential and of short duration, causing serious flooding.
- *Energy Consumption.* Houses located at the lower parts of the valley will consume more energy for heating in the winter, toward the late part of the night, and for cooling in summer than those houses located at higher elevation in the same area.
- *Orientation.* Decisions on the city's residential orientation have an impact on human health, on the degree of comfort, and on energy consumption. The degree of exposure to solar radiation is important in establishing the various land uses in a settlement and in the details of the house design. The slopes facing south receive more intensive radiation than those facing east or west. The slopes facing north enjoy more shading, and while they have enough light, they don't have much sunshine. However, a decision on site orientation should be a synthesis of the reciprocal relations among solar radiation, ventilation and heat exchange, view and landscape,

and relative humidity as related to the proximity to the body of water.

- *Land Form and Soil Condition.* Commonly known landforms resulting from climatic conditions, such as those in the hot-dry climate area—piedmont, playa, alluvial fan, flood plain, coastal plain, mesa, and the eolian—should have an influence on the welfare of the urban settlement. Each of these types has its own character. The playa, for example, must be avoided for site selection, because the combined dryness with the dust deflation introduces intolerable eye-irritating salty wind. In selecting the site, the urban design interdisciplinary team should consider soil stability under weather changes, aerodynamics of wind movement, landslide, runoff, erosion or deflation, and the soil composition. Also to be examined is the availability of satisfactory land for future expansion.[2]

## Urban Configuration

Urban design is both the art of details as well as the art of the wholistic overall harmonious form. Viewing the city with optimal thermal performance in mind, it is essential to view the design of a portion of the city as an integral of the whole. From the thermal performance point of view, our study of the historical experience led us to four distinct types of overall urban forms that can be suitable for different climates (Table 6.2):

1. Compact form
2. Disperse form
3. Clustered form
4. Combined form

### Compact Urban Form

One of the significant lessons to be drawn from the historical indigenous settlements is the introduction of the compact city form (Figure 6.2). In addition to its common historical universal justification as saving adjacent land suitable for agriculture and defense, compact city morphology re-

TABLE 6.2

*Main Climatic Types and Preferred Basic Urban Form*

| MAIN CLIMATIC TYPES (1) | PREFERRED URBAN FORM (2) |
|---|---|
| Hot–humid | Dispersed form with open ends to support ventilation |
| Cold–humid (temperate) | Mixture of open (to suit summer condition) and controlled enclosure forms (to blizzard impact) |
| Hot–dry | Compact form |
| Cold–dry | Compact and combined forms, clustered forms |
| Seashore Strips | In humid region: Moderately dispersed form especially near stormy seashore<br>In dry region: Compact form and protective toward the inland, yet open toward the seaside |
| Mountain Slopes | Semicompact form: mixture of compact and clustered |

sponded positively to the stressful climates. The history of human settlements in the Mediterranean, the Middle East, and Asia has accumulated layers of experience throughout more than five thousand years of compact city evolution.

By compact city, we refer to a city that is concentrated and firmly unified with a consolidation of land uses in a close and tight physical relationship with each other and the structures within themselves. Such a compact city certainly retains the standard conventional density of number of persons per house size unit. The residential area in particular is arranged in a neat and orderly form in a smaller interval space between dwelling units than that of a standard contemporary city with an equivalent population.[3]

Historically, most stressful-climate cities, especially those in hot-dry zones, have evolved as compact settlements in practical response to the environmental stress. Indeed, the concept of a compact city was discussed throughout this century by many planners, architects, and social scientists (e.g.,

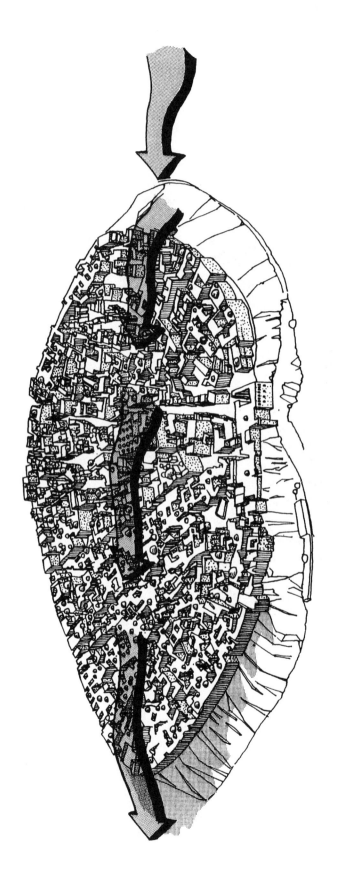

Figure 6.2   Irbil, Mesopotamia. (Reproduced from aerial photo.)

Ebenezer Howard, Frank Lloyd Wright, Le Corbusier, and Soleri). Compactness, however, does not necessarily need to be associated with high population density.

We can summarize the advantages of the compact city as follows:

1. Responds to and eases the problems posed by stressful climates, such as intense radiation, extreme diurnal temperature fluctuation, intense dryness, cold or hot winds, and dust storms
2. Consumes less energy for cooling and heating
3. Reduces the cost of design, construction, maintenance, and operation of all infrastructure networks and of tax support from the residents
4. Establishes easy and quick access within itself to the daily use, services, and business needs of residents
5. Saves commuting time and energy
6. Makes social life pleasant, especially for the very young and the very elderly residents
7. Has minimal impact on the delicately sensitive environment, especially that of a stressful climate

In short, the compact city form responds favorably in its thermal performance to regions of stressful climate, such as cold-dry and hot-dry. For both climates it provides a protective thermal environment.

*Dispersed Urban Form*

The dispersed urban form has been commonly and increasingly used all over the United States and recently in many other developed countries in Europe. It is characterized by low population density per urban unit, low-rise individual detached housing units, provision of generous space within the urban land, and by the absence of a sharp demarcation line between the built-up area at the city periphery and the open space beyond the urban area. Disperse pattern extends utilities, roads, and infrastructures, and consumes financial resources for its design, construction, and operation.

### Clustered Form

Clustered urban form is an aggregate of land use or housing in relatively small urban units integrated within very close proximity of each other. This form potentially responds favorably to stressful conditions of cold-dry or hot-dry climates.

Clustered urban forms can be fused easily with a climatically controlled environment insulated from the outside. These forms can carry within them an integrated land use or segregated land use as well. Integrated land use is a combination of different land uses that have a reciprocal relation to each other. It is usually common in cities where residents are within walking distance of most daily uses and services and often to their job. Segregated land use is primarily the dominancy of one type of use and is commonly adapted to protect the health of residents. The inner city is developed as an economic activity center and pushes residences, uses, services, and many jobs to the periphery.

### Combined Form

This is an aggregate of different forms brought together to establish a type of dispersed form and becomes a cohesive part of the urban pattern.

## CITY MORPHOLOGY AND THERMAL PERFORMANCE

The form of the city can ease wind velocity and support the increase or decrease of temperature. In addition to its velocity, air movement within the city is also a factor of the city morphology and configuration, its street design and orientation, and its form. In the indigenous city, the general skyline of the city was a straight horizontal line (Figure 6.3). In a hot-dry climate, the roofs are flat with uniform heights of two or three floors, and together they form almost one large "platform" shape. This form supports the strong wind move-

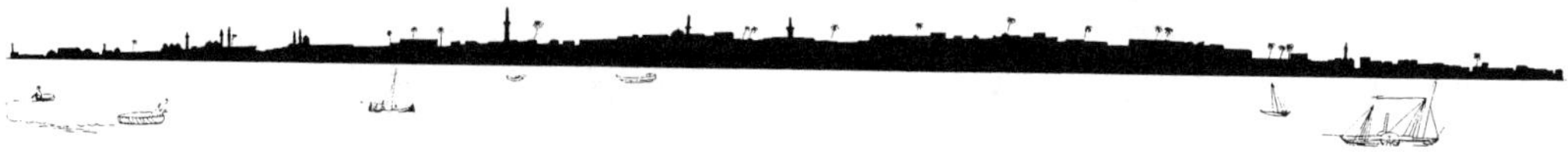

*Figure 6.3 Baghdad skyline in 1854, a uniform compact city morphology of hot-dry climate with low houses. (Drawing adapted and reproduced from Felix Jones and M. W. Collingwood, 1856, map.)*

*Figure 6.4 Lower Manhattan's nonuniform skyline, New York City. The view from Brooklyn, 1970.*

ment over the city without obstacle and therefore protects the city. In a hot-humid climate, the pitched roofs slow the wind. The modern city silhouette form is a conglomeration of the buildings with different heights and therefore they break the flow of the strong wind and divert it, in some conditions, toward the streets (Figure 6.4). Thus, construction of a single high-rise building within a low uniform skyline creates air flow diversion and may lead to the ventilation of adjacent streets (Figure 6.5). Such development is desired in highly polluted or congested streets.

Also, the amount of solar radiation returning to the air in the city is less than that occurring in the open space outside the city, since some of it is absorbed by the building walls. Thus, within the city much of the radiation is absorbed by various elements of the city. For example, vegetation within the city absorbs radiation directly and converts it through the photosynthetic process to chemical energy and, thus, reduces air temperature. In a dry-climate city, solar radiation, absorbed throughout the day by the buildings, is diffused back into the air during the evening. Due to the lack of clouds and the low relative humidity in the air, the temperature in the city will drop significantly. A densely built-up area will release this stored temperature more slowly.

Clustered urban design forms may increase the relative humidity within the city resulting from evapotranspiration and evaporation. Due to the absorbed heat throughout the day, the cooling process within the city center is slower than at its periphery. City configuration, streets' patterns, and the structure of the houses influence the velocity of wind penetration within the city. Yet, the center is supplying an increase of temperature throughout most of the day by the intensity of its human activities and car traffic. Air movement

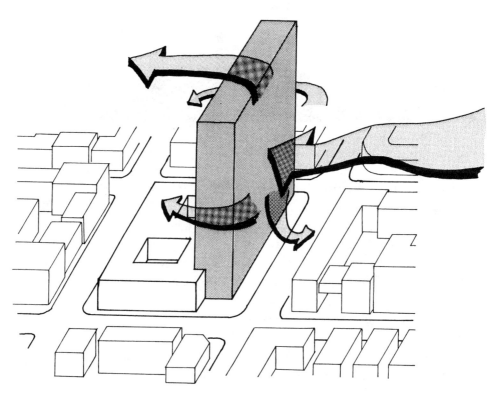

*Figure 6.5 Impact of a single high-rise building, which causes interrupted and turbulent wind patterns.*

or air turbulence also may be caused by heated air rising in the city center and drawing cooler air to replace it from the periphery through straight and open streets. Air movement can be very stormy when the street is designed diagonally to the shoreline of a sea. Improper design of city streets and configuration can make human comfort within the city even worse. Narrow and winding streets may slow down the evaporation process within their environs and have higher relative humidity than other wider streets of the same city.

The differentiation of physical forms within the city, orientations, heights, composition, conglomerates of its buildings, buildings' density, proximity to the city center or its periphery, and most importantly, the intensity of human activities create pockets of urban microclimates within the city. Consequently, each part of the city differs in its thermal performance from the other parts.

There are some basic rules to be noted concerning urban thermal performance (Table 6.3):

TABLE 6.3

*Main Climatic Types, Major Problems, and Basic Urban Design Responses*

| MAIN CLIMATIC TYPES (1) | MAJOR PROBLEMS/ISSUES (2) | BASIC URBAN DESIGN RESPONSE (3) | |
|---|---|---|---|
| Hot-humid | Excessive heat<br>High humidity | Ventilation: open ends & dispersed form<br>  Widely open streets to support wind movement<br>  Extensive shadow<br>  Dispersion of high rise buildings to support<br>    ventilation<br>  Combined variation of building heights<br>  Wide, yet shadowed open spaces<br>  Shadowing, planned tree zones | |
| Cold-humid (temperate) | Low temperature<br>Winter & summer<br>  high precipitation<br>Windy | Heating (passive and active):<br>  Mixture of open & enclosure forms<br>  Protected edges at winter windward side (with<br>    structures or trees)<br>  Uniformed building heights<br>  Medium dispersed open space<br>  Circumferential and intersecting tree strips | |
| Hot-dry | Excessive dryness<br>  combined with high<br>  day temperature<br>Dusty and stormy | Compact forms<br>  Shadowing<br>  Evaporative cooling<br>  Protected urban edges from hot winds<br>  Windward location near a body of water<br>  Narrow winding neighborhood roads & alleys<br>  Mix of building height to shadow the city<br>  Small, dispersed, and protected public open<br>    spaces<br>  Circumferential and intersecting tree zones<br>  Use of geospace city concept | |
| Cold-dry | Excessive low<br>  temperature associated<br>  with dryness<br>Stressful wind | Compact and aggregate forms, clustered forms<br>  Protected urban edges<br>  Narrow winding neighborhood roads & alleys<br>  Uniform city height<br>  Small, dispersed, and protected public open<br>    spaces<br>  Circumferential and intersecting tree zones<br>  Use of geospace city concept | |
| Seashore Strips | High humidity<br>Windy | *In humid region:*<br>  Moderately dispersed<br>    form<br>  Open urban edges<br>  Wide streets per-<br>    pendicular to the<br>    shore to receive<br>    the breeze | *In dry region:*<br>  Open toward the sea,<br>    compact &<br>    protected<br>    toward the inland<br>  High rise buildings<br>    mixed with low<br>    height |

TABLE 6.3 (CONTINUED)
*Main Climatic Types, Major Problems, and Basic Urban Design Responses*

| MAIN CLIMATIC TYPES (1) | MAJOR PROBLEMS/ISSUES (2) | BASIC URBAN DESIGN RESPONSE (3) | |
|---|---|---|---|
| | | Dispersed high rise buildings to receive ventilation | Small protected dispersed public open spaces |
| | | Variety of building heights | Shadowing planned tree zones |
| | | Wide public open space | |
| | | Shadowing planned tree zones | |
| Mountain Slopes | Windy | Semicompact form: mix of compact & dispersed Horizontal streets & alleys to enhance the view Low height buildings Small, dispersed public open spaces Nonobstructive protected tree zones Use of geospace city concept | |

- Every city creates its own microclimate, which differs from that of the outer open space of its macroregion. Aside from the city pockets of different microclimates, we can state that the central business district of the city is warmer than its surroundings due to the intensity of its activities and the proximity of its buildings. Also, the peripheral parts of the city will have a lower temperature than that of the city center. It is commonly noticeable that snow fallen in the city center melts faster than that fallen in the peripheral zone. The commonly known air heat islands associated with the city center and its industrial park is extended high to form a canopy above its site (Figure 6.6).

- Streets lined up along the prevailing wind orientation at the periphery of the city increase wind penetration deep within the city or prevent it by the city blocks (Figure 6.7). In a cold-dry climate, the periphery wind penetration will cause the city to be cooler, causing the peripheral housing zone to require more energy for heating. In a hot-dry climate, the city will receive hot

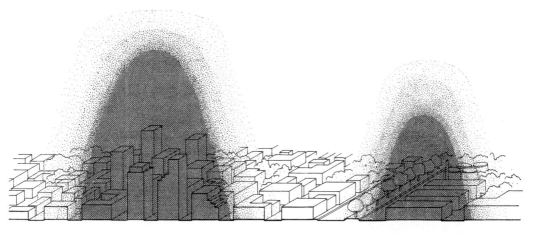

CITY CORE AND PERIPHERY

HUMAN ACTIVITIES, CAR OPERATION, HEATING OR COOLING

INDUSTRIAL PARK

MACHINES, CAR ACTIVITIES, AND POLLUTION

*Figure 6.6 Schematic diagram of city thermal generation and its canopy.*

and dusty wind in the day and colder wind toward the latter part of the night. Houses located in peripheral areas will use more energy for heating or for cooling than those located at the city center. In a hot-humid climate, such wind will certainly be welcomed, since it will be ventilating and consequently cooling the city.

## Land-Use Pattern

Much of our previous discussion has touched upon the subject of land use in some detail. Still, there are some other basic principles to be followed related to the land-use design. Both concepts of integrated and segregated land use are to be adopted alternately.

The following are some basic guidelines on land-use patterns:

- *Relation to Windward.* Allocate residential land uses so that smog and dust pollution are not carried in by prevailing wind, and noise pollution from major regional and local land uses and roads is minimized (Figure 6.8).
- *Open Space.* In regions where air turbulence is frequent, it is necessary to avoid designing large public open spaces in order to minimize dusty air turbulence, and all open spaces should be paved or planted.

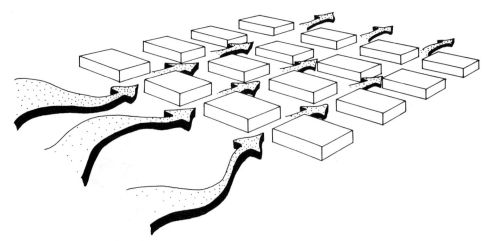

A. DESIGN FOR SWIFT URBAN VENTILATION. SUITABLE FOR HOT-HUMID CITY.

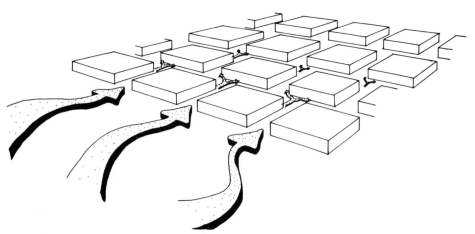

B. DESIGN FOR BLOCKING AIR MOVEMENT. SUITABLE FOR COLD-DRY AND HOT-DRY CITY.

*Figure 6.7 Two basic street configurations, orientation, and positioning within the grid system affect the prevailing winds system and the city ventilation.*

*Figure 6.8 (facing page) Smoke patterned by air movement behavior.*

- *Segregated Land Use.* In the six identified climate types, segregated land use is to be implemented for industry, transportation, storage, and all other land uses that produce any health hazard and affect the climate negatively.
- *Integrated Land Use.* For the stressful climate city, an integrated land use is suggested for residential, commercial and shopping (retail), offices and educational facilities, and public green open spaces. I believe that climate stress imposes the necessity of integrated rather than conventional land use. Integration supports proximity, climatic comfort, and social interaction; it saves land use and intensifies use by all age groups. In addi-

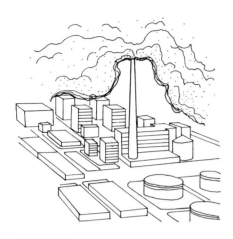

A. VERTICAL AIR MOVEMENT: DOWN.

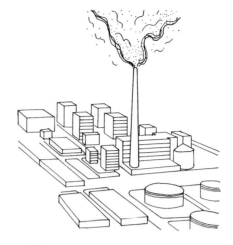

B. VERTICAL AIR MOVEMENT: UP.

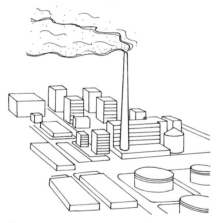

C. HORIZONTAL AIR MOVEMENT.

D. MIXED MOVEMENT (VERTICAL, HORIZONTAL, AND DOWN).

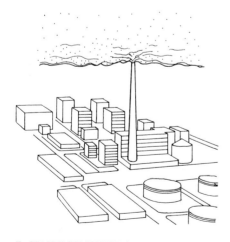

E. STABLE CONDITION (INVERSION).

F. UNSTABLE CONDITION.

tion, it reduces dependency on motor vehicles and meets the norms of developing societies.

- *Proximity of Land Use.* In the hot-humid, cold-humid, and the two stressful climates of hot-dry and cold-dry, the close proximity of daily urban services will maximize the proximity of land use and ease movement in shadowed and climatically protected spaces (such as patios and plazas), thus also reducing the length of infrastructure and energy consumption.
- *Infrastructure.* In stressful climate regions, avoid designing land uses that may encourage water accumulation or flooding. Thus, open and subsurface drainage systems should be designed for the maximum and not for the average flow. In the hot-dry region, for example, averages do not exist and design should be prepared to deal with the maximum.
- *Social Implication.* In a hot-dry climate, it is necessary to plan ample land use for indoor social activities, recreation, and entertainment to minimize the feelings of isolation in the city and compensate for the lack of conventional green countryside in the immediate environs.

## Residential Design Pattern

Street orientation determines the amount of shadowing and radiation, light and air movement, intensity of city ventilation, and duration of relative humidity in the air. In climates where wind direction and velocity change often through the day, there will be a need for spatial housing design adjustments. Also, there is a great change in temperature between day and night and a considerable variation within each time period. Therefore, it is most difficult to suggest a universal model of streets and city configuration that can respond to all these changes in an optimal way. Yet, we can adopt the following generalized assumptions as guidelines for the urban design of residential areas:

- *Street Orientation.* Streets designed straight and parallel to each other will support air movement into and within the city. The wind blowing through the unpaved sections of the city with no vegetation cover at the edges (or in the center) cause dust turbulence and garbage accumulation in addition to bringing intense heat or cold. On the other hand, streets perpendicular to each other can ease storms and dusty winds, reduce wind velocity, and bring cooler or warmer winds during the day and night. Straight blocked streets and alleys can reduce wind movement to a great extent.

- *Street Width.* Narrow, winding, or zigzagging alleys are protective against cold or hot winds, receive minimum sunshine, reduce the effect of stormy winds, and establish shadowed space throughout the day. This pattern provides a cool and comfortable microclimate and also stays relatively warm during the cold nights of a hot-dry climate. In a hot-humid climate, wide streets help ventilate the city, but the streets will need shadowing. On the other hand, wide streets will receive and absorb large quantities of solar radiation and in a stressful climate they will not encourage pedestrian use. Radiation also is increased with asphalt cover and reduced when stone paving or cement cover the streets.

- *Vegetation.* Trees at the center or along the street absorb dust and pollution, may reduce noise in the adjacent area, minimize the effect of solar radiation, reduce albedo, and establish shadowed areas. When they are narrow, streets in a hot-dry climate should be covered frequently to increase shadow. The type of vegetation and its density also has an influence on the city's thermal performance, on wind velocity, and on its relative humidity. Consequently, the vegetation influences the comfort of the residents, not to mention the impact of the aesthetic appeal of the city (Figure 6.9).

- *Evapotranspiration.* Evapotranspiration increases the relative humidity and consequently reduces air temperature when the immediate environment is warm and has low relative humidity. Also, shaded areas reduce radiation—vegetation absorbs radiation and functions as a windbreak, thereby reducing transportation of air pollution and the effects of dusty winds. Finally, soil covered with shrubs reduces dust particles floating near the ground.

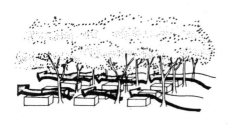

**HOT-HUMID**
DESIGN FOR: VENTILATION, AND SHADOW.
TREES: FREE HIGH TRUNKS WITH SHADOWING HIGH LEAVES

**HOT-DRY**
DESIGN FOR: SHADOW, EVAPORATIVE COOLING AND COOLED WIND BLOWING THROUGH LARGE TREE ZONE.
TREES: ACCACIA, UMBRELLALIKE

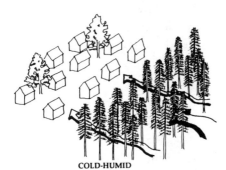

**COLD-HUMID**
DESIGN FOR: SUNLIGHT, PROTECTION AGAINST STRONG WIND.
TREES: BLACK SPRUCE, LOBLOLLY PINE. PROTECTIVE, NOT SHADOWING.

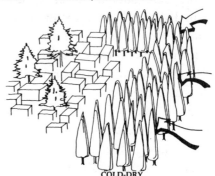

**COLD-DRY**
DESIGN FOR: PROTECTIVE TREE ZONE AGAINST STRONG WIND.
TREES: CEDAR. BARRIER PROTECTIVE WALL.

**MOUNTAIN SLOPE**
DESIGN FOR: PROTECTIVE TREE ZONE AGAINST STRONG WINDS.
TREES: RED CEDAR, BALSAM FIR. PROTECTIVE, SUPPORT VENTILATION.

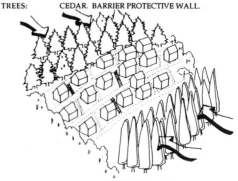

**SEASHORE**
DESIGN FOR: PROTECTION AGAINST STRONG WIND WITH FREE TRUNKS TO ALLOW VENTILATION.
TREES: BOTTLE TREE. PROTECTIVE. LIMIT THE VENTILATION.

*Figure 6.9 Contribution of tree morphology to urban design thermal performance with climatic consideration.*

## Open Public Spaces

Open space within the city, active or passive, has its own microclimate and plays an important role, especially in cold-humid and in stressful-climate cities. Open space affects heat generation or inversion, wind dynamics, and, if it is an active one, relative humidity (Figure 6.10).

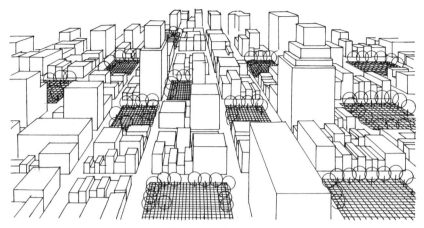

## COLD-HUMID CLIMATE CITY

OPEN SPACE GENERATES STAGNATED COLD AIR IN THE WINTER AND HUMID
AND HOT AIR IN THE SUMMER. THEY SHOULD BE COVERED WITH HIGH
TRUNK TREES TO PROVIDE SHADOW AND VENTILATION.

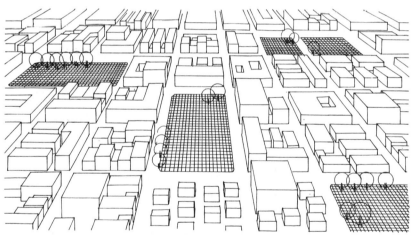

## HOT-DRY CLIMATE CITY

LARGE OPEN SPACES ARE INTOLERABLE SINCE THEY GENERATE DUSTY AIR,
HIGH TEMPERATURE AT DAYTIME (AFTERNOON), AND COLD
TEMPERATURE AT NIGHT (STAGNATED AIR), AND CONSUME LARGE
QUANTITIES OF WATER TO MAKE THEM GREEN.

*Figure 6.10 Two city
patterns of open space and
thermal performance.*

Stressful climate and public open space are strongly related issues. My findings indicate that in a hot-dry climate, a large open space in the city (especially when covered with asphalt) has a negative impact on city dwellers. In the daytime, generated heat, dust, and strong hot wind becomes intolerable. At night when the temperature decreases significantly, open spaces generate inversion. All in all, they become the bad spots of the city. Similar yet not identical development takes place in large open spaces of the cold-dry climate city as well. In a cold-dry climate, open spaces are subject to cold wind and blizzard conditions and are intolerable for pedestrians on cold nights.

My advice is that the design pattern of the stressful-climate city should avoid large open spaces and instead provide small dispersed open green spaces throughout the city. There is also a social gain from these patterns when all social classes can benefit from open spaces. Furthermore, such spots can become city landmarks for children and the elderly, whose land uses are closer to home. In a hot-humid climate city, large green open spaces are desirable, since they support ventilation and can provide plenty of shadow.


### Earth-Sheltered Habitat

Finally, there is the integration of earth-sheltered space in the stressful-climate (cold-dry or hot-dry) city. One of the major concerns of the climatically stressful city is the degree of thermal performance on the city scale and on the housing scale. It is specifically in this aspect of thermal performance where the degree of success or failure of the design will be measured. We have examined the outdoor city environment and we will discuss earth-sheltered housing and the thermal performance of the soil in Chapters Seven and Eight.

In conclusion, if the soul of urban design is to provide a pleasing and protective urban atmosphere, then environmental design becomes the central part of urban design and with it the climatic consideration. Urban design that takes climate into account is not an issue of perception and comfort only. It represents the health, social well-being, and productivity of the inhabitants as well. However, there are certain indigenous practices and ethics that concern us most.

In the indigenous houses, comfort needs were resolved by innovative passive methods (Figure 6.11). Recently these needs have been resolved by active means, such as the heating or cooling system, ventilation, evaporative cooling, and solar heat storage. The natural passive systems were developed by our ancestors who viewed the environment as a living laboratory. This historical/traditional way is worthy of our study and considerations, for much of past ethical practice can be adjusted to suit our modern norms and standards. On an urban scale, the thermal performance conditions of the city can be improved almost exclusively through the use of urban design tactics along with these natural passive systems.

Another ethic for our practice of urban design morphology and thermal performance is innovation through extensive research and study in the laboratory and in real urban cases. The education of a new generation of urban designers and architects with extensive knowledge of the correlation between urban morphology and climate performance is an essential issue. In the last two decades, many design schools have increased their research on energy savings in housing through active and passive means, but have not given equivalent attention to climate considerations on the urban scale in their curricula. It is essential that they address this issue.

The study of urban design morphology and climate reveals a correlation between them; innovative and serious study of both and their reciprocal relationship should lead to significant improvements in urban thermal performance. The comprehensive study of climate elements such as wind, temperature, and relative humidity is essential. In urban design morphology, there are a variety of urban forms and configurations to be investigated with the issue of climate in mind. Among these forms are streets (width, height, building materials), the relationship of street form and orientation to an adjacent body of water, urban silhouette and building heights and their correlation, land-use patterns, impact of open spaces, and the role of urban vegetation on urban thermal performance.

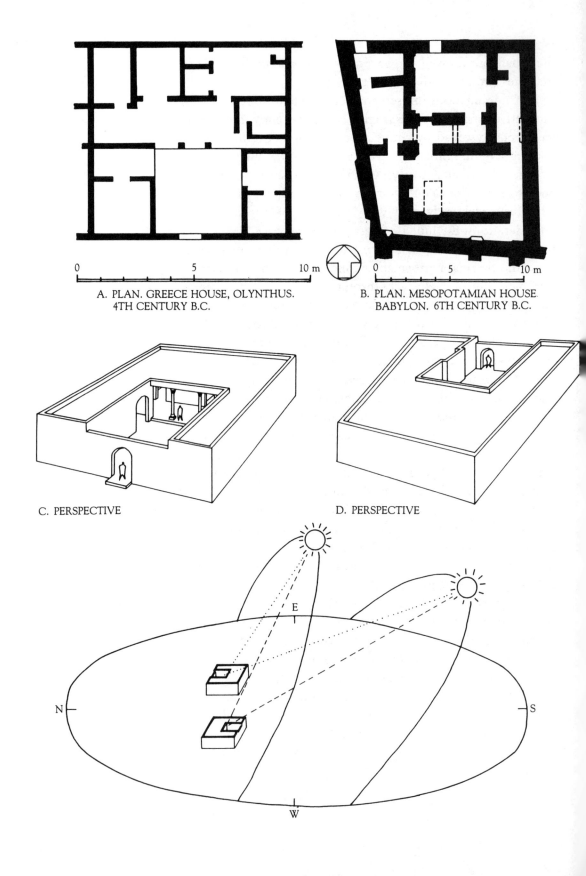

A. PLAN. GREECE HOUSE, OLYNTHUS.
4TH CENTURY B.C.

B. PLAN. MESOPOTAMIAN HOUSE.
BABYLON. 6TH CENTURY B.C.

C. PERSPECTIVE

D. PERSPECTIVE

0   5   10 m

0   5   10 m

N   E   S   W

Finally, the most sensitive of the six climates mentioned here are the extreme ones, and they require special attention. These are especially the hot-dry and hot-humid types, where a large portion of the world's population reside. We can assume that future urban population growth also will expand in both the cold or dry climatic regions, through exploitation of new natural resources or using the mountain slope, to create a new urban frontier.

In conclusion, indeed there has been reasonable and scholarly research literature introduced during the last few decades on the subject of climate and architecture, such as that of Olgay and Givoni (referenced at the end of this chapter), discussing climatic consideration and the design of single buildings. To the best of our knowledge, there is very little, if any, published work focused on climatic consideration for urban design. Since the Industrial Revolution, and even recently, we continue designing cities in a hot-dry climate, such as those of the southwestern part of the United States, with the same urban pattern on which we design and build cities in the cold-humid and blizzardly climate of the northeastern part of the United States, Canada, northern Europe, and northern Japan. Except in a sporadic few places in the world, we have not yet developed the norms and standards by which we gain the ethics of climatic consideration and of the design of urban land use, such as streets, neighborhood configurations, and other parts of the city. This is a gap that needs to be filled in the design of the school curriculum as well as within the circles of urban design team practitioners and policy makers.

*Figure 6.11 (facing page) Sunshine penetration consideration in two patio houses: one in ancient Greece with Mediterranean climate of dry and warm in summer and wet and cold in winter, and the other in ancient southern Mesopotamia, dry and mostly warm throughout the year. Note that in Greece the side of the patio facing the sun (south) is colonnaded to avoid summer sunshine penetration and still receive the winter sunshine.*

# NOTES

1. On site selection method see this author's publications:
   - "A Quantitative Method for Site Selection of a New Town," paper presented at the International Congress on New Towns: *How to Build a New Town*, Tehran, Iran, December 9-15, 1977 (69 pp.).
   - "A Quantitative Method for Site Selection of a Regional Shopping Centre," *Proceedings of the International Conference on Mathematical Modeling*, St. Louis, Missouri, August 29-September 1, 1977 (25 pp.).
   - "A Quantitative Method for Land-Use Planning," *International Technical Cooperation Centre Review* 6/2 (22), (April 1977): 11-37.
   - "Site Selection: Process, Criteria and Method," *New-Town Planning: Principles and Practice* (New York: Wiley, 1976), pp. 60-97.
   - *New Community for Virginia in the Roanoke Valley: Site Selection and Feasibility Study*. Gideon Golany Associates, State College, Pennsylvania, January 1972.
   - "Site Selection and Feasibility Study: A New Town for Roanoke Valley," In *Strategy for New Community Development in the United States* (Stroudsburg, PA: Dowden, Hutchinson and Ross, 1975), pp. 129-154.
2. On stressful climate design see this author's publications:
   - *Design for Arid Regions* (New York: Van Nostrand Reinhold, 1983), 334 pp., 173 illus.
   - *Desert Planning: International Lessons* (London: Architectural Press, 1982), 164 pp., 94 illus.
   - *Housing in Arid Lands: Design and Planning* (London: Architectural Press, 1980), 268 pp., 260 illus.
   - *Arid-Zone Settlement Planning: The Israeli Experience* (New York: Pergamon Press, 1979), 567 pp., 128 illus.

- *Urban Planning for Arid Zones: American Experiences and Directions* (New York: Wiley, 1978), 245 pp., 96 illus. Translated into Spanish: *Planificacion Urbana en Zonas Aridas* (Mexico: Editorial Limusa, 1984), 274 pp.

3. On compact urban form see this author's publications:

- *Chinese Earth-Sheltered Dwellings: Indigenous Lessons for Modern Urban Design* (Honolulu: University of Hawaii Press, 1992), pp. 144-154.

- *Earth-Sheltered Habitat: History, Architecture and Urban Design* (New York: Van Nostrand Reinhold, 1983), pp. 157-166.

- *Urban Planning for Arid Zones* (New York: Wiley, 1978), pp. 3-21.

# SELECTED READINGS

Adams, Robert, Marina Adams, Alan Willens, and Ann Willens. *Dry Lands: Man and Plants.* London: Architectural Press, 1978.

Adolph, E. F. and Associates. *Physiology of Man in the Desert.* New York: Hafner Publishing, 1969.

AIA Research Corporation. *Regional Guidelines for Building Passive Energy Conserving Homes.* Washington, D.C.: U. S. Government Printing Office. All other UNESCO series on Arid Zones; 29 published since 1953.

Amiran, David H. K., and Andrew H. Wilson, eds. *Coastal Deserts: Their Natural and Human Environments.* Tucson: University of Arizona Press, 1973.

Aronin, Jeffrey Ellis. *Climate and Architecture.* New York: Van Nostrand-Reinhold Book, Division of Litton Educational Publishers, 1953.

Barney, Gerald O., ed. *The Global 2000 Report to the President of the U.S.* New York: Pergamon Press, 1980.

Berg, Peter, Beryl Magilavy, and Seth Zuckerman. *Green City Program for San Francisco Bay Area Cities and Towns.* San Francisco: Planet Drum Books, 1989.

Berkofsky, L., D. Faiman, and J. Gale, eds. *Settling the Desert.* New York: Gordon and Breach, 1981.

Bitan, A. "The Wind Regime in the North-West Section of the Dead Sea." *Arch. Met. Geogh. Biokl.* 22 (1974):313-335.

Bitan, A. "Wind as a Negative Factor in Human Comfort and its Implications for Planning." *International Journal of Biometeorology* 3 (1976):174-183.

Botter, Robert Brown. *Ecological House.* New York: Morgan & Morgan, 1981.

Branch, Melville C., ed. *Urban Planning Theory.* Stroudsburg, PA: Dowden, Hutchinson & Ross, 1975.

Bryson, Reid A. and John E. Ross. "The Climate of the City." In *Urbanization and Environment*, edited by Thomas R. Detweiler and Melvin G. Marens. Belmont, CA: Duxbury Press, 1972.

Building Research Advisory Board. *Housing and Building in Hot-Humid and Hot-Dry Climates. Proceedings of BRAB Conference Report*, No. 5, November

18-19, 1952. Washington, D.C.: National Research Council, National Academy of Sciences, May 1953.

Chandler, T. J. *Urban Climatology and its Relevance to Urban Design.* Technical Note No. 149. Geneva, Switzerland: Secretariat of the World Meteorological Organization, 1976 (WMO—No. 438), 61 pp.

Conselman, Frank B., ed. *Frontiers of the Semi-arid World: An International Symposium*, October 14-18, 1974, No. 77-2. Lubbock, TX: Texas Tech Press, 1977, 96 pp.

Cooke, Ronald U. and Andrew Warren. *Geomorphology in Deserts.* Los Angeles: University of California Press, 1973.

Daly, Herman E. and John B. Cobb, Jr. *For the Common Good: Redirecting the Economy toward Community, Environment, and Sustainable Future.* Boston: Beacon Press, 1989.

Drew, Jane and Maxwell Fry. *Tropical Architecture.* London: William Clowes and Sons, 1964.

Eckardt, F. E., ed. *Methodology of Plant Eco-Physiology—Proceedings of the Montpellier Symposium.* Paris: United Nations, UNESCO, 1965.

Engwicht, David. *Toward an Eco-City: Calming the Traffic.* Sidney, Australia: Envirobook, 1992.

Fathy, Hassan. *Architecture for the Poor.* Chicago: University of Chicago Press, 1973.

Fitch, James Marston. *American Building: The Environmental Forces that Shape It.* Boston: Houghton-Mifflin Company, 1972.

Flavin, Christopher and Nicholas Lenssen. *Beyond the Petroleum Age: Designing the Solar Economy.* Worldwatch Paper 100. Washington, D.C.: Worldwatch Institute, 1990.

Fry, Maxwell and Jane Drew. *Tropical Architecture in the Dry and Humid Zones.* New York: Reinhold Publishing, 1964.

Gates, David M. *Man and His Environment: Climate.* New York: Harper and Row, 1972.

Geiger, Rudolf. *The Climate Near The Ground.* Cambridge, MA: Harvard University Press, 1971.

Givoni, B. Man, *Climate and Architecture.* 2nd ed. New York: Van Nostrand Reinhold, 1976.

Givoni, Baruch. *Man, Climate and Architecture.* Essex, England: Applied Science Publishers, 1976.

Givoni, Baruch. *Urban Design in Different Climates.* Geneva, Switzerland: Secretariat of the World Meteorological Organization, 1989. (WMO/TD No. 346).

*Global Report on Human Settlements.* Oxford, England: Oxford University Press for the United Nations Centre for Human Settlements (HABITAT), 1987.

Glueck, Nelson. *Rivers in the Desert: A History of the Negev.* New York: W. W. Norton, 1968.

Golany, Gideon S. *Urban Planning for Arid Zones.* New York: Wiley-Interscience Publication, 1978.

Golany, Gideon S., ed. *Urban Planning for Arid Zones: American Experiences and Directions.* New York: Wiley, 1978.

Golany, Gideon S. *Housing in Arid Lands: Design and Planning.* London: Architectural Press, 1980.

Golany, Gideon S. *Desert Planning.* New York: Nichols Publishing, 1982.

Golany, Gideon S. *Design for Arid Regions*. New York: Van Nostrand Reinhold, 1983.

Golany, Gideon S. *Urban Design and Thermal Performance*. Manuscript in progress, 1995.

Halacy, D. S., Jr. *Earth, Water, Wind, and Sun: Our Energy Alternatives*. New York: Harper and Row, 1977.

Hodge, Carle O. and Carl N. Hodges, eds. *Urbanization in the Arid Lands: A Symposium*, December 26-27, 1970, No. 75-11. Lubbock, TX: Texas Tech Press, 1974, 274 pp.

Hoschele, K., ed. *Planning Applications of Urban and Building Climatology— Proceedings of the IFHP/CIB Symposium*, Berlin, October 14-15, 1991. Karlsruhe, Germany, 1992.

International Union for the Conservation of Nature and Natural Resources (IUCN), United Nations Environmental Program (UNEP), and World Wildlife Fund (WWF). *Caring for the Earth: A Strategy for Sustainable Living*. Gland, Switzerland: IUCN, UNEP, WWF, 1992.

Jokl, Miloslav V.; with a foreword by Byron W. Jones. *Microenvironment: The Theory and Practice of Indoor Climate*. Springfield, IL: C. C. Thomas, 1988.

Jones, Felix and N. W. Collingwood. "Ground Plan of the Engeinte of Baghdad 1853-54." Copied by Bhaskerjee, 1856.

Katayama, T. and J. Tsutsumi, eds. *Cutest '92 Conference on Thermal Environment, Special in Tohwa: The Second Tohwa University International Symposium*, Fukuoka, Japan, September 7-10, 1992. Fukuoka, Japan: Dai Nippon Printing Co.

Katayama, Tadahisa, Tetsuo Hayashi, Yoshitaka Shiotsuki, Hiroki Kitayama, Akio Ishii, Masaru Nishida, Jun-Ichiro Tsutsumi, and Masayuki Oguro. "Cooling Effects of a River and Sea Breeze on the Thermal Environment in a Built-up Area." *Energy and Buildings* 15 (1990/91):973-978.

Kennedy, Declan. "Permaculture and the Sustainable City." *Ekistics* (May 1991): 210-215.

Lyle, John Tillman. *Design for Human Ecosystems*. New York: Van Nostrand Reinhold, 1985.

Manty, Jorma, and Norman Pressman, eds. *Cities Designed for Winter*. Helsinki, Finland: Building Book, 1988.

Markus, T. A. and E. N. Morris. *Buildings, Climate and Energy*. London: Spottiswoode Ballantyne, 1980.

Mazria, Edward. *The Passive Solar Energy Book*. Emmaus, PA: Rodale Press, 1979.

McGinnis, William G. and Bram J. Goldman, eds. *Arid Land in Perspective*. Tucson: University of Arizona Press, 1969, 421 pp.

McGinnis, William G., Bram J. Goldman, and Patricia Paylore. *Food, Fiber and the Arid Land*. Tucson: University of Arizona Press, 1971, 437 pp.

McHarg, Ian L. and Jonathan Sutton. "Ecological Plumbing for the Texas Coastal Plain." *Landscape Architecture* 65/1 (1975).

McLarney, William D. "Aquaculture: Toward an Ecological Approach," edited by Richard Merrill. *Radical Agriculture*. New York: Harper & Row, 1976.

McPherson, E. Gregory. "Economic Modeling for Large Scale Urban Tree Plantings." In *Proceedings of the ACEE 1990 Summer Study on Energy Efficiency in Buildings*, 4. Washington, D.C.: American Council for an Energy Efficient Economy, 1990.

McPherson, E. Gregory, and Sharon Biedenbender. "The Cost of Shade: Cost-Effectiveness of Trees versus Bus Shelters." *Journal of Arboriculture* 17/9 (1991).

Mollison, Bill. *Permaculture: A Designers' Manual.* Tyalgum, Australia: Tagari Publications, 1988.

Mollison, Bill. *Introduction to Permaculture.* Tyalgum, Australia: Tagari Publications, 1991.

Mumford, Lewis. *The City in History.* New York: Harcourt, Brace and World, 1961.

Mumford, Lewis. *Technics and Human Development.* New York: Harcourt, Brace, Jovanovich, 1966.

Mundlak, Yair and S. Fred Singer. *Arid Zone Development: Potentialities and Problems.* Cambridge, MA: Ballinger, 1977.

National Institute of Sciences of India. *Proceedings of the Symposium on Climate, Environment and Health*, No. 10, August 4-6, 1955. New Delhi, India: National Institute of Sciences of India, April 1959.

Oke, T. R. *Review of Urban Climatology 1968–1973.* Technical Note No. 134. Geneva, Switzerland: Secretariat of the World Meteorological Organization, 1974 (WMO—No. 383).

Olgyay, Victor. *Design With Climate: Bioclimatic Approach to Architectural Regionalism.* Princeton, NJ: Princeton University Press, 1963.

Olgyay, Victor and Aladar Olgyay. *Solar Control and Shading Devices.* Princeton, NJ: Princeton University Press, 1976.

Organization for Economic Cooperation and Development (OECD). *The State of the Environment.* Paris: OECD, 1991.

Rahamimoff, Arie. "Residential Cluster Based on Climate and Energy Considerations." *Energy and Buildings* 7 (1984): 89-107.

Ress, William, E. *The Ecological Meaning of Environment-Economy Integration.* Vancouver: University of British Columbia, 1989.

Reuther, Oskar. *Das Wohnhaus in Baghdad und Anderen Stadten des Irak.* Berlin: Verlag Ernst Wasmuth, 1910.

Roseland, Mark. *Toward Sustainable Communities: A Resource Book for Municipal and Local Governments.* Ottawa: University of British Columbia, 1992.

Rubenstein, Harvey M. *A Guide to Site and Environmental Planning.* New York: Wiley, 1969.

Rudofsky, Bernard. *Architecture Without Architects: A Short Introduction to Non-Pedigreed Architecture.* Garden City, NY: Doubleday, 1964.

Rudofsky, Bernard. *The Prodigious Builders.* New York: Harcourt Brace Jovanovich, 1977.

Saini, Balwant Singh. "Housing in the Hot Arid Tropics." *Architectural Science Review* 5/1 (March 1962): pp. 3-12.

Saini, Balwant Singh. *Building in Hot Dry Climates.* New York: Wiley, 1980.

Schiller, John W. "The Automobile and the Atmosphers." In *Energy Production, Consumption, Consequences*, edited by John L. Helm. Washington, D. C.: National Academy of Sciences, 1990.

Schmutz, Ervin M., ed. *Landscaping With Native Arizona Plants.* Tucson: University of Arizona Press, 1973, 194 pp.

Schneider, Stephen H. *Global Warming: Are We Entering the Greenhouse Century?* San Francisco: Sierra Club Books, 1989.

Skurka, Norma, and Jon Naar. *Design for a Limited Planet.* New York: Ballantine Books, 1976.

Smil, Vaclov. *General Energetics: Energy in the Biosphere and Civilization.* New York: Wiley, 1991.

Stearns, Forest, and Tom Montag, eds. *The Urban Ecosystem: A Holistic Approach.* Stroudsburg, PA: Dowden, Hutchinson & Ross, 1974.

Stine, William B. and John T. Lyle. *Energy Use and Conservation Practices at the Institute for Regenerative Studies.* Research Report 92-001. Pomona, CA: California State Polytechnic University, 1992.

Student-Originated-Studies Program. *Microclimate, Architecture and Landscaping Relationships in an Arid Region: Phoenix, Arizona: Final Report.* Phoenix: Arizona State University, 1977.

Thayer, Robert. "Technophobia and Topophilia: The Dynamic Meanings of Technology in the Landscape." Davis, CA: Center for Design Research, 1990.

The World Conservation Union. *Caring for the Earth: A Strategy for Sustainable Living.* Gland, Switzerland: IUN/UNEP/WWF, 1991.

Trewartha, Glenn T. *An Introduction To Climate.* New York: McGraw-Hill, 1968.

Vale, Brenda. *Green Architecture: Design for a Sustainable Future.* London; Hudson, NY: UCLA AAUP/ARTS NA, no. 2542.3, 35, 1991.

Van der Ryn, Sim and Peter Calthorpe. *Sustainable Communities: A New Design Synthesis for Cities, Suburbs, and Towns.* San Francisco: Sierra Club Books, 1986.

Victorisze, Thomas. *Design of Residences for Climate Comfort.* Cambridge, MA: MIT, 1948.

Williams, Warren, ed. *Global Change, Impacts on Agriculture and Forestry: Proceedings of the Conference Held at Science House,* Wellington, New Zealand, August 13-14, 1991. Convened by the Royal Society of New Zealand Standing Committee for the International Geosphere-Biosphere Programme. Wellington, New Zealand: The Society, 1992.

World Meteorological Organization. *Urban Climates, Proceedings of the Symposium on Urban Climates and Building Climatology,* jointly organized by the World Health Organization and WMO, Brussels, October 1968, Vol. 1. Technical Note No. 108. Geneva, Switzerland: Secretariat of the World Meteorological Organization, 1970 (WMO—No. 254 T. P. 141).

World Meteorological Organization. *Protecting the Atmosphere, Oceans and Water Resources, Sustainable Use of Natural Resources.* Geneva, Switzerland: Secretariat of the World Meterological Organization, 1992.

Wulsin, Frederick R. *Hot Climate and High Civilization.* Berkeley: University of California Press, 1953.

# 7

## SOIL THERMAL PERFORMANCE
## AND GEOSPACE DESIGN

## BACKGROUND

The earliest shelter people used as a natural form for living
was the cave. It provided an ambient protective environment
against the outside harsh diurnal and seasonal climate.
Throughout the many millennia of using this form of shelter,
people have come to recognize the significance of the soil
thermal pattern and its process and have used it to advantage
for living, food storage, working, and protection.

Today there are three major community concentrations still
using below-ground space. These communities have accumulated thousands of years of experience with below-ground
living. The largest concentration is in the loess-type soil zone
of northern China, where an estimated 35 to 40 million people
live in below-ground dwellings (*yao dong*) in rural as well as
urban communities (Figure 7.1). It is assumed that the Chinese have used below-ground space for more than four thousand years.

The second largest concentration is scattered over the
Matmata plateau, located in the southern section of Tunisia
and the northern part of the Sahara Desert, where some twenty
fortified rural communities exist. In the case of Tunisia, the

Figure 7.1 View of neighborhood cliff dwellings located at the eastern part of Yan' an City, China, where more than 60 percent of the city dwellers live below ground.

size of the communities ranges from a few thousand people, as in Matmata village, to a few hundred in the very southernmost villages (Figure 7.2).

The third largest region is Cappadocia, central Turkey, where more than forty rural and town communities exist. It is assumed that below-ground living spaces have been used here for more than six thousand years. In addition to these three ancient-contemporary below-ground living concentrations, there has been similar historical use in northern Africa, Spain, central and southern France, southern Italy, Iran, India, the southwestern parts of the United States, and in many other scattered regions of the ancient world.

The common denominator among these three major historical concentrations is their location in arid and semiarid climate regions, their lengthy accumulated historical evolu-

Figure 7.2 Geospace dwellings have been in use throughtout the history of human settlements to cope with stressful climate. Matmata pit dwellings in southern Tunisia.

tion along with their distinct architectural design, and their adjustment to the harsh environment. Their arid-climate region is characterized by temperature fluctuations between extreme highs by day and lows at night and by torrential, yet limited, rainfall. It seems that the need for protection against this climate, in a region where fuel resources are limited, has contributed significantly to the selection of this form of living. Another factor in such an arid region is the scarcity of water usually needed for construction. In all three cases, the inhabitants adapted the "cut-and-use" method that does not consume water in creating space for living. Yet another consideration is defense, especially in the cases of Tunisia and Cappadocia where fortification in below-ground communities was possible. My study of these cases provided a wealth of

*Figure 7.3  Geospace classrooms integrated with the slope and looking over the lowland. Liquan County, Shaanxi province, China.*

data concerning below-ground-space thermal performance, design form, interior microenvironmental considerations, and reciprocal indoor-outdoor relationships. It is my opinion that the study of this data can benefit our modern geospace usage.

The recent special interest in the use of earth-integrated space in the technologically advanced countries has been the result of energy-saving efforts, as well as the result of a drastic rise in urban land cost, increasing space consumption, and other pressing forces (Figure 7.3). Modern geospace is now being used for habitats, educational facilities (United States), shopping centers (Japan and Canada), industries, ports (Scandinavia), agriculture production, food and grain storage (China), hospitals, museums, restaurants, and entertainment centers (Figure 7.4).

## GEOSPACE TERMINOLOGY

Since the early use of the cave as shelter, there have been different earth-integrated spaces developed by humankind for

*Figure 7.4 Geospace restaurant, Xidan street, Beijing, China.*

various other uses. Accordingly, a long list of terminology has been adopted to represent these diverse forms. However, the variation of forms represents different degrees of relationship to the soil and patterns of thermal performance, adjustment to the local environmental conditions, and the availability of building materials (Figure 7.5).

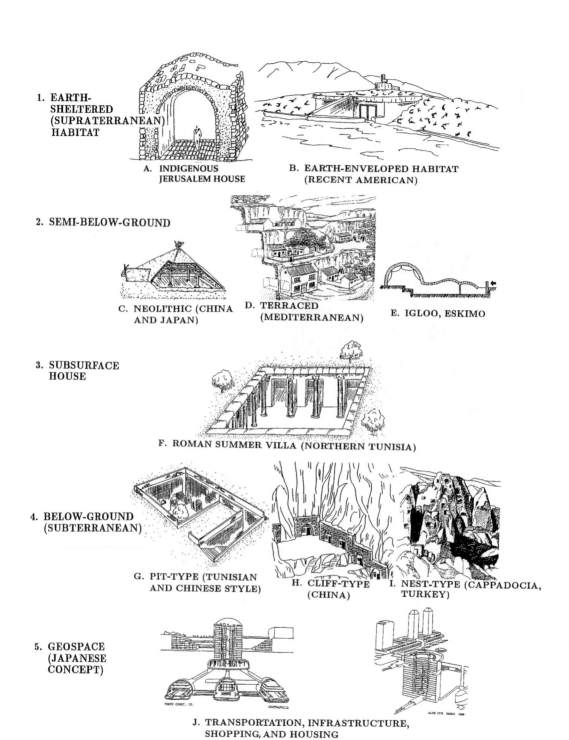

1. EARTH-SHELTERED (SUPRATERRANEAN) HABITAT

A. INDIGENOUS JERUSALEM HOUSE

B. EARTH-ENVELOPED HABITAT (RECENT AMERICAN)

2. SEMI-BELOW-GROUND

C. NEOLITHIC (CHINA AND JAPAN)

D. TERRACED (MEDITERRANEAN)

E. IGLOO, ESKIMO

3. SUBSURFACE HOUSE

F. ROMAN SUMMER VILLA (NORTHERN TUNISIA)

4. BELOW-GROUND (SUBTERRANEAN)

G. PIT-TYPE (TUNISIAN AND CHINESE STYLE)

H. CLIFF-TYPE (CHINA)

I. NEST-TYPE (CAPPADOCIA, TURKEY)

5. GEOSPACE (JAPANESE CONCEPT)

J. TRANSPORTATION, INFRASTRUCTURE, SHOPPING, AND HOUSING

*Figure 7.5 Types of earth-enveloped structures.*

The term *earth-sheltered habitat* is commonly used in the United States to indicate a habitat constructed mostly above ground, enveloped by an earth layer usually around one meter thick. The earth-sheltered habitat primarily functions as a thermal insulator between the indoor and outdoor air temperature. Its heat retention is very limited, yet it acts effectively in minimizing heat gain and loss. This form of construction is also an ancient one and is usually used in stressful-climate regions, such as hot-dry, as in the southwestern regions of the United States, in Iran, Turkey and, until a few decades ago, in Jerusalem, Israel.

*Semi-below-ground habitat* is used for a unit constructed partly below and partly above ground. This is one of the most ancient human-made housing forms and was used in the Neolithic village communities in China and Japan. This form is still in use in rural communities of Africa. The basement, commonly used throughout the world, is a similar form. Another example is the Eskimo winter igloo and summer semi-below-ground house. Another form of this type is the cliff-constructed space, where part of the house is built below and part above ground at the terrace.

*Subsurface space* is used when the distance between the below-ground space ceiling and the soil surface is very small and is constructed as part of the structure with very little coverage of soil. This subsurface house type was used by the ancient Romans at the city of Bulla Regia in northern Tunisia. The Romans built large numbers of peristyle subsurface summer villas to escape the intense heat of North Africa. Most probably, this design form was used by the native Berber tribes of North Africa before the Romans arrived. In some modern houses a basement unit is built in a subsurface style.

*Below-ground space* is applied to spaces developed at a reasonable depth below the soil—around three meters from the soil surface to the space's ceiling. Because of the soil thickness, the below-ground space is created by the cut-and-use method, where no building materials are needed. This is the most common form of earth-integrated space used throughout the history of mankind. This design form is used in cliff-terraced form as well as on flat topography in the pit-type

Figure 7.6 Below-ground dwelling permits agricultural development above its roof. Qing Long village near Taiyuan City, Shanxi province, China.

habitat (Figures 7.6 and 7.7). It is mostly developed in lime-stone or in tufa-type rock, such as in Cappadocia, Turkey, where cutting is relatively easy; or in loess-type soil, where the soil is firm and holds itself when it is dry, such as in China.

The term *geospace* is presently used by the Japanese to indicate space fully integrated deep within the earth. The Japanese designers have introduced some innovative and pioneering concepts of the geospace form for multipurpose structures in a depth of around 80 meters and combined with diverse types of daily human activities within shallower space. Here I use the term geospace in its general connotation to indicate all types of subterranean space.

However, the design of geospace to meet our modern norms and standards, especially for living, opens a new, challenging frontier for us and necessitates special considerations and treatment in the elements of form, thermal performance, natural light, sunshine, ventilation, and accessibility. This chapter focuses on the thermal performance of geospace and the related principles of the design form.

*Figure 7.7 View of pit dwelling in China where more than 30 million Chinese live below ground. Xi Feng town, Gansu province, China.*

## SOIL THERMAL PERFORMANCE

### Soil Thermal Process

One of the strongest elements influencing geospace use is the thermal performance of the soil. Generally, in the past,

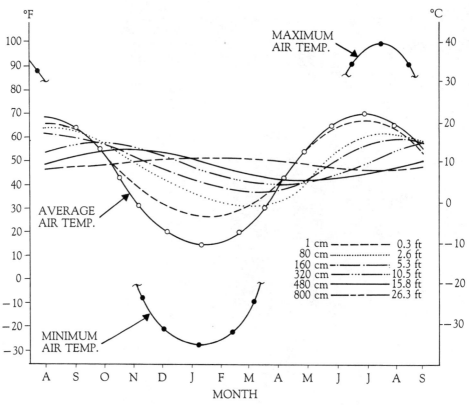

°F

100 —

90 —

80 —

70 —

60 —

50 —

40 —

30 —

20 —

10 —

0 —

−10 —

−20 —

−30 —

MAXIMUM
AIR TEMP.

°C

40

30

20

10

0

−10

−20

−30

AVERAGE
AIR TEMP.

| | |
|---|---|
| 1 cm ------ | 0.3 ft |
| 80 cm ········· | 2.6 ft |
| 160 cm -·-·-·- | 5.3 ft |
| 320 cm -··-··- | 10.5 ft |
| 480 cm ——— | 15.8 ft |
| 800 cm ----- | 26.3 ft |

MINIMUM
AIR TEMP.

A   S   O   N   D   J   F   M   A   M   J   J   A   S

MONTH

*Figure 7.8   Correlation between soil temperature fluctuation and the depth of the soil. At the depth of around 10 meters the seasonal temperature becomes stable. (Golany, 1983, p. 64. Adapted and reproduced originally from Thomas Bligh, 1975, p. 92.)*

interest in the study of the soil thermal performance process was limited to a specific zone of the soil. The agronomist's interest has been in the shallow depth that affects vegetation. On the other hand, the mining engineer has been concerned with a depth of hundreds of meters and its thermal performance. Geospace designers became interested in the zone ranging between the surface and 10 meters deep when modern geospace usage became feasible (Figure 7.8). The rediscovery of this zone has wide potential for use and has broad economic, social, and health implications.

The soil mass thermal process differs significantly from that of above-ground space. In general, we can state that down to a depth of around 10 meters the soil thermal pattern depends on the sun as the main heat supplier. Beyond that depth the effect of the earth's heat increases. However, within the 10 meters the heat gain and loss and thermal behavior within the soil depends not only on the intensity of the source of thermal supply but also on soil composition and density (rock, sandy, alluvial, etc.) and the degree of water containment.

During the day, solar heat influences the soil to a shallow depth generally ranging between 5 and 7 centimeters. Yet, there is a continued movement of this heat to a depth of around 10 meters. The basic rules are:

- Between the soil surface and this depth there is a seasonal thermal fluctuation that decreases toward the depth and increases toward the surface. No diurnal temperature fluctuation occurs.
- Around a depth of 10 meters the temperature is seasonally stable.

In short, the soil has two distinct functions. One is as an efficient insulator of heat gain and loss. The second is as a thermal retainer. To obtain thermal retention, it is necessary to have the mass of the earth. In terms of time lag, my findings show that it takes one season of around three months for the outdoor air temperature to travel to a depth of around 10 meters. Thus the summer outdoor air temperature will reach geospace at a depth of 10 meters by the winter season and the winter outdoor air temperature will reach that depth by the summer, when it is most needed.

Thermal Fluctuation

There is a strong correlation between the depth of the soil and temperature fluctuation. The governing rule is that the greater the depth from the soil surface, the smaller the thermal fluctuation. In general, at a depth of 10 meters the temperature is stable seasonally and diurnally at around 10°C with slight differentiation between the winter and the summer. In short, geospace has its own ambient microclimate independent of the outdoor air temperature fluctuation. This fact is significant especially in harsh-climate regions, where temporary or permanent settlements become necessary for the exploitation of natural resources.

It is, however, possible to minimize temperature fluctuation between the surface and 10 meters by distorting the normal thermal process through the soil. This can be achieved by placing insulation materials horizontally between the geospace structure ceiling and the soil surface. In this case, the surface temperature will travel around the insulation and take a longer time to reach the walls of the geospace habitat. Another way of distorting the thermal effect is to cover the ground surface above the geospace structure with buildings or dense forest.

Soil thermal fluctuation patterns also can be distorted when acceleration of the soil thermal process is desired so that the surface temperature will reach the geospace habitat in a shorter time than usual. To achieve such results, the soil surface above the habitat should be watered in the evening, causing the temperature received throughout the day at a depth of around 5 centimeters to penetrate deeper into the soil. The watering should take place in the early evening when the soil surface still has its maximum thermal absorption of the day and before the soil temperature is defused into the air. In repeating this action for a few evenings, the surface temperature will reach the geospace more quickly than it would by the normal process.

By observing living creatures within their natural environment, we have noticed that some creatures who live in stressful-climate regions (very hot, such as the Sahara, or very cold, such as Canada or north central Asia), or where there is an extreme diurnal temperature fluctuation, have constructed their habitats within the geospace for thermal protection.

Unfortunately, there is no universal formula available today that will identify the optimal depth at which summer temperatures will arrive in winter and winter temperatures in summer. However, taking into account the soil density, composition, and water content along with climate conditions and humidity, a reasonable estimate can be made. It may also be the case that modern dwellings would be better located at a depth where some seasonal temperature fluctuation is experienced. The primary goal is to select a site where pleasing architecture can create a space that will benefit from the thermal performance pattern of the soil and will, thus, reduce heating and air conditioning costs.

## EARTH-ENVELOPED HABITAT
## PERFORMANCE

The realization of these two functions of the soil, mentioned previously, is essential for determining geospace design and form. If insulation alone is required, we would need to build the habitat above ground and envelop it with layers of earth, as in the adobe houses of the southwestern United States. In fact, today we can achieve this with modern thin walls of high-quality insulation and can minimize heat gain and heat loss. Many modern American habitats of the 1970s and the 1980s used the above-ground earth-enveloped form to achieve high insulation, thus missing the significant advantages of the soil mass thermal retainment of geospace—the natural process resulting in coolness in summer and warmth in winter.

### Jerusalem House

In spite of what was just said, it is still possible to build the habitat above ground and establish in part the heat retention process. Throughout the historical evolution of human settlement, our ancestors realized the soil's natural seasonal thermal process and simulated it by building thick walls in the above-ground habitat. A good example of this is the indigenous Jerusalem house design type.

The Jerusalem house type practiced throughout history until half a century ago is made of thick walls formed of 1 to 2 meters of soil. The dirt-gravel wall is sandwiched between large stones on the outer side and small stones and mortar on the interior (Figure 7.5A). The climate of the region is a Mediterranean type of which the winter is cold and rainy and the summer is hot and dry. The outer wall absorbs the low winter temperature and the high humidity and travels through the soil's dirt-gravel to reach the inner wall by the summer and establish a cool ambient indoor environment. Similarly, the summer's high temperature and dryness absorbed by the outer wall permeates through to the inner wall and further to the indoor environment by the winter. In short, the interior part of the Jerusalem house is cool in the summer and warm in the winter. However, the thickness of the wall determines the heat gain and heat loss period and the heat retention capacity. To a great extent, this house design is a simulation of the thermal performance of the earth mass itself.

## Condensation

Condensation is the release of relative humidity caused by air contraction when the air temperature is reduced significantly. In geospace habitats condensation can take place in the summer when the walls provide cool low temperatures, and when the relative humidity of the air is very high, and when air exchange is minimal or nonexistent. Geospace located in rainy summer regions, such as Japan, will most probably be subject to condensation.

To minimize or eliminate condensation it is necessary to increase ventilation and air movement. Passive air movement can be achieved through the construction of vertical air shafts where, due to the temperature differentiation between the outdoors (high) and the indoors (lower), air pressure differentiation will take place. If a window or door opening onto a patio is provided, the outer air will then move downward through the shaft into the geospace habitat.

Another ambient thermal issue associated with geospace habitats is the differentiation in temperature between the outdoors and the indoors. As was mentioned previously, indoor winter temperature is relatively higher than that of the outdoors due to the summer heat retained by the soil and the time lag process. My research findings in the subterranean dwellings of the Matmata plateau, Tunisia, indicate that this indoor–outdoor temperature differentiation often causes the inhabitants of the dwellings to catch cold.

## Thermal Performance and Design Form

Do regions of different thermal performance require different geospace design forms, or is a geospace form that is applicable in the hot-dry climate, such as North Africa, an ideal one in the cold-dry climate, such as central Canada?

Geospace thermal performance observations indicate that where the summer temperature is cool and the comfort index is usually between twenty and twenty-two, a cooling system is not needed. We formulated the simplified method of determining the comfort index by dividing the combination of dry bulb and wet bulb temperatures. In this way, inhabitants can define their needs for additional heating. In the winter, a comfort index of around twelve necessitates some type of heating system. Thus, regions of hot-dry climate, where cooling is needed throughout most of the year, will require maximum surface space (walls, ceiling, and floor), since the total surface provides the cooling system of the geospace habitat. On the other hand, the major problem of the cold-dry climate region is the consumption of fuel for heating during most parts of the year and, therefore, the habitat will require minimum surface size to reduce energy consumption. Our research indicates that the most suitable design form for the hot-dry climate is the trapezoid and for the cold-dry climate, the circle (Figure 7.9).

## Significant Benefits

Geospace living is an effective way to cope with outdoor climatic conditions, especially the harsh ones. Its weather-proofing provides a comfortable ambient environment in both winter and summer. It consumes little energy and reduces heat gain and heat loss. There are other benefits as well.

Generally, the land cost is reduced, either because of the possible dual use or because of construction on low-priced sloping land. In fact, land savings can be significant since geospace habitats release other above-ground space for different purposes, such as playgrounds, recreation, or other buildings. The insulated quietness of the geospace habitats enables them to be built even near airports. Design and building cost can be minimal when large multiple units are built at the same time, or when geologically the lack of stratification enables the cut-and-use method of construction. Also, due to the paucity of exterior building materials and the low wear and tear, the price of maintenance is reduced. There is no need for new roofs every ten to fifteen years and the damage normally caused by wind, hail, rain, snow, or other natural factors is minimal.

Geospace habitats preserve the land and environment and save plenty of space for green and open areas. They provide

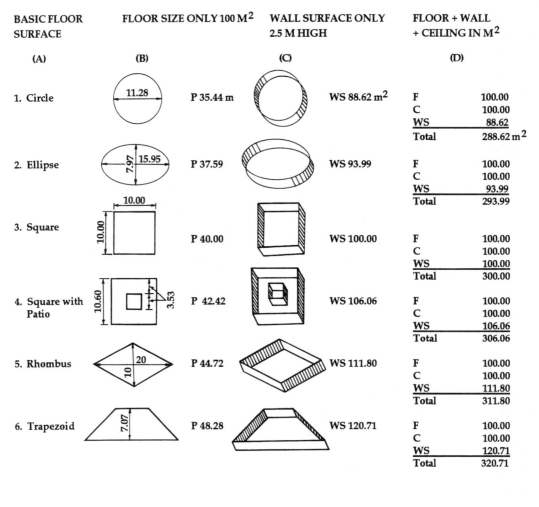

| BASIC FLOOR SURFACE (A) | FLOOR SIZE ONLY 100 M² (B) | WALL SURFACE ONLY 2.5 M HIGH (C) | FLOOR + WALL + CEILING IN M² (D) | |
|---|---|---|---|---|
| 1. Circle | 11.28<br>P 35.44 m | WS 88.62 m² | F<br>C<br>WS<br>Total | 100.00<br>100.00<br>88.62<br>288.62 m² |
| 2. Ellipse | 7.97 / 15.95<br>P 37.59 | WS 93.99 | F<br>C<br>WS<br>Total | 100.00<br>100.00<br>93.99<br>293.99 |
| 3. Square | 10.00 / 10.00<br>P 40.00 | WS 100.00 | F<br>C<br>WS<br>Total | 100.00<br>100.00<br>100.00<br>300.00 |
| 4. Square with Patio | 10.60 / 3.53<br>P 42.42 | WS 106.06 | F<br>C<br>WS<br>Total | 100.00<br>100.00<br>106.06<br>306.06 |
| 5. Rhombus | 20 / 10<br>P 44.72 | WS 111.80 | F<br>C<br>WS<br>Total | 100.00<br>100.00<br>111.80<br>311.80 |
| 6. Trapezoid | 7.07<br>P 48.28 | WS 120.71 | F<br>C<br>WS<br>Total | 100.00<br>100.00<br>120.71<br>320.71 |

Each Floor = 100 m²
All Floors are Equal in Size
All Heights = 2.5 m

P = Perimeter
F = Floor
C = Ceiling
WS = Wall Surface

*Figure 7.9 A variety of design forms with equal floor area as well as equal height to the ceiling show that the trapezoid has the greatest surface exposure while the circle has the smallest. (Reproduced from Golany, 1983, p. 106.)*

privacy, quiet, and a relaxing environment. As such, it is an ideal form for creative work, such as writing, music, composition, painting, and sculpture.

Geospace habitats can be safer than the above-ground environment when they are properly designed. They protect against storms, cyclones, tornadoes, and radioactive fallout, and there is minimal potential for a fire to spread to neighboring houses. Accordingly, insurance is expected to be lower

*Figure 7.10 Restaurant with front patio built within the cliff. Huang He River Scenic Spot, north of Zhengzhou City, Henan province, China.*

than for the conventional above-ground house. Geospace habitats can be made safer against earthquakes if protective design measures are taken, and they do not have certain problems, such as water pipes freezing and cracking. However, geospace habitats should not be designed for a site where radon exists.

Also, geospace offers diversified land use with special advantages (Figure 7.10). The temperature stability of geospace is most suitable for certain industries that require seasonal or perennial thermal stability, such as the film and wine industries. My research findings indicate that the minimal thermal fluctuation of geospace helps external wounds heal 20 percent faster after an operation, if the wet and the dry temperatures are stable.

Research conducted in below-ground living spaces in Australia revealed that living in a geospace habitat is more tranquil and healthful than in an above-ground space, especially for children. One mother indicated that her children had never slept so tranquilly as they did in the geospace habitat.

Due to its coolness in summer geospace also can be used for large-scale refrigeration and central food storage, especially for citrus fruits and vegetables. Such storage centers are used in Cappadocia, Turkey, in Ohya, Japan, and in Chongqing, China. In the Middle East, as well as in China and many other places of the ancient world, geospace has been used extensively for grain storage. Grain storage pits used in China during the Tang Dynasty (seventh to tenth centuries) were recently discovered in Luokou and in Luoyang City (Henan province), where more than 50 percent of the grain was still in good condition. Modern methods for geospace granaries are now being researched in the United States with a potential for large-scale development.

Other effective uses of geospace in the United States today are for educational facilities, such as libraries, schools, and bookstores. In universities, where space is precious and the expansion of the existing well-established library becomes essential, the nearby geospace becomes an ideal solution without interfering with the existing environment. Here too, thermal stability is an asset in preserving the books' quality. However, in the case of the library, there is a need to have stable, low relative humidity. Good examples of libraries expanded in geospace in the United States are at Harvard, Johns Hopkins, Cornell, and the University of Illinois, to name a few. Also, there are around one hundred modern earth-integrated schools in the country.

Similarly, a large number of offices, public gathering places, business spaces, religious centers, and habitats within geospace have been constructed within the last two decades. This new movement toward usage was generated in response to the energy crisis, the need to obtain ambient environment thermal conditions, or for environmental protection.

In conclusion, in many countries the image of living below ground has been associated with negative connotations, such as darkness, dampness, lack of ventilation, unhealthiness, and most important, claustrophobia. All in all, people have had a strong bias and a negative attitude against geospace living spaces. This bias is a historical one, derived from a time when the image of below-ground housing was associated with poverty and backwardness. Throughout history, the design implementation of below-ground habitats has been of poor quality in most societies. Almost all of the problems associated with geospace habitats can be considered as design or as technological ones and can certainly be solved to meet our present norms and standards. The major limitation of below-ground habitat usage is the psychological factor. The problem to be challenged is a dual one, that of claustrophobia and that of socio-psychological bias. Claustrophobia is the feeling of being afraid in confined space—children, women, and the elderly are often most sensitive.

The problem of the negative image of geospace habitats should be eased and resolved when modern versions of such habitats become commonly used by middle- and upper-class socio-economic groups. Also, increasing knowledge of the potential offered by good modern design should improve the image of geospace habitats.

Finally, the use of geospace as habitats yields more favorable results in extreme climates, hot or cold, than in temperate ones. Yet, every climate type introduces its own problems for geospace design; these need to be resolved separately. The major problem, for example, in the rainy-temperate climate zone is the humidity and with it the need to introduce an effective ventilation system along with waterproofing. As with every endeavor, the introduction of geospace habitats is a trade-off in which there are both gains and losses.

## CASE STUDIES

### Methodology for Case Studies

I had the opportunity to study selected sites in large below-ground settlements. In Tunisia (1982) and in China (1984-88), I visited all sites in both the summer and the winter. Temperatures were recorded on an hourly basis over a twenty-four-hour period.

All measurements were made with a psychrometer, which measures both dry and wet bulb temperatures. While dry bulb readings are the ones commonly used in research, wet bulb readings are valuable in desert-type conditions where humidity is low and the temperature is high. Since humidity will make an excessively dry climate more comfortable, many dry areas introduce moisture into the air to increase the comfort level. In a sense, wet bulb temperature readings create the same environment. A wick in the thermometer is kept wet and a fan moving the air will cause the moisture in the wick to evaporate. The evaporative cooling will cause the temperature to drop. When the humidity level of a space is at 100 percent, readings from both a wet bulb and dry bulb thermometer are identical. However, once the humidity drops, moisture will evaporate from the wet bulb thermometer, causing the temperature in the surrounding area to drop due to evaporative cooling.

## Case Study One: Zhang Yen Fu Family Dwelling, Shaanxi Province, China

The dwelling in this case study is located in the Ya' nan City area in Shaanxi, a province noted as the cradle of Chinese civilization and the capital of thirteen dynasties. The region is mountainous, the soil loess, and the climate cold and partly snowy in winter and warm and with limited rain in summer.

The Zhang Yen Fu dwelling is 10 kilometers east of Yan' an City in the farming village of Gao Me Wan. The village is located on a southern slope along the river and overlooks a fully cultivated valley. The cliff dwellings are built in a series of semicircular terraces with the Zhang Yen Fu home located on one directly above a major road. Recently, stone houses and earth-sheltered habitats have been built above ground, an indication of modernization. The village's improved economic circumstances are due to agricultural reforms made by the government.

The Zhang Yen Fu dwelling presented a unique case study because half of the home is within the earth of the cliff and the other half is earth sheltered. The five-room east wing of

Figure 7.11 Perspective
view of the Zhang Yen Fu
family dwelling in Gao Me
Wan Village, near Yan'an
City, Shaanxi province.
(Golany, 1990, p. 60.)

the L-shape structure is covered by 15 meters of earth (Figure
7.11). The five-room west wing is covered by only 2 meters
of earth. For comparison, two sites from each wing of the
dwelling were chosen for temperature measurements. Sites 1
and 2 are in the below-ground east wing and face southwest.
Sites 3 and 4 are in the earth-sheltered west wing and face
southeast. Site 5 is outside in the courtyard.

The four indoor sites are almost identical with hard loess
floors, brick-covered arched ceilings and interior walls, a lat-
ticed window, and a rough wooden door. Each room is about
3 meters wide. Furnishings in the occupied rooms (Sites 3
and 4) include a built-in heated bed and a stove for cooking.
The front walls of Sites 1 and 2 are made of stone and are
flooded with sunlight all afternoon. Doors and windows at
these sites were closed during the temperature readings. The
front walls of Sites 3 and 4, which were occupied at the time
of the measurements, are made of brick and receive direct
sunlight only at noon. The windows and doors of these rooms
were open throughout the measurement period.

*Thermal Performance*

The thermal performance of all below-ground spaces is affected by the soil surrounding the structure. The Zhang Yen Fu dwelling is cut into loess soil, a fine and porous soil free of stones. The nature of this soil makes construction relatively easy.

Summer wet and dry bulb temperatures at Sites 1 and 2 were well within the comfort range throughout the measurement period and were almost stable throughout the twenty-four-hour period with a differentiation of only 2.3 to 3°C (Figure 7.12). The temperatures in both rooms peaked at 21°C between 3:00 and 5:00 P.M. but remained at 17°C for most of the measurement period.

Temperatures at Site 3, one of the earth-sheltered rooms, showed much greater fluctuation and higher readings throughout the measurement period, with a longer peak between noon and 4:00 P.M.

Site 5, located outside on the patio, showed an extreme fluctuation between day and night with a low of 14°C at 6:00 A.M. to a high of 28°C in the afternoon. These temperature extremes are typical of arid environments.

Winter temperatures at all indoor sites were low enough to require some additional heating (Figure 7.13). Those at Sites 1 and 2 were, again, remarkably stable and lower than those at Site 3.

The relative humidity of all sites in the Zhang Yen Fu residence demonstrates the ability of the soil to temper that dimension of comfort (Figure 7.14). Both subterranean sites show decreased humidity during the winter while the earth-sheltered site shows little decrease between summer and winter. This can be attributed to the humidity absorbed by the outer walls during the summer. However, the humidity fluctuation at all indoor sites was moderate when compared with the courtyard.

*Figure 7.12 (facing page) Summer dry bulb (solid line) and wet bulb (broken line) diurnal temperatures, July 19–20, 1984, of the Zhang Yen Fu family dwelling. Note the differentiation in fluctuation between Sites 1 and 2 (below-ground rooms) and Site 3 (earth-sheltered). (Golany, 1990, p. 63.)*

## Case Study Two: Marhala Hotel, Matmata, Tunisia

The structure in this case study is located on the Matmata plateau in southern Tunisia. The plateau, which reaches an elevation of 400 to 600 meters, forms a ridge between the

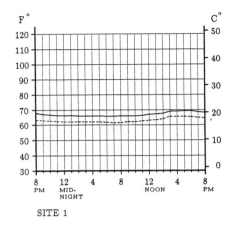

SITE 1

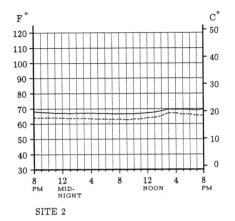

SITE 2

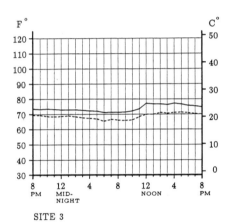

SITE 3

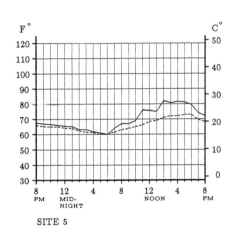

SITE 5

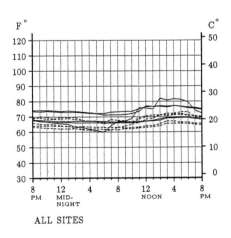

ALL SITES

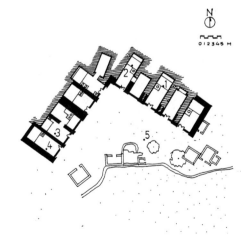

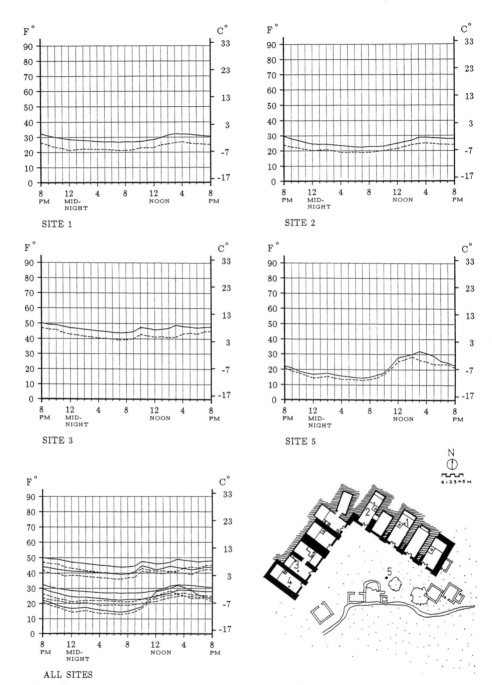

*Figure 7.13  Winter dry bulb (solid line) and wet bulb (broken line) diurnal temperatures, January 10–11, 1985, of the Zhang Yen Fu family dwelling. (Golany, 1990, p. 64.)*

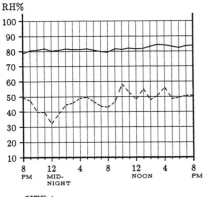

SITE 1

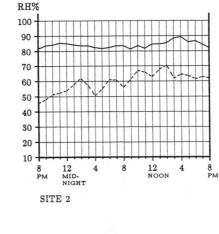

SITE 2

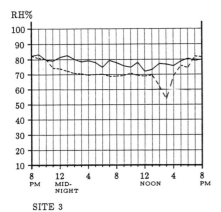

SITE 3

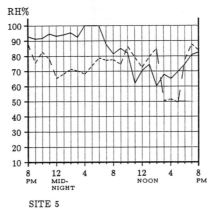

SITE 5

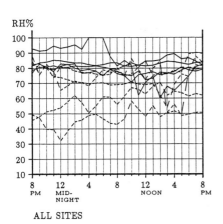

ALL SITES

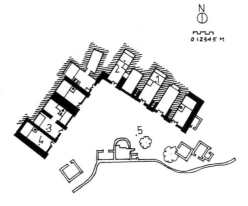

*Figure 7.14 Summer (solid line) and winter (broken line) relative humidity of the Zhang Yen Fu family cave dwelling. (Golany, 1990, p. 65.)*

Figure 7.15 Bird's-eye view of Matmata's subterranean community, facing south. (Golany, 1988, p. 48.)

alluvial plain toward the Mediterranean on the east and the lowlands of the Sahara Desert on the west. Due to its elevation, the plateau enjoys more humidity than the surrounding area, but it is still a hot, dry region with hostile and stressful climatic conditions. A true desert climate, summer temperatures exceed 40°C and winter temperatures are a more moderate 20°C.

The Marhala Hotel is located in the village of Matmata, 42 kilometers south of the city of Gabes at the northern edge of the Matmata plateau. The village rests on the lower northern slope of a large basin and is surrounded by higher hills to the north, east, and south. Both picturesque and somewhat forbidding, the village looks like a lunar landscape with rolling hills alternating with almost flat topography (Figure 7.15). The landscape also is distinguished by scattered palm trees and whitewashed buildings above ground. The last underground house to be constructed in the village was built in 1975.

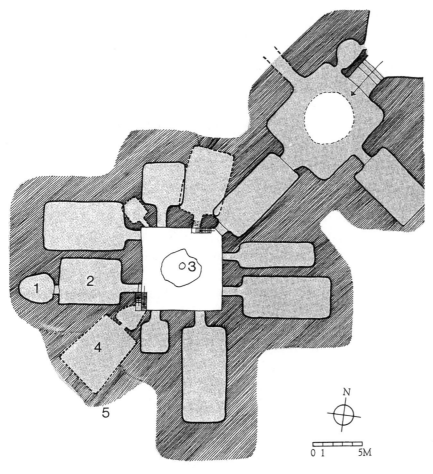

Figure 7.16 The complex of the Marhala Hotel where temperature measurements were taken. Broken lines designate second-floor rooms. The circular shape with broken lines is the partially covered opening to the sky from one of the two patios. (Golany, 1988, p. 85.)

Five sites were selected for measurements at the Marhala Hotel (Figure 7.16). Site 1, the innermost room on the ground floor, is 12 meters from the patio and 10 meters below ground. Its dimensions are small, 3.4 by 2.6 meters and 1.6 meters high. Site 2, a large room on the western side of the patio, is 6 by 4.1 meters and has a vaulted ceiling 3 meters high. There are no windows in the room, and the door was closed during the measurement period. Site 3 is outdoors in the patio and was shaded most of the time; it is located at a depth of 10 meters. Site 4 is a large room on the second floor of the hotel and measures 6.2 by 4.6 meters and 2 meters high. The earth cover over this site is 4 meters thick. Site 5 is outdoors and above ground, outside the hotel complex.

*Thermal Performance*

The thermal performance of all below-ground spaces is affected by the soil surrounding the structure. The Marhala Hotel is cut into a loess-like soil that is almost free of stones and has a reasonable amount of sand and calcium carbonate. The soil is easy to cut with simple tools and is quite dense.

Summer temperatures were most stable in the three rooms with Site 4 showing the greatest fluctuation (Figure 7.17). The temperature in the patio does have some affect on that in the rooms through the open doors. There is a noticeable difference between the rooms on the ground floor and Site 4, with the rooms on the ground floor having a more comfortable and stable temperature. Throughout the twenty-four-hour measurement period, the temperature differential between Site 1 and the outdoors was 17°C.

Winter temperatures show that Site 1, the innermost room, is the warmest and has the most stable temperature with Site 2 close behind. Site 4 is warmer than the outdoor sites except for late in the afternoon.

A comparison of the summer and winter temperatures shows that the two lower-level rooms have the most stable conditions and the least fluctuation between summer and winter.

*Figure 7.17 (facing page) Comparison of summer (solid line) and winter (broken line) dry bulb temperatures of the five sites measured diurnally in Marhala Hotel, Matmata. Note the small temperature differentiation in Sites 1, 2, and 4 between summer and winter, compared with temperature differences of Sites 3 and 5. Also, note the relative stability of both temperatures in Sites 1, 2, and 4, compared with the large temperature fluctuations in Sites 3 and 5, which indicates that the indoor climate is more comfortable in both seasons. The comfort level is greater in Sites 1 and 2 than in 4, which is closer to the surface. (Golany, 1988, p. 104.)*

## Case Study Three: The Hunt House, Bulla Regia, Northern Tunisia

While the previous well-documented two case studies included here were conducted in structures in use today, a limited study of the Roman subsurface structures in Bulla Regia offers another perspective on earth-sheltered spaces.

Bulla Regia is located about 150 kilometers west of Tunis city at the foot of Mount R' bia. The city was established on a gentle slope facing south and overlooking the large Medjerda Valley. The city had an attractive environment, cool and humid in the winter and warm and dry in the summer.

Although below-ground space had been used by the Romans in different places in the world, it was in Bulla Regia that they intentionally and systematically developed subsurface structures or a combination of space below ground and above ground in one dwelling.

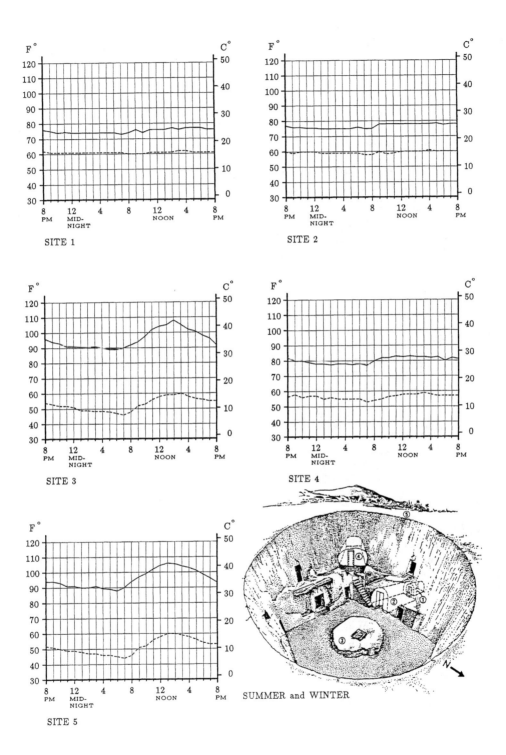

SITE 1

SITE 2

SITE 3

SITE 4

SITE 5

SUMMER and WINTER

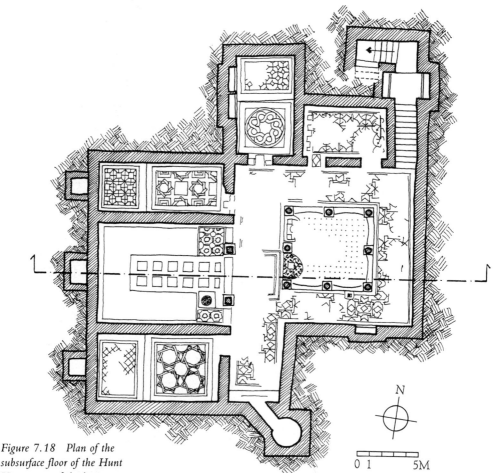

N

0 1      5M

*Figure 7.18 Plan of the subsurface floor of the Hunt House, one of the best-designed Roman buildings in Bulla Regia. Note that each room has light entering through a light shaft or the open patio. The stairway at the upper-right corner leads directly to a large colonnaded courtyard. The dining room, on the left, is also well lighted, having a partially open wall facing the courtyard. The circular form, bottom right, is the opening to the well. (Golany, 1988, p. 127; adapted and reproduced from Beschaouch, et al., 1977, p. 57.)*

Though the site is only partially excavated, the Hunt House complex is one of the best preserved, largest, and most elaborate dwellings in Bulla Regia. It is an excellent example of the use of supraterranean and subsurface space (Figure 7.18). Within the block complex of the Hunt House, there is one subsurface structure, from which the name of the house is taken. This subsurface section of the house includes five rooms opening off a peristyle courtyard. The peristyle has eight Corinthian columns and porticos on all four sides. The largest room is the dining room, which is 6.6 by 5.2 meters and, as with all of the rooms in this area, has a colorful mosaic floor. The bedrooms on either side of the dining room measure 3.4 by 6.4 meters and 2.3 by 6.4 meters. On the north side of the courtyard, a third bedroom measures 3 by 5 meters. The fifth room, which also is on the north side of the courtyard, is 2.6 by 4.4 meters. All rooms have a light shaft window at the rear of the room leading directly into a ventilation shaft that runs vertically to the surface of the ground. All rooms are approximately 5 meters below the surface and have an earth covering of less than 1 meter.

Temperature measurements were taken at twelve sites in the Hunt House, eleven in the subsurface structure and one above ground.

*Thermal Performance*

While properties of the soil surrounding an earth-sheltered structure are important in selecting the site and determining the thermal performance, at Bulla Regia it appears the Romans were concerned more with the insulating qualities of the soil and the protection of the dwelling above the subsurface structure than with the thermal retention of the soil.

Summer temperatures indicate that the subsurface section of the house was slightly cooler than the above-ground site, and there was little variation among the temperatures throughout the subsurface space. In the winter, the subsurface temperatures were cooler than above ground, thus indicating that the subsurface structure was probably used only in the summer.

However, since temperatures were taken only at one time in each season instead of over a twenty-four-hour period and the rooms were not inhabited or closed, the conclusions that can be drawn from this study are limited.

*Characteristics of Roman Subsurface Structures*

Roman subsurface structures differed from subterranean dwellings of Berbers and Arabs in southern Tunisia in a number of significant ways. All of these differences are evident in the Hunt House.

While subterranean dwellings in Matmata are 9 to 11 meters below ground, the Roman houses have an earth cover of 1 to 1.5 meters, using the earth as an insulator instead of a heat retainer. The subsurface dwelling was always part of a larger above-ground structure instead of an entire dwelling. Also, the Romans appear to have simply adapted their traditional above-ground design to spaces below ground. The units are about 10 by 10 meters and are built around an open-air court-yard with all of the rooms opening onto that space. In most cases, the ceilings of the rooms are vaulted and supported by arches and columns. The floors are decorated with colorful mosaics. The Romans solved lighting and air circulating problems by placing shaft windows at the back of each room. Outside the window the shaft opens vertically to the sky. In some cases, windows are cut into the stairways or into the wall above the columns in the courtyard.

While subterranean dwellings in southern Tunisia were created in response to the terrain, it appears that the Romans built their subsurface dwellings to create a more comfortable microclimate.

In conclusion, the data collected in the first two case studies confirms that below-ground spaces enjoy more stable and moderate temperatures than above-ground sites. The research confirms that the deeper the structure is into the earth, up to a depth of 10 meters, the smaller the temperature fluctuations between day and night and between summer and winter. The shallower the structure, or the closer it is to the surface of the ground, the greater the fluctuation between day and night and between summer and winter.

Humidity also is affected by the depth of the earth cover over a structure. Spaces at around 10 meters deep show less fluctuation in humidity within the dwelling than is true of structures closer to the surface or at outdoor sites.

It appears from these studies that a below-ground structure constructed at a depth of 10 meters and with good ventilation to control humidity would provide the most stable environment. Other significant benefits of below-ground spaces have been discussed in the body of this chapter.

Finally, geospace thermal performance introduces new dimensions into urban design and offers a challenge and therefore an opportunity for the city of the future. It is an old tradition of design ethics; we need to explore further its potentialities for urban design.

# SELECTED READINGS

OTHER WORKS ON THE SUBJECT BY THE AUTHOR

Golany, Gideon S. *Chinese Earth-Sheltered Dwellings: Indigenous Lessons for Modern Urban Design*. Honolulu: University of Hawaii Press, 1992.

—. *Design and Thermal Performance: Below-Ground Dwellings In China*. Newark, DE: University of Delaware Press, 1990.

—. *Earth-sheltered Dwellings in Tunisia: Ancient Lessons for Modern Design*. Newark, DE: University of Delaware Press, 1988.

—. *Earth-sheltered Habitat: History, Architecture and Urban Design*. New York: Van Nostrand Reinhold, 1983.

—. *Geo-Space Urban Design*. Manuscript in Progress, 1994.

—. "Soil Thermal Performance and Geo-space Design." In *Proceedings of Japan Society of Civil Engineers*, 445/III-18, 1992-1993.

—. *Urban Underground Space Design in China: Vernacular and Modern Practice*. Newark, DE: University of Delaware Press, 1989.


SOIL TEMPERATURE

Ashbel, D. et al. *Soil Temperature in Different Latitudes and Different Climates*. Jerusalem, Israel: Hebrew University, 1965.

Baggs, Sidney A. "The Dugout Dwellings of an Outback Opal Mining Town in Australia." In *Underground Utilization*, edited by Truman Stauffer, Sr., 4:573-599. Kansas City, MO: University of Missouri, 1978. Also in mimeo, University of New South Wales, Sydney, Department of Landscape Architecture, 1977.

Barney, Gerald O., ed. *The Global 2000 Report to the President of the U.S.* New York: Pergamon Press, 1980.

Bell, Daniel. *The Coming of the Post-Industrial Age.* New York: Basic Books, 1973.

Bergman, S. Magnus. "Geo-Planning—The Key to Successful Underground Construction." *Underground Space* 2 (1977): 1-7.

Beschaouch, Azedine, Roger Hanoune, and Yvon Thébert. *Les Ruines de Bulla Regia.* Rome: Ecole Française de Rome, Palais Farnese, 1977.

Blick, Edward F. "A Simple Method for Determining Heat Flow through Earth Covered Roofs." In *Proceedings: Earth-sheltered Building Design Innovations,* edited by Lester L. Boyer, 3:3-23. Stillwater, OK: Oklahoma State University, 1980.

Bligh, Thomas. "A Comparison of Energy Consumption in Earth Covered vs. Non-Earth Covered Buildings." In *Alternatives in Energy Conservations: The Use of Earth Covered Buildings; Proceedings of a Conference,* Frank L. Moreland, Editor, Fort Worth, Texas, July 9-12, 1975. Washington, D.C.: National Science Foundation, 1975, p. 92.

Bligh, Thomas P. "Thermal Energy Storage in Large Underground Systems and Buildings." In *Storage in Excavated Rock Caverns, Rockstore 77,* edited by Magnus Bergman, 1:63-71. Oxford, England: Pergamon Press, 1978.

Bodonyi, J. "Engineering Geology Related to Underground Openings." *UNESCO International Post-Graduate Course on the Principles and Methods of Engineering Geology.* Budapest, Hungary, 1975.

Boileau, G. G. and J. K. Latta. "Calculation of Basement Heat Losses." In *Underground Utilization,* edited by Truman Stauffer, Sr., 5:754-764. Kansas City, MO: University of Missouri, 1978.

Carson, James E. "Analysis of Soil and Air Temperatures by Fourier Techniques." *Journal of Geophysical Research* 68 (1963): 2217-2232.

Chambers, F. M., ed. *Climate Change and Human Impact on the Landscape; Studies in Palaeoecology and Environmental Archaeology.* 1st ed.: London; New York: Chapman & Hall, 1993.

Crabb, G. A. Jr. and J. L. Smith. "Soil-temperature Comparisons under Varying Covers." In *Soil Temperature and Ground Freezing,* 32-80. Washington, D.C.: National Academy of Sciences, National Research Council, 1953.

Davies, G. R. "Thermal Analysis of Earth-covered Buildings." In *Proceedings of the 4th National Passive Solar Conference,* edited by G. Franta, 744. Newark, DE: American Section of the International Solar Energy Society, 1979.

Davis, William B. "Earth Temperature: Its Effect on Underground Residences." In *Earth-covered Buildings: Technical Notes,* edited by Frank L. Moreland, F. Higgs, and J. Shih, 205-209. Springfield, VA: NTIS, 1979.

Druker, E. F. and J. T. Haines. "A Study of Thermal Environment in Underground Survival Shelters Using an Electronic Analog Computer." *ASHRAE Transactions* 70 (1964): 7-20.

Givoni, Baruch. "Modifying the Ambient Temperature of Underground Buildings." In *Earth-covered Buildings: Technical Notes,* edited by Frank L. Moreland, F. Higgs, and J. Shih, 123-138. Springfield, VA: NTIS, 1979.

International Union for the Conservation of Nature and Natural Resources (IUCN), United Nations Environmental Program (UNEP), and World Wildlife Fund (WWF). *Caring for the Earth: A Strategy for Sustainable Living.* Gland, Switzerland: IUCN, UNEP, WWF, 1992.

Kusada, T. and P. R. Achenbach. "Comparison of Digital Computer Simulations of Thermal Environment." In *Occupied Underground Protective Structure with Observed Conditions*. Report 9473. Washington, D.C.: National Bureau of Standards, 1966.

Kusada, T. and P. R. Achenbach. "Numerical Analyses of the Thermal Environment of Occupied Underground Spaces with Finite Cover Using a Digital Computer." *ASHRAE Transactions* 69 (1963): 439-452.

Kusuda, T. *Earth Temperature beneath Five Different Surfaces*. Report 10373. Washington, D.C.: U.S. Department of Commerce, National Bureau of Standards, 1971.

Kusuda, T. "The Effect of Ground Cover on Earth Temperature." In *Alternatives in Energy Conservation, the Use of Earth-covered Buildings*, edited by Frank L. Moreland, 279-303. Washington, D.C.: National Science Foundation/ USGPO, 1978.

Kusuda, T. and F. J. Powell. *Heat Transfer Analysis of Underground Heat Distribution Systems*. Report 10-194. Washington, D.C.: National Bureau of Standards, 1970.

Labs, Kenneth. "The Underground Advantage: Climate of Soils." In *Proceedings of the 4th National Passive Solar Conference*, edited by G. Franta. Newark, DE: American Section of the International Solar Energy Society, 1979.

Maxwell, Robert K. "Temperature Measurements and the Calculated Heat Flux in the Soil." Master's thesis, University of Minnesota, 1964.

Mazria, Edward. *The Passive Solar Energy Book*. Emmaus, PA: Rodale Press, 1979.

McHarg, Ian L. and Jonathan Sutton. "Ecological Plumbing for the Texas Coastal Plain." *Landscape Architecture* 65/1 (1975).

McLarney, William D. "Aquaculture: Toward an Ecological Approach," edited by Richard Merrill. *Radical Agriculture*. New York, NY: Harper & Row, 1976.

Organization for Economic Cooperation and Development (OECD). *The State of the Environment*. Paris: OECD, 1991.

Peters, A. *Soil Thermal Properties: An Annotated Bibliography*. Philadelphia, PA: Franklin Institute, 1962.

Pollack, H. A. and D. S. Chapman. "The Flow of Heat from the Earth's Interior." *Scientific American* 237 (1977): 60-76.

Schiller, John W. "The Automobile and the Atmosphers." In *Energy Production, Consumption, Consequences,* edited by John L. Helm. Washington, D. C.: National Academy of Sciences, 1990.

Schneider, Stephen H. *Global Warming: Are We Entering the Greenhouse Century?* San Francisco: Sierra Club Books, 1989.

Singer, Irving A. and R. M. Brown. "The Annual Variations of Sub-soil Temperatures about a 600-foot Circle." *Transactions of the American Geophysical Union* 37 (1956): 743-748.

Smith, W. O. "The Thermal Conductivity of Dry Soils." *Soil Science* 53 (1942): 435-459.

# 8

## GEOSPACE CITY CONCEPT:
### A Renewal of Ancient Tradition

## DEFINITION

Geospace city is a new urban pattern that introduces extensive and diversified urban land use into the subterranean space of the city. I believe that the fusion of this new space with the supraterranean existing city will ultimately improve the quality of urban life and be included in the comprehensive city plan. The goal of geospace city design is to address existing needs and deficiencies of the existing city and to enhance the quality of urban life by improving the five major urban problem areas of inferior location, deficient designs, social disturbances, health and environmental degeneration, and the financial burden resulting from unsuitable designs. Geospace also has the potential to solve two major urban physical problems of the future. First, it can provide a new dimension for development in cities where above-ground space is limited, especially in the center of the urban area. Second, it can provide relief for cities that have become so geographically dispersed that they cannot be managed efficiently. In both cases, geospace offers development in close proximity to all types of land use and can form a continuum with above-ground uses. For the dispersed city, it can reduce the costly spread of its infrastructure. The use of geospace also may become vital to densely populated countries, such as England, Holland, and Israel, where land is at a premium. A description of various types of geospace can be found in Chapter Seven of this volume.

## BASIC PRINCIPLES

Our geospace city concept pioneers a new urban setting that should have a far-reaching impact on the supraspace, conventional city. It introduces a new image of land use at different geo-depths and over different topographical forms. The new urban space complements but does not replace the supraspace city; its ultimate goal is to solve many existing supraspace city problems.

By definition, urban design is the synthesis of the natural and the human-made environment, where all contributing forces shaping the city are carefully considered. The focus of urban design is people and their physical, three-dimensional environment. The goal of urban design is to create the flow of a pleasing environment for all urban dwellers within the entire city. Urban designers of contemporary and future cities need to integrate basic geospace principles in their plans for the future.

The basic principles of the geospace city are as follows:

1. The ultimate removal of most, if not all, of the urban supratransportation network and above-ground utilities into the geospace levels, especially the part crossing the city center (Figure 8.1). This transfer removes a negative feature of the supracity and replaces it with life-enhancing features. An environment free from vehicles releases the urban supraspace for pedestrians, for the strong intrusion of natural landscape deep into the city, and for recreation and relaxation within a natural environment.

2. The removal of all of the city's infrastructure and its construction to the geospace level in a fully and com-

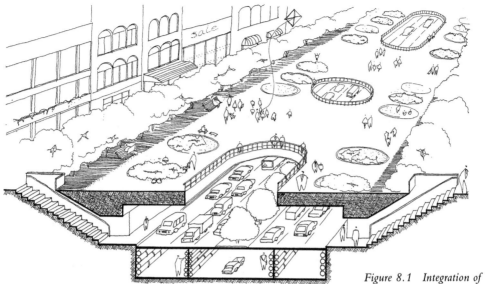

*Figure 8.1 Integration of the transportation and utilities network into the geospace and its replacement by a natural and pedestrian environment will have a significant positive impact on the social life, health, and safety of the supraspace city.*

prehensively organized plan, yet with a sophisticated and easily accessible operational space.

3. The design, implementation, and operation of a totally automated underground delivery system for the city. As with the Japanese concept, it first delivers goods underground vertically downward by elevator, then horizontally to a new location, and returning vertically upward to a receiving station.

4. To introduce the habitats into the geospace exclusively within the slopes in order to receive maximum light, sunshine, and ventilation.

5. To move all land uses that are, or potentially can be, windowless structures into the geospace (Table 8.1). Except for habitats, such land use is diverse and can include shopping centers and industries and services as well (Figures. 8.2 and 8.3).

6. Fusing the natural environment deep into the supraspace urban cityscape. Our contemporary experience of large cities reveals that the nature of urban environments is generally psychologically oppressive. Yet, urban designers have not been able to implement a city design pre-

TABLE 8.1

*Urban Windowless Buildings Most Suited for Geospace*

| EDUCATIONAL FACILITIES | STORAGES |
|---|---|
| Classrooms: schools, universities, training centers | General storage |
| | Equipment |
| Libraries | Garages |
| Museums (of all types) | Agricultural production |
| Cultural centers | Refrigeration |
| Exhibition halls | Bookstores |
| | Warehouses |

| ENTERTAINMENT & CULTURAL CENTERS | SERVICE |
|---|---|
| Theaters | Restaurants |
| Opera houses | Shopping centers (of all types) |
| Concert halls | Some offices |
| Bowling alleys | Hospitals: surgery and recovery rooms |
| Skating rinks: roller and ice | |
| Sports arenas | Grocery stores |
| Public lecture halls | Companies of all types |
| Art and creative galleries | Transportation centers |
| Schools and universities | Worship centers |
| Cultural centers | |

| AGRICULTURE | INDUSTRIES & FACTORIES |
|---|---|
| Mushroom raising | Processing plants |
| Chicken raising | Building equipment and supplies |
| | Printing industry |

dominated by a related environment that counteracts the formerly stressful features of a supracity. The introduction of a natural landscape with large plants and space will benefit all age groups and significantly improve the social quality of life.

7. The implementation of cohesive, integrated, and segregated land-use patterns into the geospace as an integral organic part of the supracity. Restructuring the supraspace city land-use pattern to readjust it to the human scale would allow the natural environment to dominate the pedestrian network throughout the city. Moreover, the integration of the geospace city with the supraspace city will bring the city, through the proximity of the combined land use, back to the human scale.

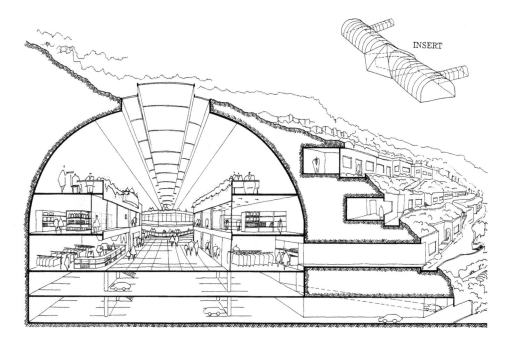

INSERT

*Figure 8.2   A geospace shopping center built within a slope-residential neighborhood has air circulation and natural light as well as a parking area with access to a subterranean transportation network.*

8. The division of the below-ground space into three levels of depth with diversified land use, following the degree of involvement of human activity and according to a comprehensive plan (Table 8.2). The basic principles of the correlation between depth and land use are: (1) The shallower the depth (0 to 10 meters), the higher the level of human activity employed. (2) The greater the depth of the geospace, the lower the level of human activities and the greater the use of an automated self-operated remotely controlled system.

However, it is not realistic to expect the implementation of the geospace city to take place within a short time. Ideally, it is easier to implement and realize our concept of the geospace city in a new town built from scratch. Since we are aware of the legislative, economic, and implementation difficulties associated with such projects, we envision its development through a comprehensive, step-by-step urban design plan. In fact, recently there have been steady and strong movements throughout the world in the utilization of the below-

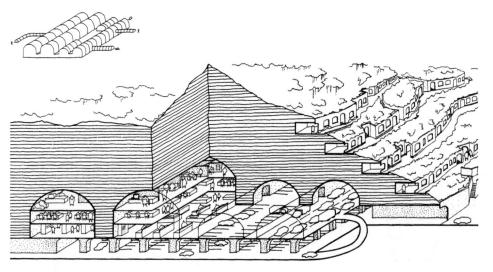

*Figure 8.3 Conceptual subterranean industrial complex developed within a slope of a geospace city. It also offers access to a major road and parking space.*

ground space within large cities. As a revolutionary concept in urban design, its merit and strength lie primarily in its long-range response to our existing urban dichotomy (Table 8.3). In all advanced regions of the world, urbanization is a strong reality of life and with it comes the drastic changes to the environment and the overall physical, social, and economic landscape. Also, this irreversible pattern of urbanization will continue to dominate the landscape of our environment and, with it, the associated increasing consumption of space, goods, and high technology and the demand for a higher standard of living. All of this leads to drastic changes in socio-economic values. Any planning system should consider these changes and the forces behind them. Under these circumstances, the role of the urban design system becomes critical and essential.

My observations and research findings regarding urban design and regional planning in many other regions of the world indicate a strong correlation between the country size, population density, and level of technology with the degree of awareness of and development of a wholistic, comprehensive national growth policy and urban design. Good examples are the cases of England (new town development), Holland (polder reclamation of land), Japan (intensive organized space) and

TABLE 8.2

*Basic Land-Use Principles, Patterns, and Human Activities of the Geospace City Related to Depth*

| LEVEL/DEPTH (1) | HUMAN ACTIVITIES (2) | SEGREGATED/ INTEGRATED LAND USE (3) | LAND USE (4) | | |
|---|---|---|---|---|---|
| **Above Ground:** height unlimited, depends on technology | Diurnally highly intensive and extensive | Selective integrated, mixed, and segregated land use | Removal of the following to below ground: Transportation network (especially from the core of the city) except for emergency cases<br>Delivery system<br>Infrastructural network<br>Increased city features: green open space, natural environment, bodies of water, childrens' playgrounds, rest areas, open markets, art displays<br>Expanded pedestrian network into all parts of the city as a comprehensively integrated network<br>Most of the traditional land use will continue to be represented | | |
| **Shallow Depth:** 0 to 10 meters | Diurnally intensive and extensive | Selective integrated and segregated land uses | Habitats (exclusively in the slope)<br>Pedestrian network<br>Special recreation<br>Surgery & recuperation rooms<br>Spiritual activities<br>Restaurants<br>Cultural centers, theaters, museums | Entertainment centers<br>Sporting activities<br>Swimming pools<br>Conferences<br>Light infrastructure<br>Light transportation<br>Parking | Hotels (for short stay)<br>Educational activities, libraries<br>Creative environment<br>Shopping centers<br>Offices<br>Public gatherings |
| **Medium Depth:** 10 to 50 meters | Selective daily human activities | Segregated land use | Subways, highways, streets<br>Parking | Nonpolluting industry<br>Delivery system<br>Storage (short range) | Infrastructural network<br>Refrigeration<br>Energy storage |
| **Deep:** 50 meters or more | Very low human activity<br>Very high automated technology | Segregated land use | High-speed transportation (intraurban)<br>Infrastructural network | High-speed delivery system<br>Special storage (long-range) | Energy storage |

TABLE 8.3

*Summary of Pros and Cons of the Geospace City*

| PROS | CONS |
|---|---|
| **HISTORICAL** | |
| Use of the geospace on a large scale proves to be feasible and implementable and can offer clues to lessons to be learned for further such development | Although individual historical cases achieve their ultimate goals, their norms of development cannot exemplify for our time norms. The new city needs an innovative design that provides sunshine, natural light, ventilation, and so forth |
| **LAND USE** | |
| Proximity of land use for daily needs | Intensifies the use of the land and may introduce congestion |
| The total separation of transportation significantly reduces human friction with the transportation network | Congestion may lead to loss of some privacy, which may not be acceptable to some cultures |
| Shortens utility length | |
| Increases use of pedestrian network | |
| Brings proximity of daily human activities into nature | |
| Enhances integrated land use with the existing city by bringing a fusion of the two cities | |
| Mix integrated land use offers more comfort to the users | |
| Increases the ratio of green open space within the city | |
| **SOCIAL** | |
| Enhances social interaction among age groups through the introduction of intensive-mix land uses | Cultural bias may cause acclimatization difficulties |
| Improves urban self-image | Possible claustrophobia |
| | Difficult to eliminate psychological resentment |
| | Requires adaptability and takes time |
| **ECONOMIC** | |
| Reduces urban land price by dual land use | Initial investment cost is high |
| Geospace brings compactness to the city and reduces the length of the infrastructure, expenditure in its design, construction, and maintenance | Land price may escalate after initial development is made |
| Slow city land price speculation | New design may be costly and require research |
| Increases housing options and employment | Construction duration cost may be high |
| Geospace saves energy, resists temperature fluctuation, has comfort-ambient temperature, is quiet, and stimulates creativity | |

TABLE 8.3 (CONTINUED)

*Summary of Pros and Cons of the Geospace City*

| PROS | CONS |
|------|------|
| TRANSPORTATION | |
| Increases the usage of nonpolluting mass transportation, such as subways | Requires a major change in the system |
| Reduces the use of private transportation | |
| Makes commuting time shorter | |
| ENVIRONMENT | |
| Provides a pleasing and generous, yet relaxing urban environment | May introduce some environmental constraints and need adjustments |
| Provides a livable, yet active city plus a relaxing environment | Potential increase of noise generated from public spaces |
| Provides creative environment | |
| Protects against stressful climates | |
| QUALITY OF LIFE | |
| Improves quality of life significantly by moving all transportation below ground | Air pollution may become a problem unless passive or active ventilation is designed or electric cars become common |
| Provides a wide, natural environment plus a pleasing green space | |
| Will ease mental pressure on individuals and groups | |
| Provides proximity to land use | |
| Living environment free from pollution | |
| Introduces wide pedestrian network throughout the city and total separation and safety from motor ways | |
| Reduces transportation noise and pollution | |

Israel (population integration and distribution), which are geographically small, have a high population density, and are limited in natural resources but are able to establish a cohesive and wholistic national urban development policy and effective spatial urban design.

## FUSION OF THE TWO CITIES

The fusion of the supraspace city with the geospace city should be accomplished by following land-use design principles for a given urban site, especially those of the city centers:

- The fusion should take place primarily between the two adjacent levels of the supraspace and that of the immediate, shallow-depth geospace level (up to 10 meters).
- Above-ground and below-ground land uses should complement (not conflict with) each other in their functions and should introduce continuity throughout the space.
- Activity periods for adjacent city-level land uses should be the same. In other words, planners should avoid placing land uses that are active only at night adjacent to land uses that are active only during the day.
- Land-use integration rather than land-use segregation is most desirable for sites where there is human activity. It provides an atmosphere of urbanity and creates a livable environment.
- The design of the two levels should enable a flow of movement between them without indicators marking the change in the level.
- Lights and colors of the two levels should be similar or identical to one another, rather than contrasting to each other, in order to support the feeling of continuity among users.

In short, the design should be introduced as one unified whole rather than two distinct levels.

## GEOSPACE HABITAT

The treatment of habitat in the geospace needs a special and innovative approach. Any such treatment should consider, among other things, the elements of sunshine and natural light penetration; psychological perception as related to claustrophobia; environmental and health aspects; safety; comfort; and air circulation. To consider these issues, the treatment of the habitat should be on two distinct levels—site selection and design.

### Habitat Site Selection
The optimal site for a geospace habitat is the slope (Figure 8.4). Compared with the flatland or the lowland, the slope

*Figure 8.4 Using slopes for housing and other construction to save land suitable for agriculture was a central ethic of the indigenous community. Students' dorm at Yan' an University, Shaanxi province, China.*

provides good ventilation, low risk of air inversion, unobstructed sunshine and natural light, clean and healthful fresh air, and a dust- or pollution-free environment. In addition, the slopes are close to the natural environment, which provides an attractive view to the lowland and ensures privacy and solitude. They also provide good drainage, low water table, low risk of flooding, and lower temperature than the adjacent lowland, and consume less energy for heating and cooling. Finally, they save the lowland for agriculture. Although initially slope development may cost more than flatland development, in the long term it is cost effective when one considers the health benefit. Any development should be viewed in its long-range context with all contributing factors.

Contrary to the common development of the above-ground slope where housing is usually provided with approximately 10 percent gradient, a geospace slope habitat using an innovative design method can be constructed with a gradient of up to 80 percent (Figure 8.5). While the habitat will occupy the slope face, access to the community through roads and

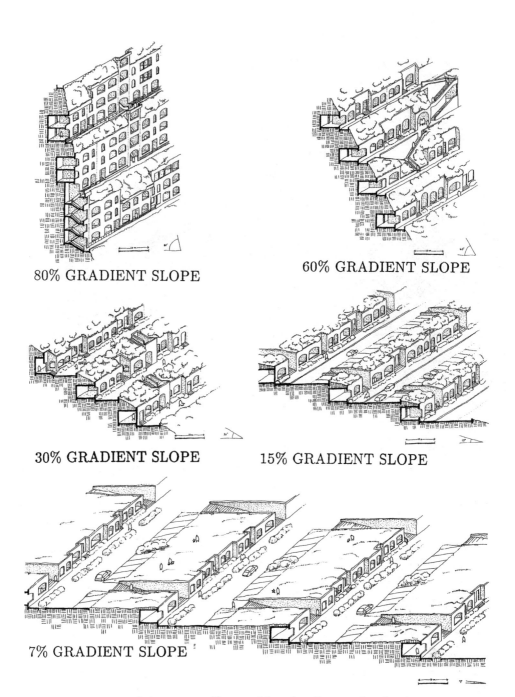

80% GRADIENT SLOPE

60% GRADIENT SLOPE

30% GRADIENT SLOPE

15% GRADIENT SLOPE

7% GRADIENT SLOPE

subways, as well as parking, loading and unloading, and emergency needs, will be served through the below-ground space at the back of the habitat (Figure 8.6). Similarly, the shops and shopping centers will be developed at the back of the habitat.

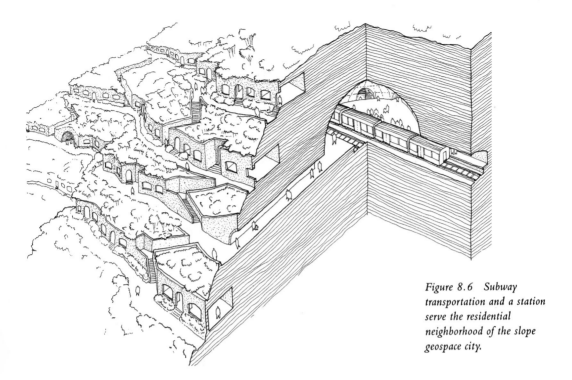

Figure 8.6 Subway transportation and a station serve the residential neighborhood of the slope geospace city.

## Habitat Design

Slope geospace habitats can be designed as single houses, as a complex of apartments in extended terraced arrangements, or lined up in a row. Any one of the three types can be designed to be completely earth integrated, partly earth integrated, or combined with above-ground sections. The variety of combinations is endless (Figure 8.7).

Windows of the habitat are limited to the front (in the case of the fully below-ground habitat) where the facade can be designed to be longer than the depth penetrating into the cliff. Or, windows can be added to the right and left side of the structure parts that are projected to the front and not covered by earth, when the structure is partly below ground. In the latter case, an additional skylight can be added to the roof section not covered by earth.

Careful design calculation can provide sunshine and natural light deep into the room (Figure 8.8). At the latitude of

*Figure 8.5 (facing page) The slope for geospace habitats can range from a 7 percent to 80 percent gradient. The habitats introduce difficulties in construction and accessibility, but offer many benefits, such as ventilation, light, sunshine, attractive view to the surrounding environment, tranquillity, and privacy in the neighborhood. Note the correlation between slope gradient and habitat lot size.*

ETHICS AND URBAN DESIGN | 231

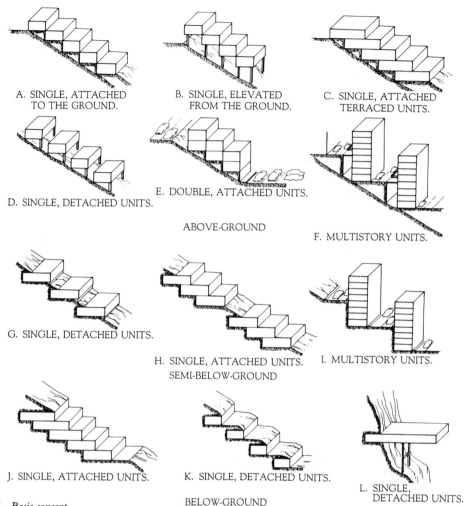

A. SINGLE, ATTACHED
TO THE GROUND.

B. SINGLE, ELEVATED
FROM THE GROUND.

C. SINGLE, ATTACHED
TERRACED UNITS.

D. SINGLE, DETACHED UNITS.

E. DOUBLE, ATTACHED UNITS.

ABOVE-GROUND

F. MULTISTORY UNITS.

G. SINGLE, DETACHED UNITS.

H. SINGLE, ATTACHED UNITS.
SEMI-BELOW-GROUND

I. MULTISTORY UNITS.

J. SINGLE, ATTACHED UNITS.

K. SINGLE, DETACHED UNITS.

BELOW-GROUND

L. SINGLE,
DETACHED UNITS.

*Figure 8.7  Basic concept of various possible relations of the building units to an acute slope.*

*Figure 8.8 (facing page) Sun radiation changes in the summer and winter as we move north from the equator. The sunshine penetration decreases in summer and increases in*

24°N with a ceiling height of 3 meters, the winter sun penetrates to the depth of approximately 3 meters (42° angle), while at the latitude of 44°N, with the same ceiling height, the winter sun penetrates to the depth of 6 meters (winter angle 22°). Sun penetration increases as latitude (traveling away from the equator) and height of the ceiling increases. The positioning of the window is also important. High and large windows allow more sun and light penetration.

The most important principles in the design of the slope geospace habitat are the following:

6 METERS HEIGHT          3 METERS HEIGHT

SCALE

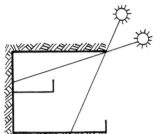 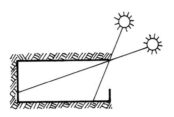

- LATITUDE: 48°N
- SUMMER ANGLE (MAX.): 66°
- WINTER ANGLE (MAX.): 18°
- EXAMPLES: MUNICH (GERMANY),
  BUDAPEST (HUNGARY),
  SEATTLE (WASHINGTON),
  MONTREAL (CANADA)

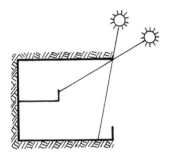 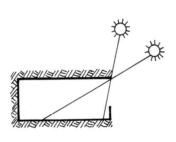

- LATITUDE: 36°N
- SUMMER ANGLE (MAX.): 78°
- WINTER ANGLE (MAX.): 30°
- EXAMPLES: TOKYO (JAPAN),
  TEHRAN (IRAN),

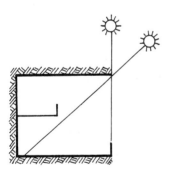 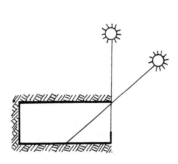

- LATITUDE: 24°N
- SUMMER ANGLE (MAX.): 90°
- WINTER ANGLE (MAX.): 42°
- EXAMPLES: CALCUTTA (INDIA),
  MIAMI (FLORIDA),
  MONTERREY (MEXICO)

- *Site.* Selection of the site should be exclusively on the slope and not on flat land.
- *Orientation.* The habitat should face south, southeast, or southwest.
- *Accessibility.* The design should ascend, not descend, into the habitat in order to overcome a feeling of claustrophobia.

winter as latitude increases. The maximum summer (June 21) and winter (December 21) sunshine penetration in a slope geospace habitat is 7 meters deep. The increase of the ceiling height from 3 to 6 meters also increases the sunshine penetration. City locations are approximate.

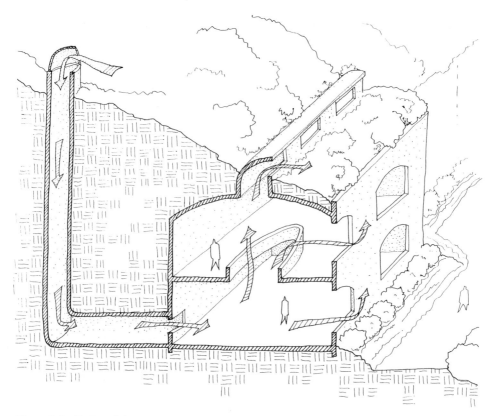

Figure 8.9 Design of the ventilation system is an essential requirement of the slope geospace habitat. Passive ventilation is supported by the air dynamic typical of the slope.

- *Perception.* Direct eye contact should be unobstructed between the indoor and the outdoor environments so that the inhabitants can feel the rhythm of nature and be a part of their environment.
- *Ventilation.* Air flow should be passive and increase air exchange (Figure 8.9).
- *Height and Color.* Ceiling-to-floor dimensions should be higher than that commonly used in above-ground houses (4 meters or more), including within corridors; offering generous width and length is recommended. Light and pleasing colors will be very helpful.

Finally, the slope geospace habitat is tranquil, soundproof, and vibrationless, and provides a healthy environment for good uninterrupted sleep. Also, spaces within the habitats should have plenty of natural vegetation.

In conclusion, the use of below-ground space is an ancient practice dating from the early sheltering of humankind. Yet, the concept of a geospace city as a unified, comprehensive entity is a pioneering one and should be integrated with the existing city. My research findings lead me to believe such integration is essential for revitalizing the existing city. A great deal of my analysis and proposals are inspired by extensive research I conducted on indigenous below-ground space use in Tunisia, China, Cappadocia (Turkey), and the modern one in Japan. In practice, my concept of a geospace city can be fully constructed within existing cities located near slope sites. A new town located primarily on the slope of a mountain will be an ideal case for implementing the geospace city concept.

My research findings indicate that a large-scale use of the geospace significantly shrinks the complex of all of the infrastructure and the road network, and thereby saves the taxpayer money. By combining geospace with compactness and slope, which I developed as the Trinity Concept, a city will reduce the length of its total utilities by 75 percent.

An ideal development of the geospace city combined with the supraspace city can be achieved by designing and constructing a completely new town located on or adjacent to the slope. Yet, it is feasible that an existing city located on flat land may benefit significantly from this concept, without constructing geospace habitats. Although historically the geospace is frequently used for one type of land use, the contemporary techniques of the complete geospace city concept have yet to be implemented in a comprehensive and cohesive city.

The project of the geospace city should be initiated by a professional team within the existing city, such as the city planning commission. There are issues that require the special attention of the existing city planning commission at the very early stages in their exploration of the geospace city.

- *Legal Issues.* Various countries legally define the depth limits of land ownership. Also, some countries make a distinction between land ownership and the resources of that same given land. In Japan, for example, a land owner legally controls the land to the center of the earth, as well as the air above it. On the other hand, in Israel, the land owner controls the land while the resources of the land are owned by the public. Therefore, when developing the geospace city, there may be a need to amend the legislation and limit private land ownership to a 50-meter depth, as the Japanese have suggested. This depth satisfies the structural needs of the foundation of an above-ground high-rise building. In most cases, such a depth will include the bedrock. Space below the bedrock can be used by a larger geospace city. However, the legal limit of depth should differ among cities and countries. It depends on the geological structure of the site.

- *Geological Survey.* A comprehensive survey of the environmental geology of the city is essential. It should include stratification, composition, structural strength and constraints, existence of radon, and degree of humidity within the soil.
- *Water Table.* It is necessary to survey the level of the water table fluctuations, its seasonal changes, and its possible impact on the geospace structure at the potential site.
- *Accessibility.* A geospace city will consume a large tract of land for diversified use. It is therefore necessary to study the possibilities of the potential geospace network and the feasibility of comfortable accessibility from existing above-ground public spaces to the geospace city.

The Japanese have explored the usage of below-ground spaces as a public project by creating a parallel network of geospace below the existing supracity roads. Their practice applies primarily to shopping centers and subways (Figure 8.10). Being a pioneering endeavor, these are all public enterprises. Japanese private enterprise developed geospace shopping centers and other land uses below supraspace private buildings. Private enterprise proves to be more innovative, flexible, generous in design, and prolific in its exploration of the geospace. The geospace city has the potential to upgrade

*Figure 8.10  Modern Japanese geospace shopping centers proved to be successful in their engineering system construction, management, and quality, and offer an attractive and comfortable environment. Osaka Shopping Center, Osaka, Japan.*

the quality of urban life, to introduce innovative dimensions into large cities, and to bring vitality to the urban environment.

The introduction of diversified land use into the slope, where an extensive use of below-ground space should take place, provides an enriching addition to the slope habitats. The combination of these two dimensions brings far-reaching health and environmental benefits with little or no destruction of the physical environment.

As with any design endeavor where the contributing forces are diverse and sometimes conflicting, the final product of this geospace city project has its compromise. Aside from the "cost-benefit analysis" approach often used by economists, there is also a price to be paid for upgraded social quality of life, improved health conditions, and mental well-being; on the other hand, there is the degree of discomfort in living in an existing, congested urban flatland site. The slope geospace habitat is a trade-off and with it may come a compromise between gain and loss; but it offers new hope for upgrading our quality of life. Our contemporary practice is certainly limited, yet with our historical experience and our modern, sophisticated technology in urban design, we can do wonders in this endeavor.

Finally, the geospace city endeavor requires vision, long-term strategies for urban design, a comprehensive approach, and strong determination. Our globe is too small (and is the only home) for its fast-growing population of already five billion inhabitants. It is too precious to waste.

# SELECTED READINGS

## CITY PLANNING

Birkerts, Gunnar. *Subterranean Urban Systems*. Ann Arbor, MI: University of Michigan, Industrial Development Division, Institute of Science and Technology, 1974.

Botter, Robert Brown. *Ecological House*. New York: Morgan & Morgan, 1981.

Culther, Lawrence Stephen and Sherrie Stephens. *Recycling Cities for People: The Urban Design Process*. Boston, MA: Cahners Book International, 1976.

Golany, Gideon S. "Geospace Urban Design." Manuscript in Progress, 1995.

Golany, Gideon S. "Integration of Underground Placement within Urban Design." In *Earth-Sheltered Habitat: History, Architecture and Urban Design*. New York: Van Nostrand Reinhold, 1983, pp. 145-214.

"House 'Revealed' Itself on Slope (case study)." *Earth Shelter Digest and Energy Report* 11 (September/October 1980): 11-14.

Jansson, Birger. "City planning and the Urban Underground." *Underground Space* 3/3 (1978): 99-115.

Moreland, Frank L. "Earth-covered Habitat—An Alternative Future." *Underground Space* 1 (1977): 295-307.

Moreland, Frank L., ed. *Earth-covered Buildings and Settlements*. Springfield, VA: NTIS, 1979.

Mumford, Lewis. *The City in History*. New York: Harcourt, Brace and World, 1961.

Reissman, Leonard. "The Visionary: Planner for Urban Utopia." In *Urban Planning Theory*, edited by Melville C. Branch. Stroudsburg, PA: Dowden, Hutchinson & Ross, 1975.

Rowe, Peter G. *Design Thinking*. Cambridge, MA: MIT Press, 1987.

Van der Ryn, Sim and Peter Calthorpe. *Sustainable Communities: A New Design Synthesis for Cities, Suburbs, and Towns*. San Francisco: Sierra Club Books, 1986.

SOCIO-ECONOMIC

Bell, Daniel. *The Coming of the Post-Industrial Age.* New York: Basic Books, 1973.

Berkowitz, Bill. *Community Dreams.* San Luis Obispo CA: Impact Publishers, 1984.

Kennedy, Declan. "Permaculture and the Sustainable City." *Ekistics* (May 1991): 210-215.

Mollison, Bill. *Permaculture Two.* Tyalgum, Australia: Tagari Publications, 1979.

Mollison, Bill. *Permaculture: A Designers' Manual.* Tyalgum, Australia: Tagari Publications, 1988.

Mollison, Bill. *Introduction to Permaculture.* Tyalgum, Australia: Tagari Publications, 1991.

Mumford, Lewis. *Technics and Human Development.* New York: Harcourt, Brace, Jovanovich, 1966.

Renner, Michael. *Jobs in a Sustainable Economy.* Worldwatch Paper 104. Washington, D.C.: Worldwatch Institute, 1991.

Roseland, Mark. *Toward Sustainable Communities: A Resource Book for Municipal and Local Governments.* Ottawa, Canada: University of British Columbia, 1992.

Toffler, Alvin. *Powershift: Knowledge, Wealth and Violence at the Edge of the 21st Century.* New York: Bantam Books, 1990.

Walter, Bob, ed. *Sustainable Cities.* Los Angeles: Eco-Home Media, 1992.

Wilson, J. "Permaculture's Role in Southern and Eastern Africa." *Permaculture Edge* (April 4, 1994): 17-18.

ENVIRONMENT

Barney, Gerald O., ed. *The Global 2000 Report to the President of the U.S.* New York: Pergamon Press, 1980.

Bateson, Gregory. *Mind and Nature.* New York: E. P. Dutton, 1979.

Carleton, Joseph G. "An Environmentalist's Views on Underground Construction." In *Underground Utilization, A Reference Manual of Selected Works,* 8 vols., edited by Truman Stauffer, Sr. Kansas City, MO: University of Missouri, 1978, vol. 6, pp. 894-899.

Commoner, Barry. *Making Peace with the Planet.* New York: Pantheon Books, 1990.

Daly, Herman E. and John B. Cobb, Jr. *For the Common Good: Redirecting the Economy toward Community, Environment, and Sustainable Future.* Boston: Beacon Press, 1989.

Dasler, A. R. and D. Minard. "Environmental Physiology of Shelter Habitation." *Transactions. Proceedings of the ASHRAE Semiannual Meeting,* Chicago, Illinois, 1965. Chicago: American Society of Heating, Refrigerating & Air-Conditioning Engineers, 71, Part I 1965, pp. 115-124.

Frederick, Douglas D. "Water Resources: Increasing Demand and Scarce Supplies." In *America's Renewable Resources: Historical Trends and Current Challenges,* edited by Kenneth D. Frederick, and Roger A. Sedjo.

Washington, D.C.: Resources for the Future, 1991.

Freudenberger, Dean. "The Agricultural Agenda for the Twenty-first Century." *KIDJA, Israel Journal of Development* 7/8 (1988).

Geyer, John, Robert Kaufmann, David Skole, and Charles Vorosmargy. *Beyond Oil: The Threat to Food and Fuel in the Coming Decades.* Cambridge, MA: Ballinger, 1986.

*Global Report on Human Settlements.* Oxford, England: Oxford University Press for the United Nations Centre for Human Settlements (HABITAT), 1987.

International Union for the Conservation of Nature and Natural Resources (IUCN), United Nations Environmental Program (UNEP), and World Wildlife Fund (WWF). *Caring for the Earth: A Strategy for Sustainable Living.* Gland, Switzerland: IUCN, UNEP, WWF, 1992.

LaNier, Royce. "Earth Covered Buildings and Environmental Impact." In *Alternatives in Energy Conservation: The Use of Earth Covered Buildings,* edited by Frank Moreland. Washington, D.C.: National Science Foundation/USGPO, 1978, pp. 269-278.

Lovelock, James. *The Ages of Gaia: A Biography of our Living Earth.* New York: W. W. Norton, 1988.

Moreland, Frank L., ed. *Alternatives in Energy Conservation: The Use of Earth-covered Buildings.* Washington, D.C.: National Science Foundation/USGPO, 1978.

Organization for Economic Cooperation and Development (OECD). *The State of the Environment.* Paris: OECD, 1991.

Rapoport, Amos. *House Form and Culture.* Englewood Cliffs, NJ: Prentice Hall, 1969.

Schiller, John W. "The Automobile and the Atmosphers." In *Energy Production, Consumption, Consequences,* edited by John L. Helm. Washington, D. C.: National Academy of Sciences, 1990.

Smil, Vaclov. *General Energetics: Energy in the Biosphere and Civilization.* New York: Wiley, 1991.

Stearns, Forest and Tom Montag, eds. *The Urban Ecosystem: A Holistic Approach.* Stroudsburg, PA: Dowden, Hutchinson & Ross, 1974.

Stine, William B. and John T. Lyle. *Energy Use and Conservation Practices at the Institute for Regenerative Studies.* Research Report 92-001. Pomona, CA: California State Polytechnic University, 1992.

Thayer, Robert. "Technophobia and Topophilia: The Dynamic Meanings of Technology in the Landscape." Davis, CA: Center for Design Research, 1990.

Walter, Bob. "Gardens in the Sky." In *Sustainable Cities: Concepts and Strategies for Eco-City Development,* edited by Bob Walter, Lois Arkin, and Richard Crenshaw. Los Angeles, CA: EHM Publishers, 1992.

Wells, Malcolm. "To Build Without Destroying the Earth." In *Alternatives in Energy Conservation,* edited by Frank Moreland. Washington, D.C.: National Science Foundation/USGPO, 1978, pp. 211-232. Also in *Underground Utilization, A Reference Manual of Selected Works,* 8 vols., edited by Truman Stauffer, Sr. Kansas City, MO: University of Missouri, 1978, vol. 4, pp. 546-552.

World Resources Institute (WRI). *World Resources; A Guide to the Global Environment 1992-93.* New York: Oxford University Press, 1992.

ECOLOGY

Altieri, Miguel A. *Agroecology: The Scientific Basis of Alternative Agriculture.* Boulder, CO: Westview Press, 1987.

Gliessman, S. R., ed. *Agroecology: Researching the Ecological Basis for Sustainable Agriculture.* New York: Springer-Verlag, 1990.

Gore, Albert. *Earth in the Balance: Ecology and the Human Spirit.* New York: Houghton-Mifflin, 1992.

*Green Pages: The Local Handbook for Planet Maintenance.* Berkeley: Green Media Group, 1990.

National Research Council (NRC). *Alternative Aquaculture.* Washington, D.C.: National Academy Press, 1989.

Ress, William, E. *The Ecological Meaning of Environment-Economy Integration.* Vancouver: University of British Columbia, 1989.

PSYCHOLOGY

Collins, Belinda L. "Review of the Psychological Reaction to Windows." In *Underground Utilization*, edited by Truman Stauffer, Sr. Kansas City, MO: University of Missouri, 1978, vol. 4, pp. 532-540.

Paulus, Paul B. "On the Psychology of Earth-covered Buildings." In *Alternatives in Energy Conservation: The Use of Earth-covered Buildings*, edited by Frank L. Moreland. Washington, D.C.: National Science Foundation/USGPO, 1978, pp. 65-69. Also printed in *Underground Space* 1 (1976): 127-30.

Seybert, Jeffrey A. "Psychological Factors and Future Expansion of Underground Space Utilization." In *Underground Utilization*, edited by Truman Stauffer, Sr. Kansas City, MO: University of Missouri, 1978, vol. 7, pp. 1018-1019.

Wunderlich, Elizabeth. "Psychology and Underground Development." In *Underground Utilization*, edited by Truman Stauffer, Sr. Kansas City, MO: University of Missouri, 1978, vol. 4, pp. 526-529.

DESIGN WITH HOT-DRY CLIMATE

Baggs, Sydney A. "The Dugout Dwellings of an Outback Opal Mining Town in Australia." In *Underground Utilization*, edited by Truman Stauffer, Sr. Kansas City, MO: University of Missouri, 1978, vol. 4, pp. 573-599. Also in mimeo, University of New South Wales, Sydney, Department of Landscape Architecture, 1977.

Behr, Richard, Ernst Kiesling, and Gary Boubel. "Earth Sheltered Housing Potentials for West Texas." *Earth Shelter Digest and Energy Report* 5 (September/October 1979): 24-25.

Gelder, John. "Underground Desert Shelter." B. Arch. thesis, University of Adelaide, Australia, 1977.

Golany, Gideon S. "Subterranean Settlements for Arid Zones." In *Earth Covered Buildings and Settlements*, edited by Frank Moreland. Springfield, VA:

NTIS, 1979, pp. 174-202. Also in *Housing for Arid Lands*, edited by G. Golany. London: Architectural Press, 1980, pp. 109-122.

Labs, Kenneth. Terratypes: "Underground Housing for Arid Zones." In *Housing in Arid Zones: Design and Planning*, edited by G. Golany. London: Architectural Press, 1980, pp. 123-140.

Langley, John B. and James L. Gray. *Sun Belt Earth Sheltered Architecture*. Winter Park, FL: Sun Belt Earth Sheltered Research, 1980.

Van Der Meer, Wybe J. "The Possibility of Subterranean Housing for Arid Zones." In *Housing for Arid Lands: Design and Planning*, edited by G. Golany. London: Architectural Press, 1980, pp. 141-150.


## INDUSTRY AND COMMERCIAL USES

"Building Underground: Factories and Offices in a Cave." *Eng. News Rec.* 20/166 (1961): 58-59.

Callahan, S. J. "The Development of Limestone Mines Into Underground Warehouses and Manufacturing Plants." In *Underground Utilization, A Reference Manual of Selected Works*, 8 vols., edited by Truman Stauffer, Sr. Kansas City, MO: University of Missouri, 1978, vol. 1 pp. 22-26.

Carlier, R. "Design of Windowless Factories in Belgium." *Institut Technique du Batiment et des Travaux Publics, Annales* 22/262 (1969): 1441-1483.

Chryssafopoulos, Nicholas. "Employee Attitudes." In *Underground Utilization, A Reference Manual of Selected Works*, 8 vols., edited by Truman Stauffer, Sr. Kansas City, MO: University of Missouri, 1978, vol. 4, pp. 530-531.

Fairhurst, Charles. "U.S. Develops New, Commercial Uses for Earth-Sheltering." *Underground Space* 5/1 (1980): 31-35.


## UTILITIES, HIGHWAYS AND PARKING

Alders, Charles. "A Study of Earth Covered Buildings by an Electric Utility Company." In *Alternatives in Energy Conservation*, edited by Frank Moreland. Washington, D.C.: National Science Foundation/USGPO, 1978, pp. 107-115.

Berg, N. "Aspects on Underground Location of Urban Facilities—Power Supply, Oil Storage, and Sewage Treatment." *Symposium on Geological and Geographical Problems of Areas of High Population Density*, October 1970. Washington, D.C.: Association of Engineering Geologists.

Brown, Verne. "Underground Location of Utilities as Part of Underground Development." In *Underground Utilization, A Reference Manual of Selected Works*, 8 vols., edited by Truman Stauffer, Sr. Kansas City, MO: University of Missouri, 1978, vol. 2, pp. 254-256.

Homes and Narver, Inc. *Engineering Study of Underground Highway & Parking Garage & Blast Shelter for Manhattan Island*. Oak Ridge, TN: Oak Ridge National Laboratory, March 1966.

Hunt, F. R. "Underground Power Transmission." *Underground Space* 3/1 (1978): 19-33.

Lowe, Marcia. *Alternatives to the Automobile: Transport for Livable Cities.* Worldwatch Paper 98. Washington, D.C.: Worldwatch Institute, 1990.

Meyer, Kirby. "Utilities for Underground Structures." In *Alternatives in Energy Conservation,* edited by Frank Moreland. Washington, D.C.: National Science Foundation/USGPO, 1978, pp. 165-181.

Rosander, A. "Underground Sewage Treatment Plant." *Underground Space* 2/1 (1977): 39-45.

Smith, Wilbur and Associates. *Transportation and Parking for Tomorrow's Cities.* New Haven, CT: Automobile Manufacturers Association, 1966.

## SHELTERS

Fathy, Hassan. *Architecture for the Poor.* Chicago: University of Chicago Press, 1973.

Givoni, B. *Man, Climate and Architecture.* 2nd ed. New York: Van Nostrand Reinhold, 1976.

Turner, John. *Housing by People: Towards Autonomy in Building Environments.* New York: Pantheon Books, 1977.

Vale, Brenda and Robert Vale. *Autonomous House.* New York: Universe Books, 1977.

Vale, Brenda. *Green Architecture: Design for a Sustainable Future.* London; Hudson, NY: UCLA AAUP/ARTS NA, no. 2542.3, 35, 1991.

Wells, Malcolm. *Underground Buildings.* Brewster, MA: Malcolm Wells, 1990.

## SCHOOLS

Bailey, Edwin R. "Alternatives to Educational Space Needs." In *Underground Utilization, A Reference Manual of Selected Works,* 8 vols., edited by Truman Stauffer, Sr. Kansas City, MO: University of Missouri, 1978, vol. 2, pp. 180-183.

Carter, Douglas N. "Terraset School." *Underground Space* 1/4 (1977): 317-323.

Carter, Douglas N. "Terraset Elementary School, Reston, Virginia." In *Alternatives in Energy Conservation,* edited by Frank Moreland. Washington, D.C.: National Science Foundation/USGPO, 1978, pp. 135-149.

Carter, Douglas N. "Community and Building Official Reaction to Earth Covered Buildings: A Case Study Terraset Elementary School, Reston, Virginia." In *Earth Covered Buildings and Settlements,* edited by Frank Moreland. Springfield, VA: NTIS, 1979, pp. 78-81.

Demos, G. D. Controlled Physical Classroom Environments and Their Effect Upon Elementary School Children (Windowless Classroom Study). Riverside County, CA: Palm Springs School District, 1965.

Larson, C. Theodore. *The Effect of Windowless Classrooms on Elementary School Children.* Ann Arbor, MI: Architectural Research Laboratory, University of Michigan, Nov. 1965.

Lutz, Frank W. "Studies of Children in an Underground School." In *Alternatives in Energy Conservation,* edited by Frank Moreland. Washington, D.C.:

National Science Foundation/USGPO, 1978, pp. 71-77. Also in
*Underground Space* 1/2 (1976): 131-134.

Lutz, Frank W., Patrick D. Lynch, and Susan B. Lutz. *Abo Revisited: An Evaluation of the Abo Elementary School and Fallout Shelter* (Final Report). Washington, D.C.: Defense Civil Preparedness Agency, Contract #DAHC20-72-C-0155, June 1972.

Platzker, J. "The First 100 Windowless Schools in the U.S.A." Paper presented at the *Twenty-Eighth Annual Convention of National Association of Architectural Metal Manufacturers*, 1966.

Tikkanen, K. T. "Window Factors in Schools." In *Overhead Natural Lighting*, Part 2. Helsinki, Finland: University of Technology, February 1974.


CASE STUDIES

Ben-Hamza, Kacem. "The Cave-Dwellers of Matmata: Ritual and Economic Decision-Making in a Changing Community." Ph.D. diss., Indiana University, 1977.

Beschaouch, Azedine, Roger Hanoune, and Yvon Thebert. *Les ruines de Bulla Regia*. Rome: Ecole Francaise de Rome, Palais Farnese, 1977.

Haan, Herman. "Matmata." In *Architects Yearbook*, edited by David Lewis, 2:126-128. London: Elek Books, 1965.

Hou Ji-Yao. "Cave Dwellings in North Shaanxi Province." *Knowledge of Architecture* 2 (n.d.). (In Chinese.)

Inaba, Kazuya, et al. "Investigation and Improvement of Living Environment in Cave Dwellings in China." In *Proceedings of the International Symposium on Earth Architecture, November 1–4, 1985, Beijing*. Beijing, China: Architectural Society of China, 1985.

Louis, Andre. "L'habitation troglodyte dans un village des Matmata." *Cahiers des Arts et Traditions Populaires; Revue du Centre des Arts et Traditions Populaires* (Tunis: Secretariat d'Etat aux Affaires Culturelles et a l'Information), 1968, vol. 2, pp. 33-60.

Louis, Andre. "Aus Matmatas et dans les ksars du sud, l'olivier et les hommes." *Cahiers des Arts et Traditions Populaires; Revue du Centre des Arts et Traditions Populaires* (Tunis: Ministere des Affaires Culturelles), 1969, vol. 3, pp. 41-66.

Qian Fu-yuan and Su Yu. "Research on the Indoor Environment of Loess Cave Dwellings." In *Proceedings of the International Symposium on Earth Architecture, November 1–4, 1985, Beijing*. Beijing, China: Architectural Society of China, 1985.


OTHER

Petrova, Elena. "Rooftop Gardening in Russia." *Permaculture Edge* (April 4, 1994): 8-9.

# CONCLUSION

Throughout this book, I have reviewed some selected case studies, introduced theories and concepts, analyzed their input, and outlined the lessons to be drawn from their ethics for future urban design. As much as I would like to, I am unable to fully introduce the details of the urban design of the future city. The five urban expansion frontiers, which are detailed in the introduction, should be envisioned as relevant and implementable examples for the future city. I have finished research and writing a new manuscript titled *Geospace Urban Design*, which is expected to be published shortly, and another manuscript on the subject of slope urban design will be finished shortly. Here, too, the theme of both books is the future city. My conviction is that urban designers should pay more attention to the comprehensive design of future cities than is currently practiced.

The other theme of this book is to study the lessons learned from the past and to present the evolution of human settlements. Our ancestors considered socio-cultural values when designing their homes, neighborhoods, and cities. Their cohesive social values introduced a balance within the society and produced an equilibrium in their natural, social, as well as physical human-made environment. A collaboration between the community and individuals provided for consumable needs on one side and maintained the survival of the natural environment and the community on the other side.

For the sake of my argument, I confined the past, present, and future generically by distinctive landmarks that highlighted radical changes in human settlements. In chronological terms, the past was defined as the period from nomadism to the evolution of villages, to regional development, and finally, to the classical form of the past city system. The start of the present era was marked by the beginning of the Industrial Revolution in the nineteenth century, which is associated with a radical physical, social, economic, and environmental change within the city. Finally, the beginning of the future city era has been marked by the recent increase in the communication information system.

The history of human settlements covers more than ten thousand years. In the case of Mesopotamia, for example, the rise of the village took place around the eighth millennium B.C. The cradle of the city began to evolve during the middle of the fourth millennium B.C. with the classical city reaching its peak at the beginning of the Industrial Revolution. This lengthy period of human settlements provides us with a wealth of knowledge about the classical village and city living from which we are able to draw lessons.

Past indigenous community ethics encompassed all facets of life. The community had sustainability, which maintained a social balance, and gave security and safety to its people. The ethics of social behavior were explicit, and expectations for the individual and the community were clear. Among indigenous societies, the community offered security for its sensitive elderly. When persons of the extended family came of age, their clan assured them of their future, their survival, and eliminated homelessness, thereby diminishing the mental stress that our existing modern society has not been able to accomplish for everyone.

As the case studies of the past reveal, it was in both the transition from nomadism to the village, and later, from the village to the city, that the community was fully assimilated with the social ethics by which they conducted their lives. In the transition from nomadism to the settled village society, the strong social ethics that were already shaped determined the pattern of the physical configuration and form of the new settlement. The community was able to fuse its social ethics with the new human-made physical environment without discrepancies and conflicts between them. Merging these two entities established the harmony of the village's physical aesthetics within itself and with its surrounding natural landscape. Also, both the nomadic society and the newly settled villages retained their communal settings and their inherited, indigenous collaborative-collective working systems. A similar but not identical evolutionary process took place during the "urban revolution" when some villagers established the city. Individuals from the rural communities who came to the city were still strongly rooted in their inherited collaborative-collective working systems. The city was established by individuals of diverse origins who were seeking new opportunities other than agricultural practice but who were still imbued with their village collective social ethics. Here, too, the ethics of the new urban dwellers became part of their new human-made physical environment. In the four case studies of the past that are used, namely, the indigenous cities of Mesopotamia, Egypt, Indus Valley, and China, the communities, similar to the village settlements, responded to their natural environment and its constraints for improving their cities. Due to these constraints, city dwellers adopted a compact physical form, propinquity, and narrow shaded streets as protection against hot-dry winds. Also, they selected proximity to the river as a source of life and to preserve land for agriculture. These indigenous city dwellers, however, as those of the village settlements, succeeded in responding to their environment with respect. Until the nineteenth century, the city existed with the human scale expressed through propinquity, which is social and physical proximity. As with any change, those two transitional periods were not problem free before they established an equilibrium.

However, the message to be gained from the past is to understand and recognize its lessons for our current and future practice. These lessons should not be viewed as conflicting with our modern practice, but as complementing it and accepting them as welcome input for future urban design. The strength of the past is in its ethics of cohesive social values, which introduced a social balance within the society and produced an equilibrium in the natural, social, as well as physical human-made environments. The achievements on these three levels were a product of collective-collaborative cooperation between community and individual needs, with consumption on one side and survival of the natural environment on the other.

The present, as defined here, covers almost two centuries since the rise of the industrial city and offers a reasonable accomplishment from which wisdom can be gained. The major lessons of present achievements lie within the ethics and codes of advanced technology. No doubt, technology will continue its accelerated achievement and impact in the future. However, the present is not free from major problems that seriously threaten the achievements based on the social ethics of the past.

The "miscommunication" between the ethics of technology and those of human values in the present has introduced confusion instead of fusion, the dominance of technological ethics, and has diminished the significance of social cohesive values. The overriding materialistic values have dominated our urban society, introducing social instability and creating a lack of social equilibrium. The result is the dehumanization of the community and the individual. Social problems are more prominent than all other elements of our urban environment, and they demand more attention from urban designers, who are not being trained to challenge such issues. In the past, the city was a gravitational center for culture, art, and an enhanced social quality of life all provided in a safe environment. Today our cities, or reasonable portions of them, are not safe. They breed homelessness, individual loneliness, insecurity, delinquency, abandonment of the elderly, crime, a filthy environment, pollution, noise, congestion, a deteriorating physical environment, and mental anxiety. The greater the cities' congestion, the more likely these negative social environmental phenomena are to occur. We have loaded our socio-cultural system and our environment beyond its ability to support itself and its carrying capacity. We have been unable to conceive of reciprocal relations among the factors that have evolved into these new conditions, which have not created the desirable equilibrium. However, a comparison of the present and the past lessons indicates that in the past, technology and social values coexisted with minimal conflict.

In a dynamic era of accelerated change, we have not been successful in fusing the social equilibrium of past ethics with the norms of present technology. The disassociation of these two ethics will further dehumanize our society and mold the future citizens, imbued with materialistic values, into tools rolling the machinery of technology. A dehumanized society is a source of social disorder, mental frustration, dissatisfaction, diminished self-image, social disintegration, individualism and selfishness, and a lost sense of community, which frees citizens from public responsibility. Potential social conflict and discontent becomes the norm. Our challenge is to balance technological dominance with human needs into a workable ethic where communities and individuals can feel at home in this world.

Urbanization will continue to increase in the future. An urban lifestyle offers benefits, such as social and economic opportunity, a greater chance for interaction, a variety of choices in all facets of life's excitement, and many more. Yet recently, urbanization has become associated with almost uncontrollable negative qualities, such as diminished safety and security, crime, mental and physical disturbance, unemployment, and increased individual isolation and loneliness. These social problems will continue to be more prominent than all other elements of our urban environment and will demand more attention from urban designers, sociologists, philosophers, anthropologists, historians, and policy makers. The evolution and acceptance of a large-scale urban type seems to minimize community feasibly, supports social disintegration, increases tension, and creates a loss of self identity. Some urban designers accept the dominance of technology as a given fact in its absolute form. Others conceive of this dominance as a threat to our urban social quality of life if it is not integrated with socio-cultural ethics which enhance a community's well-being.

Future urban designers, decision makers, and politicians should seek to create pleasing environments and make urban dwellers the center of attention. With new technology, we are venturing into a new socio-economic phase arising from the *global information communication revolution*. The challenge of our urban design lies in solving the conflict between the rising ethics of information technology and the long-evolved ethics of socio-cultural values. This conflict continues to dominate the urban environment and is of concern to urban designers and social scientists. It carries with it a challenge and an opportunity to emphasize enhancing socio-cultural ethics and norms, diffuse conflicts, and search for humanistic and spiritual values.

Throughout the history of human settlements, education has proven successful in improving society. Indeed, in every civilization, the historical religious education has been an effective tool in teaching ethics and behavioral conduct. In contrast, modern, formal education, which we value, has never been commonly available to all inhabitants of the world as the historical one has been. On the other hand, in spite of the overriding recent technological, materialistic ethics, I view education for social ethics within a pluralistic society as the cardinal key for enhancing the future quality of urban life. The question, then, is what values and ethics should our children be taught now in order to secure a better future city? Should the focus be on materialism and technological ethics? The isolated ethics of sophisticated technology, alone, cannot create a healthy community without the ethics for social sustenance based on spiritual and social values.

As a comprehensive urban designer, my conviction is that future urban design ethics should fuse the agro-urban pattern with nature, agricultural production, and an urban lifestyle. The future urban pattern should rely heavily on socially balanced urban communities with a sense of individual attachment, freedom of privacy, and self recognition. The new urban design approach is to be centered around community ethics and individual needs rather than on the dominance of physical design form and its aesthetics, only.

Globally, as we face the future, a uniform cosmopolitan urban physical environment is being imposed upon us. We are heading more and more toward an international urban lifestyle as well. This new urban setting may carry the threat of loss of socio-cultural identity and ethnicity and the assimilation of community within the universal culture. Urban society tends to accept such evolution more than village society does. However, socio-cultural identity, self-reliance, and social sustainability should lead to self-recognition and self-identity. Similarly, we can anticipate the rise of ethnic identity throughout the world, and with it, the enhancement of the human rights movement, a condition that has the potential to lead to ethnic friction and conflict within the future urban society.

In the past, our ancestors set the limits on the use of resources and thereby shaped their environmental ethics. We, in our new ethic, have crossed this threshold and have seriously threatened the resources of our socio-cultural environment as well as the natural one.

The subject of the future city should be of concern to all people. For the sake of improving the ethics of future urban design, this book has analyzed the lessons of the urban past and the present. Neither the Eastern countries, which are still rich with socio-cultural values, nor the Western world, which has introduced impressive, sophisticated technology, have been able to fuse these two ethics. It is by this fusion that our success or failure will be measured.

# INDEX

historical perspective and, 67
human-made environment and, 13, 15–17
natural environment and, 10–13
in the Netherlands, 138
summarized, 6–7
Equilibrium, natural environment and, 13
Ethic. *See also* Environmental ethic
city and, 60
defined, 1–2
education and, 252
Evaporative cooling, site selection, climate types and, 152
Evapotranspiration, thermal performance, city morphology and, 167

Fishing village:
described, 53–54
valley theory and, 111
Floating city, future uses of, 3–4
Flood, site selection, climate types and, 153
Folk, regional concept and, 115–120
Food storage. *See also* Agriculture
geospace and, 200
and seminomadism, 47–48
towns and, 55–56

Gardening, Chinese perspective on, 23–24
Gate, *see* City gate
Geddes, Patrick, 102–103, 107, 115–120
Geology, natural environment and, 12, 13, 14
Geospace. *See also* Soil thermal performance
defined, 190
terminology of, 186–190
Geospace city, 219–238
defined, 219–220
habitat, 228–238
design, 231–238
site selection, 228–230
principles of, 220–227
supraspace city fusion, 227–228
Glickson, Artur, 116, 119, 120
Growth centers, *see* Regional growth centers

Han Dynasty, 84
Harappa City, 75
Hinduism, 19
Holland, *see* Netherlands
Hot-dry climate, 149, 150, 155, 161, 168, 169, 173
Hotel, Matmata, Tunisia, soil thermal performance

case study of, 204, 208–210
Hot-humid climate, 149, 150, 155, 161, 168, 173
Houses, *see* Residences
Howard, Ebenezer, 157
Huang He River Valley, 83, 84, 91
Human-made environment. *See also* Environment; Natural environment
Chinese perspective on, 19–24
environmental design and, 17–19, 220
environmental ethic and, 13, 15–17
Western perspective on, 24–26
Hunt House, Tunisia, soil thermal performance case study of, 210, 212–214
Hydrology, valley theory and, 109

Indigenous past:
city and, 56–58
community and, 37–38
of nomadism, 43–46
presettlements and, 41–42
and regional growth centers, 55
and regional site activity, 49–50
of seminomadism, 46–49
social factors and, 37–38, 247–253
towns and, 55–56
urbanization and, 38–39
village and, 50–54
Indus Valley, 38, 41, 51
comparison of indigenous forms of early urban centers in, 89–94
described, 73–78
map of, 74
Interdisciplinary approach, urban design and, 6, 102
Interinfluence, natural environment and, 11
Irrigation:
in China, 84
and comparison of indigenous forms of early urban centers, 90–91
in Egypt (ancient), 80–81

Japan, environmental perspective of, 19–24
Jarmo, Iraq, 49
Jeanneret, Charles–Édouard (Le Corbusier), 157
Jerusalem house, soil thermal performance of, 195–196
Judaism, 19

Kinship:
architecture and, 71
nomadism and, 45

Regional concept, comprehensive design and, 115–120

Regional growth centers:
  described, 55
  towns and, 56

Regional site activity, described, 49–50

Religion:
  Asian perspective, on environment, 19–24
  in China, 86–87
  comparison of indigenous forms of early urban centers and, 92–93

Residences:
  in China, 87
  earth-sheltered habitat, 170–173
  in Egypt (ancient), 81
  in Indus Valley, 76
  in Mesopotamia, 71, 72
  soil thermal performance case study, Shaanxi Province, China, 202–204
  thermal performance, city morphology and, 166–168

Resource village, valley theory and, 111

Rivers:
  comparison of indigenous forms of early urban centers and, 90
  village and, 51–52

Roman structures, soil thermal performance case study of, 210, 212–214

Sarab, Iran, 49

Sea frontier, future uses, 3–4

Seashore breeze, site selection, climate types and, 153

Seashore strip climate, 149, 150, 155, 161–162, 168

Seasonal cycle, seminomadism and, 47–48

Semi-below-ground habitat, defined, 189

Seminomadism, regional site activity and, 49–50

Shang Dynasty, 84

Shintoism, 19

Site activity, *see* Regional site activity

Site orientation, site selection, climate types and, 153–154

Site selection:
  climate types and, 151–154
  geospace city and, 228–230

Slope, site selection, climate types and, 153

Social factors. *See also* Community; Culture
  agriculture and, 90–91
  in China, 84, 87
  city and, 56–58
  in Egypt (ancient), 80–81

geospace city, 237–238

indigenous past and, 37–38, 247–253

nomadism, 43–46

regional concept and, 115–120

regional site activity and, 49–50

seminomadism, 48–49

urban design and, 6

village and, 53

village/city dichotomy, 58–60

Soil(s), site selection, climate types and, 154

Soil thermal performance, 183–214. *See also* Climate;
  Thermal performance
  background, 183–186
  case studies, 201–214
    of family dwelling, Shaanxi Province, China, 202–204
    of hotel, Matmata, Tunisia, 204, 208–210
    of Hunt House, Tunisia, 210, 212–214
    methodology for, 201–202
  earth-enveloped habitat performance, 195–201
    benefits, 197–201
    condensation, 196
    design form, 196–197
    generally, 195
    Jerusalem house, 195–196
  geospace terminology, 186–190
  thermal fluctuation and, 193–194
  thermal process and, 191–193
  urban design and, 144–145

Soleri, Paolo, 157

Song Dynasty, 84

Space frontier, future uses, 4

Street plans:
  of China, 86
  of Egypt (ancient), 81–82
  of Indus Valley, 75, 76, 77
  of Mesopotamia, 71–72
  thermal performance, city morphology and, 162–163, 164, 166–167

Subsurface space, defined, 189

Tang Dynasty, 84

Taxation, city and, 58

Technology:
  agriculture and, 52
  environment and, 1
  human-made environment and, 15–16

Thermal fluctuation, soil thermal performance and, 193–194

Thermal performance, 147–173. *See also* Climate;